The Mousse and the Man from the Michelin

My doomed attempt to become a celebrity chef in the 80s

By Kent Austin

Text copyright ©2015 Kent Austin

All Rights Reserved

All characters and events in this publication, other than those clearly in the public domain, are fictitious and any resemblance to real persons, living or dead, is purely coincidental.

To Seemah

CONTENTS

PART ONE 1

THE 1970s – CRIMES AGAINST FOOD 1

MOUSSE DE FOIE DE VOLAILLE 3

THE MOUSSE.. 5

BOVINGTON 1970... 7

CHAPTER 1 13

CHAPTER 2 49

CHAPTER 3 105

CHAPTER 4 121

CHAPTER 5 141

CHAPTER 6 155

CHAPTER 7 181

CHAPTER 8 199

PART TWO 213

THE 1980s – THE MOUSSE 213

CHAPTER 9 215

CHAPTER 10 245

CHAPTER 11	267
CHAPTER 12	287
PART THREE	**315**
THE MAN FROM THE MICHELIN	317
SIX MONTHS LATER	331
POSTSCRIPT	337

It all happened. Although not necessarily in the order in which it is told.

Some names of people and places have been changed.

PART ONE

THE 1970s – CRIMES AGAINST FOOD

MOUSSE DE FOIE DE VOLAILLE

'The evolution of this recipe was quite tortuous and many-sided. It was originally based on the world-famous chicken liver mousse from the Auberge du Père Bise, the 3-star restaurant in Tallories on Lake Annecy. It evolved via Michel Guérard's famous terrine fondant de foie volaille and was adapted by me on many different occasions. It has finally ended up in a period of great stability where the recipe is executed faithfully to the last little milligram of each ingredient concerned. The end product is such a fragile and delicately smooth mousse. There is an extraordinary tension in the kitchen each time it is ordered.'

From *My Gastronomy* (1986) by Nico Ladenis, chef-proprietor, Chez Nico, London (2 Michelin stars)

THE MOUSSE

The year was 1980. The age of nouvelle cuisine was upon us, and it had taken us completely by surprise. Determined not to be left behind in the scramble for recognition, we followed the example of every other chef with delusions of grandeur and bought ourselves a food processor. From that day onwards anything that couldn't be made into a mousse had no chance of getting on the menu: fish, poultry, game, vegetables, as well as every kind of fruit, you name it – perfectly good food, all rendered to the consistency of baby goo, and all in the cause of gastronomic advancement. If not a mousse, then we'd settle reluctantly for a puree, but pulp it we would. It was if we were catering for a nation without teeth.

BOVINGTON 1970

Nestling in a wooded cleft of the South Downs, a patchwork of lanes and meadows set about a picture-book church, Bovington was the model of an English country village, as timeless as tea and scones, as predictable as a summer shower.

On the surface at least.

Look twice and you would discover a community rotten at the core. In fact Bovington barely qualified as a community, at least not in the sense that its inhabitants perceived themselves as belonging to a unified group. They didn't. Yes, Bovington had all the trappings of a community: alongside a church it had a rectory, a pub, a manor house, a school, a post office, a foxhunt, a cricket club, a racing stud, a bus service, a tea room ... It even had its own council estate, in the form of a neat row of unpresumptuous flint cottages that lined the main road. Yet nothing was as it seemed.

Of the fifty or so houses and cottages that made up the village, many lay empty, derelict – front doors swinging from hinges, windows grimed and broken, gardens choked with weeds. The majority of the properties were owned by a reclusive Greek shipping magnate named Spiros Stephanides, whom no one ever saw (some theorised that he didn't exist). Although he lacked an official title, the mysterious Mr Stephanides was the de facto lord of the manor, in that he owned Bovington Place, an imposing medieval pile set in the heart of the village, as well as the Bovington Estate and several hundred acres of prime grazing. Mr Stephanides' properties were administered by his estate manager, a mild-mannered, benevolent man named Reginald Todd. Reginald was happy to let a cottage at a peppercorn rent to anyone who wanted one, on the proviso they gave it a lick of paint and fixed the roof – all it took was a handshake; no fussy leases or paperwork. Sadly there were few takers. Most of the properties were former tied cottages, labourers' dwellings once occupied by the small army of workers it had taken to maintain the estate – the Bovington Estate had once included several farms, but by now there were just two working farms in the village. The remainder lay abandoned and, along with much of the housing stock, unsellable and virtually worthless. The exodus from the land that had begun after the Second World War had reached its peak and, as in so many other English villages, most of the inhabitants had long since upped sticks and left for a brighter future in the towns.

With the exception of a few of the grander houses, which were in private ownership, the remainder of the homes in

The Mousse and the Man from the Michelin

the village belonged to a racehorse trainer named Jimmy Cowman. A newcomer to the village, Jimmy was a moneyed thug whose main activity since his arrival had been to intimidate his sitting tenants (most of them long-standing Bovington families, reluctantly acquired by Jimmy as part of the estate when he purchased the local stud). His strategy was to harass them into leaving their homes which he would then reoccupy with his overworked and underpaid staff. When he wasn't making his tenants' lives a misery or abusing his stable lads, Jimmy was to be found drinking and holding forth at volume in Bovington's only pub, The Twelve Cups, where he was also master of foxhounds to the local hunt (an unruly band of vandals who reserved the right to trample underfoot any obstacle that came between them and their quarry – ranging from pet rabbits and children's pushchairs to newly-dug graves).

When landlords Les and Nancy Foamer acquired the tenancy of The Twelve Cups, sometime in the late 1960s, it was an outstandingly preserved 18th century inn. Among its many original features were a fine inglenook fireplace and a centuries-old oak bar which ran the length of the saloon. So beguiled were Les and Nancy by their inn's unique heritage that they immediately set about tearing the heart out of it. This involved removing the unsightly wooden bar and replacing it with a sleek new one in stylish wood-grain-effect Formica. The inn's walls, bare and rough-hewn, were plastered over and lined with flock wallpaper; its flag-stoned floor rendered and carpeted, while any remaining antique features such as shelves and doors were replaced with modern off-the-peg equivalents, or simply painted over. All that was left to achieve was the tasteful addition of a bank of gambling machines, complete with buzzers and flashing lights. The cumulative effect resembled something between a tyre-fitter's waiting room and a provincial French brothel, with an atmosphere to match. Yet, curiously, it resulted in a dramatic improvement in business.

In the absence of an indigenous population, The Twelve Cups relied for its survival on a growing clientele of urban car owners, whose newfound distraction was to drive into the country at the least pretext, especially to pubs. Some of the many new regulars to The Twelve Cups even thought it would be a nice idea to revitalise the long-defunct Bovington Cricket Club. So they banded together, laid new turf on the pitch and refurbished the pavilion. As not one of the new cricket club's members was a village resident, the field remained off-limits to locals, padlocked behind a sturdy five-bar gate.

Another victim of the dwindling population was the village church which, for want of a congregation, had reduced the number of Sunday services it held to one a month. (Al-

The Mousse and the Man from the Michelin

though, being obscenely picturesque, it continued to enjoy a brisk turnover on weddings.) The diocese responded by relocating the rector to a neighbouring village and selling off the vacant rectory to a wealthy philanthropist, who converted it into a refuge for victims of domestic abuse. As most of the rectory's new occupants were young mothers, Bovington's population of school-aged children rose, literally overnight, to its highest level since the 19th century. Sadly, however, the village school had long since closed (inexplicably becoming home to a commune of hippies), so the children were left to amuse themselves. Nor could the young mothers readily draw their benefit payments, the money upon which they relied to survive, due to the post office-cum-village store having gone out of business. They lived in hiding, stranded in a remote, alien environment (declining passenger numbers meant the village bus service had been cut to just one bus a week), in permanent fear of being hunted down by their brutal ex-partners. With little to occupy their time, many of the young mothers sought consolation in the willing arms of the patrons of The Twelve Cups. This made for a lively, if frequently violent, social mix – the wife-battering ex-partners, it turned out, had an uncanny knack for discovering the whereabouts of their fled women, and were only too happy to batter a few errant lovers into the bargain when they caught up with them.

It was around this same time that Bovington saw the arrival of new blood. It began as a trickle. Arriving in their Volvos from Kensington and Fulham, they sniffed around the village, tentatively peering through windows of empty houses, knocking on doors, interrogating neighbours. *Who owned this delightful little cottage? Was it perhaps for sale? Yes! What was the asking price? How much! No, obviously we wouldn't hold you to it. What did you say the owner's name was? Spiros who? We'll be back on Monday. We must show Araminta. I just know that Giles is going to be swept away. Such a delightful little cottage. So much potential. Perfect for the weekends. And such a good price!*

The market was stirring.

Bovington's property slump that had lasted so long was coming to an end. Within a year, much of the village's available real estate had been snapped up. One especially enterprising young couple even bought the ailing tea room, with a view to turning it into a high-class restaurant. So it was that The Mute Swan Tea Room – a former monastic dwelling fronting onto the dusty B-road that snaked its way through the village – metamorphosed to be reborn as The Mute Swan Restaurant. And it was about to open its doors to a very hungry public.

CHAPTER 1

Oblivious of the looming food revolution that was set to destroy us in its path, we spent the 1970s at The Mute Swan catering for the undiscerning palate of the British diner in the only way we knew. Our brand of cooking pre-1980 could be described as bastard French, in that it had Gallic pretensions but was of doubtful heritage. The reality was that most of the menu was pure invention, and it was a very hit and miss affair. The rule of thumb was that for any dish to sell successfully it must have an exotic name, or at least possess a suggestion of foreign glamour. For instance, a starter made from a blend of cream cheese, bacon and onions flavoured with honey, was called Pousse Bedaine (slang for 'fatso' in French). Slimy on the palate and sickly rich, it sold like, and somewhat tasted like, hot cakes.

Another favourite starter was a mixture of chopped melon, cucumber and tomatoes infused with vegetable oil, malt vinegar and bottled mint sauce. This went by the name of Desert Island Cocktail. That not one of its ingredients was likely to be found on a desert island did not, at the time, present an irony.

Then there was Poulet Parisienne, a culture clash of ingredients that included boiled chicken pieces, tinned orange segments, bamboo shoots and bean sprouts, blended with curried mayonnaise and served on a bed of German pumpernickel. Unsurprisingly, a starter called Salami Provençale – a potent stew made from Danish salami, tomato puree and powdered garlic, served on slice of fried bread – had little to associate it with the region after which it was named. Ditto Frogs' Legs Biarritz; ditto Snails Bourguignon.

The low point of our inventiveness, however, was the, for once, unambiguously named Lemons Filled with Sardine Butter. If a single dish epitomised the era, this was it. Even I, in my profound culinary naivety, suspected there was something not quite right about this one. It involved hollowing out a lemon, stuffing both halves with a concoction of mashed tinned sardines and softened butter, before squashing the two halves together again – thus forcing the excess filling to escape and form a greasy band around the fruit's circumference. The end result resembled the planet Saturn, complete with gaseous rings, though with the addition of nipples at both poles. The challenge for the diner was to extract the content of the lemon and eat it with toast. I could only speculate on how it tasted because, despite being charged with its production, I hadn't the stomach to try it. One might have thought that diners would be warned off by the name alone, yet Lemons Filled with Sardine Butter sold

The Mousse and the Man from the Michelin

astonishingly well – too well. So to spare us the chore of hollowing out a fresh lemon for each new order, we simply rinsed the previously used lemon halves under a hot tap and refilled them. We repeated this process until the lemon skin finally disintegrated.

Compared to the rampant eclecticism of our starter menu, our system for creating main courses was simple. We just married whatever meat or fish we were using with at least two additional, and preferably improbable, components. The functional words when writing any menu therefore became 'with' and 'and'. For instance: Halibut *with* Bananas *and* Mango Chutney; Pork Chop stuffed *with* Figs *and* Almonds; Braised Duck in Red Wine *with* Chestnuts *and* Pineapple; Grilled Sirloin of Beef *with* Snails *and* Anchovy Butter...

You get the idea...

Bold juxtapositions such as these, we believed, were the hallmark of sophistication. As a chef in the 1970s one's reputation lived or died on the capacity to invent a relentless progression of new and evermore outrageous combinations. No two menus must ever be the same. It was originality at any price, and The Mute Swan was at the cutting edge. Perhaps the most worrying thing of all was that we genuinely believed we were serving good food. But we did, after all, merit an entry in *The Good Food Guide*, *The Egon Ronay Guide* and even *The Michelin Guide*, so I suppose we could be forgiven for misleading ourselves.

For Gerald and Arabella Golightly, the proprietors of The Mute Swan, there was only one person on the planet more feared and revered than the Good Food Guide inspector and that was The Man from the Michelin – for it was He who had the power to confer that ultimate accolade, the coveted Michelin star. Each year without fail, on the day of publication, and following a sleepless night, Gerald would visit the Eastbourne branch of WH Smith at 7 am sharp to acquire his copy of the new *Michelin Guide* in the vain hope of discovering that we had won our first star. The odds of it ever happening were on a par with being struck by a meteorite, but it didn't prevent us from dreaming, if only fleetingly. Nor did it soften the blow when inevitably we failed.

Gerald would perform the same annual ritual for the publication of both *The Egon Ronay Guide* and *The Good Food Guide,* the latter being an especially emotionally charged event. For unlike *The Michelin Guide, The Good Food Guide* (referred to among foodie types as the GFG) featured a hard-hitting critique of every restaurant it stooped to include in its pages, of which there were few – at the time The Mute Swan was just one of maybe three restaurants in the Brighton post code district to merit an entry. So elitist

The Mousse and the Man from the Michelin

was the GFG that simply to feature among its pages was considered an honour, even if you received a lousy review. The downside was that its inspector-cum-writers pulled no punches: sarcasm, hyperbole, innuendo, personal insult – all, we discovered, were considered legitimate in their avowed crusade against mediocrity and pretention. *The Good Food Guide* prided itself on its rigorous impartiality and, unlike less respected guides, it was free from advertising and consequently editorially independent.

Sadly for The Mute Swan, *The Good Food Guide* was offended by just about everything we stood for: our heavy, flour-infused sauces; our profligate use of cream and butter; our 'ridiculously generous' portions (designed to please what the GFG once referred to derisively as 'BFFs' – 'Big Fat Farmers'); our 'ridiculously mean' portions (introduced as a kneejerk reaction to the former accusation); our practice of chalking the menu on 'scruffy' blackboards (an affectation the Golightlys had borrowed from the bistros of Chelsea, and previously unheard of in the provinces); and our 'gimmicky' *prix compris* menu that included a complimentary glass of 'thin' port. But they especially hated us because we were successful. Because The Mute Swan wasn't just ordinarily busy, it was heaving-insanely-packed-to-the-beams busy, and had been so ever since the Golightlys first opened their doors to the public. And for the hair-shirted, bean-eating purists at the GFG it rankled.

Perversely, considering how much energy we invested in attempting to please them, adverse criticism from the guides made no obvious impact on business. If anything we just got busier. And our appeal was universal – from the local plumber and his wife on their wedding anniversary through to international opera stars from nearby Glyndebourne. Throughout that decade, to secure a table at The Mute Swan typically involved a six-week wait. We turned away at least as many people as we ever fed. It was not unusual for diners to make the one hundred mile round trip from London just for the experience, despite there being many better restaurants in the capital. We routinely received telephone reservations from locations as far flung as New York and Rio de Janeiro; and were once visited by Queen Sofia of Spain. All of this just to eat at a small country bistro, buried away in a sleepy Sussex hamlet. Small wonder that we'd become blasé.

The runaway success of The Mute Swan was not easy to explain. Its popularity could certainly not be attributed to the food alone, nor did it have much to recommend it on aesthetic grounds. Other than a scab of crazy paving, wishfully alluded to as 'the patio', and a small area of scrubby bushes and herb beds, it had no garden to speak of, and the car park – ill-lit, surfaced with lumpy shingle and pitted with

The Mousse and the Man from the Michelin

waterlogged potholes – was so small that customers were regularly obliged to park their cars in the public car park at the opposite end of the village. The shell of the building comprised a row of ancient yet unremarkable flint cottages fronting directly onto the main road; the interior walls had been knocked through to form an interconnecting warren of cramped rooms, in which any person over five-foot-eight was in danger of striking their head on the beamed ceilings.

But what the restaurant lacked in opulence it made up for in character. And The Mute Swan had it in spades. Before relocating to pursue a new life in the country, the Golightlys had been habitués of The Chelsea Arts Club, the favoured haunt of London's elite artist set (It exists to this day, and remains notoriously stuck-up about whom it allows to join.) and, unofficially at least, it had become the template for The Mute Swan's trademark bohemian shabby-chic decor. The walls of the restaurant were lined with an eccentric collection of drawings and oil paintings (including works by Duncan Grant and Clive Bell – acquired from nearby Charleston Farmhouse, the country retreat of the Bloomsbury Group); while on arrival diners were obliged to pick their way through a jumble of salvaged curios and objet d'arts that included antique polyphons, chaotic stacks of antiquarian books and a disproportionate number of ill-matched, broken and threadbare sofas. Taken individually, not one of The Mute Swan's constituent parts would have caused much of a stir. But experienced side-by-side, and with their myriad blemishes subdued by the forgiving glow of log fires and a few judiciously placed candelabra, they colluded to powerful effect. Add to this the enticing tang of roasting game, fine red Burgundy and freshly ground coffee, and upon setting foot in the restaurant it was difficult not to fall victim to a touch of artfully contrived magic. There was nowhere else quite like it.

In contrast to *The Good Food Guide*, *The Michelin Guide* was an organ of few words. Rather than engage in criticism, it preferred to grade a restaurant by a complex, if charmless, system of symbols – the definitive award being three stars. This way it was able to maintain an aloof detachment while at the same time enforcing its unquestionable stamp of authority. To place our quest in perspective, at this time the idea of any restaurant in the United Kingdom acquiring three, or even two, Michelin stars would have been unthinkable. So far as I'm aware, there was but a tiny handful of restaurants in possession of a single star, most of these in the capital, and none without a French chef. (In case you were wondering, at the time of writing, in 2013, in the UK there are 138 one-star restaurants, as well as 20 with two stars and four with three stars. It's fair to suppose we've moved on.) *The Michelin Guide* at this time was a dyed-

The Mousse and the Man from the Michelin

in-the-wool French institution, and to call the French culinary establishment parochial in its attitudes is to call Santa Claus jolly. In the 1970s the mere mention of 'British' and 'chef' in the same breath, in the presence of a Frenchman, was guaranteed to provoke a gust of incredulity tinged with barely concealed contempt. I know this from humiliating personal experience. It would have helped had we known exactly what we were striving for to earn our star, but the behind-the-scenes machinations that governed the Michelin star system were kept deliberately inscrutable. The Man from the Michelin was a fickle master. Nobody knew for certain how to please him. And even if for a rare moment we thought our tormentor was beginning to soften towards us, the rules, so far as they existed, would mysteriously cease to apply. It wasn't that the goal posts had been moved; they were never there in the first place.

You might have thought that The Man from the Michelin didn't like us, in which case we doubtless would have given up trying to impress him. But this wasn't entirely true because, while we may have lacked the fabled Michelin star, we had at least been awarded a not-to-be-sniffed-at Michelin 'Red M'. This, in the eyes of *The Michelin Guide*, positioned The Mute Swan among the top fifty restaurants in the British Isles. Clearly we weren't *all* bad. Like an abused wife with self-esteem issues, it was this glimmer of approval that kept us hanging on and allowed us to tolerate the cruelty of our repeated rejection.

Meanwhile, Gerald's love-hate relationship with *The Good Food Guide* had developed into a full-blown persecution complex. Being offended by *The Michelin Guide* for the withholding of an abstract symbol was one thing but, for Gerald, being publicly insulted by an anonymous food hack with literary pretensions and a grudge to bear was quite another. One year, following a particularly savage drubbing, something in him snapped.

'Those bastards have gone too far this time,' sputtered Gerald, striding into the kitchen and brandishing his newly acquired GFG as if it were a warrant for his execution. He was newly returned from his annual expedition to WH Smith and, as was customary on these occasions, the entire restaurant staff had gathered respectfully in the kitchen to receive the critics' verdict, in the full expectation that our hopes were about to be summarily dashed. We were not to be disappointed. 'That does it. I'm going to write to these sandal-wearing evangelists and tell them I don't want to be in their bloody guide ever again.'

'Can you really do that?' someone asked.

'I can do what the bloody hell I like,' said Gerald, twitching with indignation. 'It's my restaurant. Who needs

The Mousse and the Man from the Michelin

them anyway? Bunch of jumped up yogurt eaters – failed cooks the lot of 'em. You know what they say about a critic, don't you? He's a man who knows the way but can't drive the cart. My only consolation is that every review we've had from these people so far has clearly been written by an ill-informed idiot. Were it not for this one redeeming coincidence I think I'd happily go out and shoot myself.'

We scoured our entry in the GFG for a second and a third time, reading between the lines for any crumb of comfort. But it was not to be. As usual, our review was unremittingly negative. The general thrust was that The Mute Swan valued style over substance, preferring to rely on populist gimmickry as a substitute for serious cooking. But our worst crime, paradoxically, was that we were simply too busy.

Having slept on the problem, it occurred to Gerald that, even if the GFG agreed to exclude us from future guides, readers would inevitably conclude that we'd been dropped on account that we weren't good enough, rather than us having opted out voluntarily. It seemed that we were trapped in our uneasy alliance. As a compromise, Gerald settled for the less radical course of writing a letter of complaint to the editor – a swingeing offensive that cast doubt on his qualifications to play judge and jury with the livelihoods of struggling restaurateurs. The editor's reply, when it eventually arrived, was curtly to the point and suggested that if we really wanted to be taken seriously as a restaurant, the first thing we need do was cater for fewer customers. But not only did this advice fly in the face of Gerald's red-blooded capitalist instinct, it also raised the question of how one measures success, for, as the editor helpfully pointed out in his letter, if 'bums on seats' were the only gauge of a restaurant's worth, then The Mute Swan was undeniably up there with the best. But, sadly for us, popularity did not rate highly among the GFG's criteria for judging a restaurant.

With hindsight, even Gerald would have admitted they had a point. The dining room at The Mute Swan contained just eight tables and seated 25 diners at a push – not nearly enough to turn a healthy profit. Gerald astutely circumvented this problem by operating a multiple (and highly contentious) sittings system. This enabled us to fill each table three times during the course of an evening, between the hours of 7 and 10pm. Upon arrival diners would be ushered into one of several lounges for pre-dinner drinks while they chose from the menu. They would then be shown to their table as it became vacant. But while such a system might be workable in theory it failed to take into account the vagaries of human timekeeping, and the potential for disaster was ever present. Even on those occasions when things went according to plan, the waiting staff were still faced with the sensitive task of demanding that people vacate their tables and retire

The Mousse and the Man from the Michelin

to the lounge 'for port and coffee', so as to clear the way for the next wave of diners. With some justification, people did not take kindly to being asked to move. This was their table; they'd reserved it and paid handsomely for the privilege.

But despite the logic of their argument, Gerald dismissed the advice of *The Good Food Guide* out of hand, convinced he knew best. Gerald inevitably knew best about most things. Sometimes I loved him for it. Occasionally I hated him for it. But I was perpetually in awe of the fact, and had been so ever since our first meeting...

***

It was an early autumn's evening in 1971, the occasion of my interview for the post of trainee assistant chef. ('No previous experience necessary as full training will be given. Live in'.) I was 18 years old. Anxious to make a good impression, I'd arrived at the restaurant early. I was greeted at reception by a stiffly-permed thirty-something woman of indeterminate nationality. She was wearing an exceedingly tight lime green trouser suit which lent the impression that her voluptuous contours had been poured in while liquid and then set fast.

'Allo, I'm Betsie, ze man*a*geress', the woman informed me, a ribbon of cigarette smoke leaking from the corner of her mouth. 'Mr Golightly is expecting you, but 'e's bin 'eld

– 25 –

up...you may av to vait a bit.'

Betsie gestured distractedly towards the bar with the tip of her cigarette and told me to find a seat. Without further word, she turned her back on me to join three other thirty-something women who were huddled around a table in a corner of the bar. They were drinking wine, and, judging by their intermittent fits of giggling, appeared to be slightly drunk. I perched self-consciously on the edge of a chaise longue and pretended to leaf through a copy of *Country Life*, my mouth dry with nerves.

It was now past seven o'clock and the first customers were beginning to arrive. Removed from their reverie, the women stubbed out their cigarettes and fell instantly into meet and greet mode, busily distributing menus and wine lists and taking drink orders. As the bar filled, I found myself alone at the centre of a small crowd, enveloped in a fog of cigarette smoke and heavily applied perfume, a dozen animated conversations rattling in my ears. My most vivid recollection of that night, however, is the rich cocktail of cooking aromas that wafted enticingly from the restaurant kitchen. At that moment something in me clicked – I like to think it was a kind of primal reaction occurring between synapse and taste-bud, inexplicably dictating my future vocation, but it was more probably due to the fact that I hadn't eaten since breakfast and my stomach was rumbling. Either

The Mousse and the Man from the Michelin

way, I was hooked.

Some 45 minutes later, and just when I was beginning to feel that I'd been left for dead, a sleek silver-grey sports coupé roared ostentatiously to a halt outside the bar window. The driver, a tall, boyish-faced man in his late twenties, strode proprietarily into the bar and approached me, hand outstretched, beaming effusively as if greeting a long-absent friend. Taken aback at the force of this welcome, I found myself reflexively checking over my shoulder, convinced that he was addressing somebody else. Looking me full in the eye, he shook my hand firmly and protractedly.

'Gerald Golightly. So good to meet you ... so very good to meet you. And sorry to have kept you waiting. What can I get you to drink?'

'But I've, erm, come about the job,' I stammered, 'the job of trainee assistant chef?'

By now I was in no doubt there had been a case of mistaken identity, and with some justification. Even as early as 1971, The Mute Swan was by far the most celebrated restaurant in the area. Since opening two years earlier it had acquired a reputation locally as something of a phenomenon. I should add that 'locally' in this context refers to Eastbourne, our closest town and a destination more noted for its preponderance of care homes than its contribution to fine food, so thankfully the bar was set low. If only by default, The Mute Swan reigned supreme, as did Gerald Golightly, who in his role as pioneering restaurateur had become a minor celebrity among the chattering classes of the Sussex Weald; he'd even been interviewed by our local newspaper, *The Eastbourne Gazette & Herald*, which where I came from was a sure sign that you'd arrived. And now here I was in the presence of this entrepreneurial demigod, clearly being mistaken for somebody else and well on my way to blowing my chances of getting a desperately needed job.

Gerald towered over me where I sat, flamboyantly confident in yellow corduroy slacks, Gucci loafers, red sleeveless sweater, dog tooth shirt with gold cufflinks, all topped off with a paisley cravat. His presence dominated the room in every sense.

'Yes, yes, of course, the job. You are, erm...Kent Austin, aren't you?' he said, squinting down at a crumpled scrap of notepaper in his hand. As he spoke his tousled mop of auburn hair bounced luxuriantly in time with his words.

'Yes, that's me – '

'Jolly good then. So what's your poison, red or white? Or perhaps you'd prefer a little stiffener, help ease the nerves?'

'Stiffener?'

The Mousse and the Man from the Michelin

'Scotch? Gin? Tio Pepe? What do you normally drink?'

I'd seldom drunk anything stronger than lemonade shandy. Unable to think of a worthy response, I named the first drink that entered my head. 'Oh, in that case I'll have a brown ale, please.'

No sooner had I said it, then I realised I'd committed my first indiscretion. Gerald seemed bemused. 'Brown ale, you say? Hmmm, not sure we stock such a thing ... I think I know what you'll enjoy.' As if on some hidden cue Betsie the manageress materialised at Gerald's side, a curl of cigarette smoke escaping from her heavily rouged lips. She fixed my gaze, expressionless. 'Betso, would you get Kento here a glass of the new Sauvignon Touraine '70, please. Actually, make it two glasses and bring the bottle. We'll be in the snug.' (It was Gerald's custom, I was to discover, to attach an 'O' suffix to any person's name that would bear the load.)

I followed Gerald into a cramped lounge at the back of the restaurant, one of a labyrinth of rooms that served as an overspill to the bustling dining room. Returning with an ice bucket and two glasses, Betsie poured the wine. 'Vil zer be anysing else, Gerald?' As she spoke, her head rocked detachedly from side to side. I thought of Lady Penelope from *Thunderbirds*.

'No, that's fine, thank you, Betso. Although you could

put another bottle on standby.'

'But of courze.'

As Betsie left the room she gave me a broad wink and ran her tongue suggestively beneath her upper lip. I loosened my collar and swallowed hard.

Gerald took a lengthy gulp of wine. I followed suit, wincing involuntarily. The wine was tart, aromatic, like nothing I'd experienced.

'You don't like it?' Gerald seemed mildly hurt.

'No, no. I do. It's fine,' I said, attempting to recover my composure. 'It's just that I've never had wine before. The taste came as a bit of shock.'

'You've never drunk wine?' said Gerald, his expression of incredulity dissolving into one of pity. 'So what on earth do you drink when you eat?'

'Erm, water, I suppose, or sometimes tea...or orange squash.'

'No, I mean when you eat out. In restaurants.'

'I don't eat in restaurants,' I said, a note of panic edging into my voice.

'Never? Surely you eat out on special occasions? Don't your parents ever take you out?'

The Mousse and the Man from the Michelin

It was a sad fact. I was eighteen years old and, Wimpy Bars and my father's Christmas sherry aside, I'd never set foot in a restaurant or drunk wine. I was feeling increasingly out of my depth. 'Er, no, not really.'

'That's a shame. But not to worry. So what do you like to cook?'

'Cook?'

'You know, when you're at home. If you don't dine out, then surely you must cook?'

Odd as it may seem, I hadn't anticipated this question. I thought hard. 'Let me see...I've cooked eggs...popcorn...sausages...custard – '

'Ahhh, custard! Egg custard? Crème brûlée?' said Gerald, clapping his hands approvingly.

'No, I don't think so, just, you know, ordinary custard.'

'I see. Well that's all very commendable, but when I say *cook* I mean something a little more ambitious. Do you have a signature dish?'

I was puzzled by this line of enquiry. *Was I now expected to supply my own cookware?* But I suspected it could be the clincher. 'Well,' I finally ventured, opting for a course of damage limitation, 'I don't have a signature dish, as such, but I could always get one. And I've lots of other kinds of dishes. I've a butter dish. A Pyrex dish with a glass lid. A dish shaped like a fish. A – '

'Have you ever cooked anything at all?' said Gerald, by now speaking as if he were dealing with a simpleton.

'Well, I've cooked eggs, popcorn, sausages – '

'Yes, yes, so you say.' Gerald slapped his thighs and consulted his wristwatch. So, first things first. What star sign are you?'

'Star sign?'

'Yes, you know. What sign of the zodiac were you born under?'

'I don't know.'

'When's your birthday?'

'October. The second.'

'Ah, now, let me see, yes, that makes you a Libran. Oh, we'll get along just fine together. I'm Leo, by the way. Can't see any worries there. Can you start tomorrow?'

'Tomorrow? You mean I've got the job?' I was dumbfounded. To my mind, as interviews went it couldn't have been more disastrous.

The Mousse and the Man from the Michelin

'Yes, you do want the job, don't you?' I'll need to know now. As you can imagine, we've been overwhelmed with applicants. I've a waiting list of hopefuls and, it has to be said, many with a good deal more experience than yourself, but the wrong star sign, sadly.'

'Yes, yes, I do want the job. Thank you. Thank you so much – '

'The starting wage is fifteen pounds a week, plus a long-service bonus of one hundred pounds, paid once a year.'

'Fifteen pounds.' I was shocked. It was at least twice as much as I'd been expecting.

'Well, I know it doesn't sound like much money, but it's a live-in position, food and accommodation all found,' said Gerald, taking a defensive tone. 'This is reflected in the salary, of course. And, needless to say, it's a very valuable training, an apprenticeship, if you like. One needs to take a long-term view. You'll learn a lot here.'

I returned home that night in a state of high excitement, infatuated with the prospect of beginning a new life. Home was a sprawling and dilapidated maisonette in the seedier end of Eastbourne, where I lived with my father and 12-year-old sister. Damp, crumbling and insanitary, the building should have been condemned long ago. There was no central heating or hot water and it had a faulty sewage system. The place was an irredeemable dump, but my father insisted on staying because the rent was cheap. We lived on the brink of squalor, and I hated it. The punishing cold in winter, the stench of sewage in summer, uncarpeted floors, no decent furniture, no refrigerator, no phone, a broken TV set. Our only source of heat was a gas cooker. The knobs had dropped off long ago and we were obliged to turn it on and off with the aid of a pair of pliers. My mother had walked out three years earlier, unable to stomach any more hardship. Since then we'd existed on a seven-day diet of spam and chips, with the occasional boiled egg or can of Irish stew thrown in by way of a treat.

I could cope with the diet. I could put up with my father watering down the milk when he thought I wasn't looking. I could even tolerate watching him eat his food off of newspaper with a knife while dressed only in his vest and underpants. But what really stuck in my craw was that he could allow us to live this way, because he had the money to change everything – had he chosen. I knew he had the money to make things better for us, and he knew that I knew but, plead as I might, he insisted on making do. The will to change just wasn't there. He no doubt had his reasons for living the way he did, but whatever they were he kept them to himself. When he died, some twenty years later, my sister and I were not entirely shocked to find in excess of forty

The Mousse and the Man from the Michelin

thousand pounds in used bank notes stuffed into a trunk beneath his bed. We squandered every last penny with relish.

I found my father seated at the kitchen table. He was busy trimming his toe nails, while alternately soaking each of his feet in a bowl of steaming water, as was his habit.

'Dad, I got the job.' I tried to sound casual but was unable to contain my delight.

'I'll rent your room out then,' replied my father sullenly, at the same time attacking a particularly horny toe nail with a pair of industrial wire clippers.

'Is that all you can say? Aren't you pleased for me?'

'Why should I be pleased? Now I've got to find someone else to do your job. Don't they even want a reference from me?'

'Didn't ask,' I answered brightly.

'More's the pity. I'd have told them what a bloody shirker you are.'

Not only had Gerald not asked for a reference, he'd also neglected to ask me what I currently did for a job, which came as a relief because, had I been truthful in my reply, I would have had to tell him that I sold and exchanged second-hand pornographic magazines from a market stall.

Kent Austin

Or, more precisely, I worked for my father, who sold and exchanged second-hand pornographic magazines from a market stall (mostly to ageing men in shabby raincoats, the magazines' pages much dog-eared and vaguely sticky), and had been doing so ever since leaving school without any qualifications, aged fifteen. My weekly wage was eight pounds, four pounds of which my father withheld in lieu of board and lodging. Vocations didn't come less promising, and any mention of it in the presence of polite company had so far proved an unreliable icebreaker. All I could think of was escape. And now my time had come.

But for all my dissatisfaction with my lot in life, I'd never harboured an ambition to become a chef. Quite the contrary: it had been drummed into me by my teachers at school that catering was the last word in dead-end jobs. The received wisdom was that only academic failures became chefs. In an age of Jamie Oliver and Heston Blumenthal, where cooking has supplanted rock and roll in the public imagination and turned chefs into television personalities and multi-millionaire superstars, it's clear my teachers had badly misread the zeitgeist. But they couldn't be blamed, because in its dour mediocrity British catering at the time had attained a special kind of low. No person in their right mind would want to become a chef. It was the undisputed career of last resort.

The Mousse and the Man from the Michelin

But change was in the air. Emboldened by its newfound relative affluence, the British public in the 1960s had become fixated with the idea of self-improvement. Nowhere was this more apparent than in attitudes towards eating. Where for generations we'd thought ourselves lucky to have enough food on the table to fend off hunger, we were now curious to experiment. And for inspiration we looked to the colourful, and at times disturbing, world of the TV chef.

Throughout the 1960s, the only cooks of note to appear on television were a preppy American named Graham Kerr, aka The Galloping Gourmet, and our very own Fanny Craddock. There'd been TV cooks before her, but she was the first to achieve real success, not least because she was rude, aggressive and supercilious – in fact in every way the prototypical celebrity chef.

As bizarre acts go, Fanny Craddock remains hard to beat. With her formal frocks, pancake makeup and wild gleaming eyes her stage persona hovered somewhere between a pantomime dame and a highly strung schoolmistress. She was assisted on set by her husband, Johnnie, who – with his quaint monocle and meekly henpecked manner – provided the perfect foil to her bombastic style. Fanny made it her business to educate and patronise her viewers in equal measure. The premise of her programme, so far as I ever made out, was that as a nation we were so barbaric in our eating habits that we required coaching at even the most elementary level, like Amazonian tribesmen who'd never set eyes on a dining table. Alongside delivering sound culinary advice, such as 'how to solve the problem of a dry bird', Fanny would lecture us on such cultural niceties as how to use a napkin without looking like one is blowing one's nose; or selecting one's cutlery from the outside in, while being careful not to brandish a table knife as if it were a dagger.

Fanny had a fondness for culinary dyes, which she recommended we use liberally in everything from sauces to puddings, to add sophistication to our cooking. One such dish was Green Cheese Ice Cream: ice cream made from Gruyère cheese, dyed green. Another was Jelly à la Zizi: a multi-coloured, multi-layered road-kill of a pudding that paid fitting homage to the psychedelic age in which it was conceived. Unfortunately, this was still the era of black and white television so we had to take Fanny's advice at face value. It was only years later, when her programmes were finally broadcast in colour, that we were presented with the unsettling truth: I recall on one occasion her making a blancmange that contained so much yellow dye that it was actually painful on the eyes.

Other Fanny staples were veal brains cooked with cream and brandy; pigs' kidneys flambéed in brandy with cream; *Homard Mélanie*: lobster in a cream and brandy sauce;

The Mousse and the Man from the Michelin

Crêpes Suzette: pancakes drenched in cream and brandy; and a 'flotilla' of meringue swans, served floating on an upturned mirror, each swan paddling regally in its own reflection and piped liberally with brandy-fortified cream. As if in sullen resistance to a trend, a dish known as Maypole Chicken (a roasted chicken stabbed through with a kebab skewer and adorned with whole peeled oranges that gave it the appearance of a shamanic talisman) remained inexplicably dairy and alcohol-free.

And for the kids there were hard-boiled eggs – hard-boiled eggs festooned with anchovies to resemble beer barrels; hard-boiled eggs studded with coiled and sculpted pipe cleaners to resemble (still more) swans; and hard-boiled eggs with lettuce-leaf wings and halos fashioned from pasta hoops to resemble angels – all washed down with lashings of extravagantly pink milk.

Only many years later was it discovered that Fanny's outlandish ideas and unpredictable personality were most likely due to a lifelong addiction to amphetamines. It would explain a lot.

In our cynical postmodern age it is easy to sneer at Fanny Craddock and her genteel pretensions, but in her day she was to exercise a profound influence, if not on our routine eating habits then on our capacity to aspire to better things.

Kent Austin

As well as filling the Royal Albert Hall with admirers, who flocked in their thousands to witness her live cookery demonstrations, Fanny published more than a hundred best-selling cookery books. In the process she introduced us to such enduring staples as the prawn cocktail, deep fried brie, duck a l'orange, beef bourguignonne and cheesecake – recipes destined to burn their way into our collective psyche, and to be served with wildly varying degrees of success at dinner parties to this day.

In 1970 the dinner party was for the majority of us a previously alien concept, and as such remained open to broad interpretation. It nevertheless adhered to a number of unwritten rules. In the first place, it was essential to commence your meal with an aperitif. A typical dinner party might begin with the ladies sipping a Babycham (essentially fizzy pear juice with a suggestion of alcohol), while the men would drink a pint or two of Party Seven bitter (weak, frothy and innocuous, and a pale shadow of its traditional counterparts) poured from an unwieldy seven-pint (why seven?) reinforced steel can that required the muscles of a navvy to puncture a hole on either side to extract the contents. If you were feeling especially adventurous you might even opt for a Cinzano or Martini cocktail, but that was as far as it stretched. Drinks would be accompanied by an array of nibbles. Alongside assorted bowls of Twiglets, crisps and nuts

The Mousse and the Man from the Michelin

(olives were out because nobody liked them – the one exception being to complement the above-mentioned Martini cocktails) you might find cheese and tinned pineapple on sticks, pinned for convenience and aesthetic impact onto the backs of grapefruit hedgehogs. Another classic standby was Ritz Crackers – most usually piped with Primula (a curiously moreish savoury toothpaste that is still widely available) and topped with a sprinkling of microscopic tinned prawns. For starters there was salmon mousse – made from tinned salmon and cream cheese, set with plenty of gelatine for maximum rigidity. You could judge a well-prepared mousse by striking it briskly with the back of a spoon. Ideally the spoon should bounce cleanly off the mousse while leaving its surface unblemished. Other firm favourites were melon balls, curried eggs (cold hardboiled eggs halved and served with curry sauce) and Melba toast with Gentleman's Relish. But the undisputed king of dinner party starters was avocado dressed with prawns and Marie Rose sauce. The avocado pear had not long made its debut in British shops (at the time it was generally unobtainable above what is now known as the M4 corridor, although it continued to creep northward at a rate of some ten miles annually, eventually to arrive in Accrington circa 1990) and as such was possessed of a mystique that a twenty-first century diner might reserve for, say, the fugu fish, and there was always a hushed reverence whenever one was served. Sadly, in the absence of modern supply chain management – these days so easily taken for granted – which practically guarantees a perfectly ripe and unblemished fruit every time, the 70s avocado was inevitably too hard, too soft or too discoloured to eat – and on occasions could even achieve a combination of all three states simultaneously. But reluctant to waste such a rare delicacy, we'd tuck-in without complaint.

For the main course you could bank on being served any one of the following: chicken Kiev, steak, cheese fondue, spaghetti bolognaise. End of story. Why mess with a perfectly good formula by introducing the tyranny of choice? For pudding – or dessert, as Fanny would have us call it – if you were really pushing the boat out there was of course no substitute for Black Forest gateau, served with an obligatory dollop of whipped cream. Alternatively there was chestnut Mont Blanc: sweetened chestnut purée buried beneath a tower of whipped cream. Another favourite was syllabub: basically sweetened whipped cream laced with Jiff lemon juice. Dessert was infinitely flexible, just so long as it involved cream, which, Fanny's influence aside, held an irresistible allure due to it being perceived as the last word in decadent luxury and, as our parents never failed to remind us, it had been rationed during the war. Whatever dessert you served, however, it must in no way resemble anything that

The Mousse and the Man from the Michelin

might have been eaten by your parents' generation – sadly ruling out some of the best puddings known to man. Finally, no self-respecting 70s dinner party would be complete without a bottle or two of wine, the variety of which was boundless, just so long as it came in an amusingly-shaped bottle and was called Blue Nun, Black Tower, Mateus Rosé, Bull's Blood or Ruffino.

During your meal – which would be liberally dispersed with cigarette breaks; not just between courses but also during courses – the conversation was likely to drift on to the pressing issues of the day: was it really pea soup they used in the film *The Exorcist* to simulate vomit, or had the director somehow managed to obtain real ectoplasm? (Most of us were convinced of the latter.) Was Dr Alex Comfort's *The Joy of Sex* destined to change our approach to lovemaking forever? And was the practice of big-toe sucking, as promoted by the author without a hint of irony, really a legitimate form of sexual gratification or was it possibly a bit overrated? (These are the women talking here. For the men, conversation was strictly confined to football or the relative merits of the Morris 1100 and Vauxhall Viva Estate.) Or was it right that women should hold managerial positions, or would it render subordinate males sexually impotent? Our musings would be complemented by the anodyne strains of Andy Williams and the Carpenters playing on the gramophone in the corner of the room. Although it was just as likely that the television would be left on, at full volume, throughout the meal; not only did this prevent us from missing our favourite programmes – *Starsky and Hutch, The Dukes of Hazard, Randall and Hopkirk Deceased...* – but it also provided a welcome point of refuge in the event of a conversational bottleneck. Everyone was happy.

To facilitate our sophisticated new lifestyles we acquired an armoury of indispensible hi-tech gadgets. These included the Sodastream siphon, the Goblin Teasmade, the Hostess heated serving trolley, the Chopomatic vegetable dicer and the Kenwood electrically operated carving knife – a few of which items we used more than once before stashing them at the back of a cupboard to gather dust indefinitely. My friend Ronnie Patterson's parents, who were ostentatiously wealthier than anyone else I knew, even had a bar (yes, a bar!) installed in their front room – complete with shelf-mounted bottles and optics – at which Mr Paterson mixed cocktails (cocktails!). Ronnie and I would look on in awe as his father demonstrated his technique with a shaker. Mr Paterson called it his 'world's best father shaker' because it was engraved with the words 'Arthur Paterson – World's Best Father'. At the time, he was working his way methodically through a book of cocktail recipes with the aim of making a different new cocktail every day.

The Mousse and the Man from the Michelin

According to Mr Paterson, the success of a cocktail depended on the quality of the shake. And he certainly had a knack for it. 'Who's the world's best father?' he would ask, once all the ingredients were mixed together with ice cubes and ready to be shaken.

'You are, Dad!' Ronnie and his mum would chorus in reply. It was their little ritual. They would then laugh and clap appreciatively while Mr Paterson performed a special dance, shaking his cocktail shaker above his head and behind his back as if it were a percussion instrument. It was at times like these that I wished I had a family like Ronnie's. There was no denying it, these people had style.

But while Mr Paterson enjoyed mixing cocktails, he had no appetite for drinking them (he preferred beer), and the task of judging his creations fell to his wife. Mr Paterson would adopt an expression of mock trepidation as she took her first sip. Unfailingly, following a pregnant pause, she would nod her approval. This was the cue for a further round of applause from Ronnie and his mum, while Mr Paterson looked on, smiling modestly and evidently basking in his family's adoration. Despite this, Ronnie and I noted, Mrs Paterson seldom got beyond the first sip of any of her husband's cocktails. With hindsight, this was understandable because Mr Paterson's cocktails were, if nothing else, adventurous. One of his recipes involved taking equal quantities of rum, grapefruit juice and Campari, adding a dash of Worcester sauce and a shot of Jagermeister, and topping the finished cocktail with a blob of mayonnaise; another called for vodka, tomato juice and cream cheese.

If the 70s dinner party now strikes us as unimaginative (cocktails excepted), it's with good reason. For while we may have taken a vicarious pleasure in watching TV chefs prepare evermore elaborate dinner parties for their studio guests, the reality was that for the most part we were content merely to watch. Then, as now, we were simply too exhausted, too lazy or too poor to attempt any real cooking. The 1970s had also heralded a major shift in family life. With some 60 percent of housewives now out at work, many were faced with juggling full-time jobs with the task of cooking for their families (few men cooked). Demand for convenience foods rocketed, as Britain fell in love with the TV dinner. Not that anyone objected. In fact the more of the stuff you could consume the better. Convenience food was good, not least because it was an American invention.

The first rule when planning your convenience menu was that nothing should be fresh – fresh produce of all types was distinctly passé. Liberated from the shackles of cooking meat-and-three-vegetables seven nights a week, housewives relied instead on a growing number of tinned, frozen, boil-in-the-bag and dehydrated ready meals. Many of these make

The Mousse and the Man from the Michelin

periodic comebacks to this day, among them Vesta curry, Bird's Eye boil-in-the-bag cod steaks in cheese sauce, Mr Brain's faggots, Findus crispy pancakes, Spam, Angel Delight and Arctic Roll, to name just a few.

To make such advances possible, food scientists were increasingly turning to synthetic ingredients, a trend that was to meet with massive popular approval. Because, of course, additives and preservatives were a good thing, an expression of our modernity, of how far we'd come as a civilisation. After all, it was only a year earlier that the Americans had put a man on the moon, and we were reliably informed by the newspapers that in the near future all of us would be living on an 'astronaut's diet', which consisted exclusively of life-enhancing pills and supplements. Food in its crude form – messy, inconvenient and time-consuming – was set to become a thing of the past.

As well as a cocktail of nourishing additives, many convenience foods contained high proportions of fat and sugar. Once again, this knowledge was generally received with nods of approval because, as everybody knew, fat and sugar were good for you. They gave you energy on which to do a day's work. They were rationed during the war – therefore they *had* to be good for you. The result, however, was an unprecedented outbreak of mass obesity. But rather than concede that convenience foods were responsible, government dieticians blamed the problem on bread and potatoes. Concerned about their burgeoning waistlines, people everywhere replaced unhealthy real bread with Nimble – an airy and guiltless approximation of bread that necessitated eating double the quantity to compensate for its lack of substance. And thankfully the potato hazard was nipped in the bud with the advent of Cadbury's Smash – freeze-dried instant potato resurrected with boiling water to form a paste that was judged to taste not only identical to real mashed potato, but better. Our belief in the power of science to improve our quality of life was beyond question. And as a generation we felt privileged to bear witness to such momentous times.

It was against this backdrop that I became a chef.

I'd applied for the job at The Mute Swan not because I wanted to cook for a living, but out of desperation. I could think of no other way of escaping my domestic predicament. Initially, it was the live-in element that had clinched it. But now, in the light of my successful interview, to my surprise I was beginning to warm to the idea of a career in cooking. Who knows, one day I might even appear on television like Fanny Craddock? The morning after my interview I packed a suitcase, loaded my dilapidated Austin A30 with my few worthy possessions and left to begin a new life. I would never spend another night beneath my father's roof.

CHAPTER 2

I'd been asked to report for work at 8 am. It was a Sunday and the restaurant was eerily quiet. Unable to get a reply at the front door, I ventured to the rear of the building. I peered cautiously around the kitchen entrance, suitcase in hand.

'Yes, what do you want?' It was more of a challenge than a question. The man who spoke was clearly as startled by my arrival as I was by his appearance: in one hand he wielded a meat cleaver and in the other an indeterminate fleshy object that might have been an internal organ, clutched in a fold of a disturbingly blood-stained apron. Stretched full length on a table behind him was a partially disembowelled deer, its head lolling at a macabre angle above a blood-filled metal pail.

'Erm, I'm meant to be starting work here today. My name's Kent...Kent Austin? I was told to report to Mark, the head chef.'

'I *am* Mark the head chef. Starting work? As what?'

Mark did not conform to my notion of what a head chef should look like. For some reason I'd expected to be welcomed by a distinguished middle-aged man dressed in starched chef's whites and a tall hat. Mark, by contrast, was wearing a tie-dye granddad vest and purple cotton loon pants, and, unshaven and dishevelled, he looked anything but distinguished. 'Trainee chef?' I ventured.

'Are you sure? Nobody mentioned it to *me*. I'm always the last fucking person to be told anything in this place. I've already got the shift covered,' he snapped, running a blooded hand through his hair and pushing his spectacles further up the bridge of his nose, from where they immediately slipped down again. 'I can't fucking believe this.'

'Would you like me to go away and come back later?' I said, crushed.

'I don't fucking believe it, I really don't.' Mark, who was in his mid twenties and bore an uncanny resemblance to Elton John, complete with premature bald patch, reached for a half-burnt cigarette that was balanced on the corner of a windowsill and took a deep lungful of smoke. 'Well, as you're here I suppose you'd better stay. You can clear this lot up for a start. Here, put this on. You'll need it.'

Mark tossed me an apron and went back to his work, shaking his head and muttering expletives under his breath. He was slashing skilfully at the viscera of the deer with a boning knife, apparently in an effort to detach it from its

The Mousse and the Man from the Michelin

abdominal cavity. Without warning, a glistening bundle of purple intestines broke free from the carcass and began to slide floor-wards.

'Quick, grab the bucket and catch the guts as they drop out,' ordered Mark, while pushing forward with his forearms in an effort to hold the intestines in place. A warm effluvia of blood and excrement assaulted the back of my throat making me want to vomit, a sensation that was intensified by the humidity in the kitchen.

'Where shall I put my suitcase?'

'What's in it?'

'Well, my things...clothes – '

The viscera could hang on no longer. Like the stillborn birth of some otherworldly creature, the deer's innards slithered intact from its abdominal cavity and, with a moist slap, hit the floor.

'Shit! Grab the bucket! What, you living in as well? Well I don't know where they're going to put you. There are no rooms free, you know. I don't fucking believe it.'

And so I began work at The Mute Swan. As inductions went it was rudimentary and, with hindsight, didn't bode well for the future, but I knew no different.

My first job that Sunday lunchtime – indeed, my first ever task as a chef – was to clean up the intestinal spillage. Armed only with a mop and bucket, I was unsure where to begin. I poked ineffectually at the carnage on the floor with the head of my mop, while still fending off an urge to retch. *Surely Mark didn't expect me to pick up a heap of raw guts with my bare hands?*

'Is there a shovel or something I can use?' I asked.

'No. Just pick it up.'

'Rubber gloves, perhaps?'

'No.' Mark had his back to me. He was stabbing impatiently at something in the bottom of a vast blackened pot that was simmering on the stove.

'Then how do I –?'

'Just pick it up. Like this.' With a hiss of irritation, Mark spun on his heel and manhandled the offending mess from floor to bucket in one deft sequence, before wiping his hands down the flanks of his apron. 'You won't last five minutes in this job if you're a squeamish type,' he said, shaking his head despondently. 'I don't fucking believe it. I really don't.'

I wondered whether Mark's seemingly open-ended capacity for incredulity was reserved for me alone, or if it was borne of some more deeply ingrained disillusionment. Ei-

The Mousse and the Man from the Michelin

ther way, I had the uneasy feeling that I'd already failed some crucial test.

My first shift at The Mute Swan could not be described as a success.

Following my feeble encounter with the deer's intestines, I was assigned to vegetable peeling duties. The peeling machine was housed beneath an open-sided lean-to at the rear of the kitchen, sandwiched between a row of foul-smelling swill bins and a half-dead privet hedge. It was a crude contraption, comprising a barrel-shaped steel cylinder with a lid at the top and a ridged rotating disc at the base, driven by a powerful electric motor. The inside of the cylinder was lined with a harsh abrasive coating, designed to denude any root vegetable of its skin in a matter of moments.

'And while you're waiting for each load to finish peeling, you can get on with scaling the sea bass,' said Mark. 'No standing around. Think time management. I want to see a sense of urgency, got it?'

'Yes, got it,' I said. Although I was far from certain that I had. Next to the peeling machine was an outdoor sink, beside which, stacked on a table, were several large fish. Gaping mouthed, blank eyed, they glinted silver in the morning sun.

'Just grab it by the tail and scrape downwards with the

blade of the knife towards the head, like this,' said Mark. He struck deftly at the fish's flank while a thousand translucent scales exploded into the air with every stroke of his knife. Insistently sticky, the scales adhered to any surface with which they made contact, and in a matter of seconds our clothes and skin were coated with a crusty film of circular discs which, in their near invisibility, resembled so many lost contact lenses. 'Keep the tap running to wash off the scales as you scrape, and be careful not to cut into the skin or you'll spoil the flesh. Here, you have a go.' Mark stood back, arms folded.

To my relief, I proved quite adept at fish scaling, and by the time I'd completed my first sea bass Mark seemed satisfied that I could cope unsupervised. He then gave me a perfunctory lesson in operating the peeling machine. My task, while physically demanding, was hardly complicated. Filling the machine involved lifting a fifty-six-pound bag of potatoes to chest level and pouring half the contents into a hole at the top. Then one simply turned on a tap which fed water via a hose into the cylinder to act as a lubricant, flung the switch and waited, opening the lid periodically to check progress. Apart from this there was nothing to do, other than open the door of the machine and allow the freshly peeled potatoes to tumble out into a bucket. The potatoes were considered ready when all the skin had been removed but not,

The Mousse and the Man from the Michelin

Mark warned, the eyes. While tempting, as it saved time digging them out later, waiting for the eyes to disappear was wasteful, as they frequently extended deep into the potato. Keen to learn the finer points of food preparation, I immediately made a note to this effect in a small notepad that I'd brought with me for the purpose. Mark gave me an odd look but said nothing.

Satisfied that my first load of potatoes was revolving safely in the peeler, and with Mark returned to the kitchen, I continued with my task of fish scaling. In the light of Mark's advice, I made a special effort to move as quickly as possible. *What was the term he'd used? 'Sense of urgency', that was it.* Well, I'd go one better than that; I'd be a time-managing, multi-tasking human dynamo.

The French for sea bass is *loup de mer* – 'wolf of the sea'. I've no idea how it earned such an intimidating name but, as I was about to discover, it is indisputably a fish to be reckoned with. Mark had neglected to mention that the sea bass is armed with a phalanx of vicious needle-like spines ranged along the central part of its body. When fully extended the upper row of spines resembles a fan-like sail, several centimetres in height. But when folded against the body the spines are all but invisible to the unsuspecting eye. Midway through scaling my second fish, a hidden spine entered the middle finger of my right hand on the downward thrust, penetrating deeply into the fleshy area between nail and finger tip. (I later discovered that this is a part of the body favoured for attention by professional torturers, selected for its potential to inflict maximum prolonged agony.)

Like some demented Morris dancer, I hopped, jigged and gyrated on the spot, my body convulsed with pain. My fingertip was growing visibly larger by the second, as a pinprick stream of blood pumped rhythmically from my wound. In an effort to stem the flow, I wrapped my injured finger in a corner of my apron and squeezed tightly. After what seemed like several minutes, the bleeding had subsided sufficiently for me to inspect the damage. The tip of my finger had doubled in size, turned purple and continued to pulsate, but apart from this I was unscathed. I was, however, faced with another altogether less soluble problem: during my lapse of concentration I'd somehow managed to cleave a deep incision into the body of the sea bass. I was reflecting on the implications of this discovery when I remembered the contents of the peeler. And something wasn't right. The familiar rumbling sound of the potatoes as they tumbled inside the cylinder had diminished to a feeble purr. I opened the lid of the machine and, with trepidation, peered inside. Where once had been half a sack of sturdy King Edwards, each the size of my fist, there now revolved a small handful of perfectly spherical white marbles, ranging in size from a

The Mousse and the Man from the Michelin

walnut to a pea. The remainder of the potatoes had disappeared without a trace, ground to a pulp and flushed away down the drain.

My first instinct was to destroy the evidence. Glancing furtively over my shoulder, I poured the remaining potatoes from the sack into the mouth of the machine, engulfing what little remained of the previous batch. All being well, Mark need never know what had happened.

I returned to the kitchen with my freshly peeled potatoes. Looking into the pot, Marked seemed puzzled. 'You weren't listening. I said peel the whole bag,' he said.

'This is the whole bag.'

'That never is a whole bag of potatoes. And what the hell have you done to your hand?' Mark was staring aghast at my purple throbbing finger, shaking his head in disbelief. 'We've got sixty covers booked for lunch. This will never make enough roast potatoes to feed them. Go and peel the rest.'

I returned lamely to my post at the peeling machine and my now empty bag. The only way out of my predicament was to find another bag of potatoes. I was in luck. To the side of the lean-to was a shed, stacked with assorted bags of potatoes. My original potatoes had been labelled King Edward, but try as I might I was unable to identify another such bag. There were, however, several bags of a different variety called Jersey Royal. Surely one variety of potato is much the same as another, I reasoned. And besides, this was an emergency. I heaved a bag off the top of the pile and proceeded to fill the machine.

Had I not cunningly disguised the Jersey Royals by burying them beneath what remained of the King Edwards (to my dismay I'd discovered the former was a much smaller variety of potato), my subterfuge would have been exposed. But Mark was clearly under pressure of his own, surging around the kitchen, bouncing dynamically from task to task: one moment chopping onions with machine-like dexterity, the next making pancakes in four pans simultaneously – like some multi-limbed Hindu deity. So as it was, he simply instructed me to trim, cut and par-boil the potatoes in preparation for roasting, with barely a glance in my direction.

With the potatoes roasting safely in the oven, I was now assigned to pot washing duty, a task that demanded clearing the contents of two large sinks, each filled to collapsing point with an unruly stack of pots, pans and sundry cooking utensils. Next to the sinks was a work-top, also piled high with burnt and grease-encrusted pots. I had no idea where or how to begin, for whenever I attempted to move any item from the pile, the entire edifice threatened to collapse around me, and there was no space to spread out. Noting my

The Mousse and the Man from the Michelin

paralysis, Mark came grudgingly to my aid. 'The first rule of working in a professional kitchen is to use your initiative,' he said. As if by way of a demonstration, Mark then proceeded at superhuman speed to unload the contents of the left-hand sink onto the floor. When he'd finished, the entire floor area of the scullery – a small, windowless room annexed to the main kitchen – was obscured by pots and utensils, me standing at the centre, a wretched human island. 'There, now you can get started,' said Mark. It's easy when you know how, isn't it?'

To frustrate matters, by this time the waitresses had begun to show up for work (always waitresses, never waiters – Gerald made a rule of employing exclusively female staff front-of-house; it was also stipulated in his job advertisements that only 'attractive girls' of 'good breeding' need apply). They were now forced to tip-toe their way, tut-tutting and snickering through the chaos on the floor to reach the entrance to the dining room. I felt ridiculous.

I may have been in a state of shock at the prospect of the task before me, or perhaps it was just my routinely lethargic approach to physical exertion. Whatever the reason, some thirty minutes later I'd made no detectable impact on the washing up. Predictably, it wasn't long before I once again attracted Mark's ire.

Kent Austin

'The second rule of working in a professional kitchen,' said Mark, leaning over my shoulder and fixing me with a dangerous smile, 'is dynamism. And, if you don't mind my saying, so far today you've been about as dynamic as a sloth on barbiturates. What has just taken you thirty minutes would have taken me five. Now, I want to see you scrubbing that pan as if your life depends upon it because I assure you, as far as the life of your job goes, it does. We've a full house for lunch, the first customers will be placing their orders in less than an hour, and you haven't even started on your *mise en place* yet.'

I was just wondering what a meezongplas was (a type of fish, perhaps?) when a man appeared at the scullery door. A few years older than me, he had an unwashed, dishevelled appearance and smelled strongly of stale sweat. He was dressed in greying chef's whites.

'Kent, this is Kevin,' said Mark. 'Kevin, meet Kent. Kent, Kevin was your short-lived predecessor. Kevin, Kent's taking your job.' Mark sounded so bored it was a miracle he reached the end of the sentence.

If anyone could accurately be described as gormless, it was Kevin. In fact, if there were ever such a thing as a gormlessness contest (not unimaginable in an age of reality TV), then Kevin would be a shoo-in for gold. Stooped, gawky

The Mousse and the Man from the Michelin

and tongue-tied, his every mannerism seemed stalled somewhere between confusion and self-pity. One's first impulse was to feel sorry for him, but it was a sentiment that was swift to pass.

'What d'yu mean he's taking my job?' said Kevin, looking incredulously from Mark to myself and back again, as if expecting us to burst out laughing and let him in on the joke. 'I ain't bleedin' left yet.'

'Technically speaking, no,' said Mark, 'but – '

'But what?' said Kevin, apparently on the edge of tears.

Surreptitiously catching my attention, Mark raised his eyebrows, as if to say, '*You can see what we're dealing with here. Just humour him.*' (At least that's how I interpreted it.) Eager to win Mark's approval, I reciprocated with what I intended to be a knowing smile, although in my enthusiasm I suspect it might have come across more as a mocking sneer.

'You taking the piss?' said Kevin, noticing my expression. 'What's going on?'

Kevin had one of those unfortunate mouths that seem to be populated with too many teeth. As he spoke he generated an abnormally large volume of saliva which, if he continued speaking long enough, would begin to escape from the corners of his lips, forcing him to wipe each cheek repeatedly with the back of his hand.

'It's not like that, Kevin,' said Mark. 'Nobody's taking the piss. Gerald just hadn't bothered to tell anyone that Kent was starting today, that's all. Now calm down. It's not as if you didn't know this was coming. Anyway, laughable as it may seem to have the blind leading the blind, we need you here to show Kent the ropes. You're still on the payroll so you may as well do something for your money. You can start by helping him with the pot wash. So just get over it, alright?'

'Yeah, well...'

Cowed into submission, Kevin joined me at the sink and proceeded aggressively to scrub at a pristine non-stick baking sheet with a pad of wire wool. Somehow between us we managed to clear the backlog of washing up. I was left grimy and exhausted, yet my day had scarcely begun. With service approaching, Mark instructed Kevin to take me through the basics of *mise en place,* meaning literally – Kevin had been proud to enlighten me – 'putting in place'. On this occasion the 'putting in place' involved nothing more complicated than preparing a large quantity of salad and vegetables, but the very foreignness of the term invested the task with a special importance, and I jotted it down in my notepad – m-e-e-z-o-n-g-p-l-a-s (it was the first of many misspelled

The Mousse and the Man from the Michelin

and mostly redundant French culinary terms that I was to acquire over the coming months).

Apart from the occasional muttered instruction from Kevin, we worked side-by-side, chopping and slicing in virtual silence. Eventually, if only to be polite, I decided to risk a question. 'So how long have you worked here?' I asked breezily.

'A month,' said Kevin, clearly still wounded, although seeming to invite further enquiry.

'Is that all? So why are you leaving so soon?'

'I would have been gone before now, but nobody answered the advert for the job, at least not until you came along.'

'That can't be right. Gerald told me at my interview that he'd had lots of applicants.'

'Did he? Yeah, well, he hasn't. He told me he'd only had one reply, and that's you. That's why I'm still here, isn't it. There's been no one else to take on my job. Did he ask you what your star sign is?'

'Yes, he did.'

'Yeah, he did that to me too...said we'd get on well, 'coz our signs are right.'

'And do you?'

'Do I what?'

'Get on well?'

'Yeah, really well, as a matter of fact. I like it here.'

'Then why are you leaving?'

'They made me join the army.'

'Join the army? Who made you join the army?'

'Mr Golightly said I should join the army. He drove me to Aldershot Barracks and made me sign up for five years with the Para Brigade. Then he drove me back here again. I report for duty in Aldershot next month.'

'Did you *want* to join the army?'

Kevin shrugged noncommittally. 'Never thought about it, I suppose.'

My final task before service was to whip the cream. This involved pouring a gallon of whipping cream into a free-standing mixing machine, fitted with something called a balloon whisk, and watching over it like a hawk until it attained precisely the right texture: too little whipping would leave the cream limp and inconsistent, I was informed, while a moment too long and the cream would curdle. Mark entrusted my tuition in this respect to Kevin; apparently it was

The Mousse and the Man from the Michelin

one of the few skills he had managed to acquire during his spectacularly brief career as a chef. Considering his ignominious status, Kevin took an impressive pride in his role as mentor, hovering at my shoulder and scrutinising my every move. We'd just thrown the switch on the mixing machine when there was a roar from the opposite end of the kitchen. Mark, it seemed, had encountered a problem.

'Kent, come here, please.' Mark's voice was calm, yet at the same time oddly unsettling. Fearing the worst, I made my way sheepishly to the end of the kitchen, Kevin trailing diligently in my wake like some hapless court jester. Mark was stood over the oven, staring in disbelief at the contents of a roasting tray, as if doubting his own sanity. A small purple vein pulsed rhythmically at his temple.

'These aren't King Edwards,' said Mark. 'These are new potatoes. You can't roast new potatoes. They're all mixed in with the old potatoes. How did this happen?'

Mark had a point. Whereas the King Edwards had acquired a crispy-golden crust to be proud of, the Jersey Royals looked like giant brown suppositories – hard, oily and glassy-smooth. Faced with no alternative, I provided Mark with a concise account of the events and thought processes that had led to my present position, convinced that once he knew the facts I would be vindicated.

'But why?' beseeched Mark. 'Why the hell didn't you just tell me what had happened? Then we could have done something about it, but now it's too late.'

'I was, erm, using my initiative?'

'Your what?'

'You did say it was the first rule of working in a professional kitchen – '

'Are you trying to be funny?'

'Yeah, coz it ain't funny,' chipped in Kevin, who, clearly smelling blood, had positioned himself strategically at Mark's elbow.

'Shut the fuck up, Kevin,' said Mark. 'I'll deal with this – '

As luck or misfortune would have it, I was rescued from the obligation to explain myself further by the occurrence of an unrelated but equally ill-timed incident. Mark had frozen mid-sentence. Turning around I followed his horrified line of vision to the opposite end of the kitchen to where what can only be described as a dairy-based tempest was raging with full fury. In the distraction of the moment, Kevin and I had neglected to watch over the whipping cream. When cream separates it loses its unified consistency and breaks down into its component parts – known to cheese makers as

The Mousse and the Man from the Michelin

curds and whey, but more recognisable to the layman as butter and milk. An industrial food mixer operates at hundreds of revolutions per minute, and now with each turn of its mighty whisk it propelled a high-velocity shower of greasy popcorn-shaped missiles halfway across the kitchen. They collided with walls, ceiling, refrigerators and everything else in their 360 degree path, lingering momentarily before oozing slowly floor-ward, like pus escaping from a wound.

'Now look what you've gone and done,' said Kevin, jabbing a forefinger into my ribs.

'Look, I'm really sorry about this,' I said, turning to Mark.

'Well don't just stand there,' said Mark, 'go and switch the bloody thing off.'

'*Me* switch it off?' I said, reluctant to face the inevitable dousing that would result from getting within six paces of the machine. 'But it was Kevin who switched it on.'

'Yeah, but it was you what left it,' said Kevin.

'No, you left it,' I said, feeling decidedly picked upon. 'Mark asked to see me, not you. You should have stayed to watch over it.'

'Yeah, but it was your responsibility. I'm just your mentor.'

'Kevin, you couldn't mentor a fucking lemming to take its own life,' said Mark. 'Now go and switch it off before the whole kitchen gets swamped.'

'I'm not getting anywhere near it,' said Kevin stubbornly. 'I'll get smothered.'

'Jesus fucking aitch Christ, it's like working with Laurel and Hardy,' said Mark, taking off his apron. 'I'll switch it off myself then.'

Wielding his apron before him like a toreador's cape, Mark charged full tilt at the out-of-control machine. It was at this exact moment that an unsuspecting and sartorially pristine Gerald entered through the kitchen door, directly into the line of fire. In a noble display of self-sacrifice and lightning-fast thinking – and with a *pas de deux* worthy of Nureyev himself – Mark instantly positioned his apron between Gerald and the machine, allowing himself in the process to become inundated. All went well for a moment, until Mark's glasses became too spattered to see out of. Gerald, meanwhile, had clearly decided that retreat was the best option. But as he turned to make his escape he collided with the back of a disorientated Mark who, rendered blind, was now left staggering in a confused circle. Deprived of the cover of Mark's apron, Gerald took the full impact of the curds and whey, his tailored cashmere blazer receiving a

The Mousse and the Man from the Michelin

particular pasting. With nothing now left to lose, he strode coolly up to the mixing machine, heedless of the soaking he was receiving, and switched it off. The ensuing calm was eerie. The only sound was the steady pitter-patter of curdled cream as it detached itself from the ceiling and landed on the floor. It was Gerald who broke the silence.

'Goodness me, that was invigorating. I don't suppose you've a towel have you, Marko? I'd better spruce myself up a bit. I'm taking orders in half an hour.' Gerald spoke as if he'd suffered but the mildest inconvenience. 'Actually, I'd only dropped by to let you know we've a new trainee chef starting today.' Gerald dabbed ineffectively at his tie with the corner of a dampened tea towel. 'It had completely slipped my mind. Can't recall his name, though...Ken somebody? Anyway, I hope he works out for you.'

***

Twelve hours later I'm sat on the edge of my bed. It's past midnight. I ache all over. My head is buzzing with exhaustion and I can barely summon a coherent thought. There's a part of me that wants to burst into tears, but it's all too much effort. Instead I find myself transfixed by a framed print that is hung on the wall above the washbasin. Executed in muted shades of pink, it depicts a teenage girl walking through a sun-dappled arbour, chiffon-clad, golden haired, a doe-eyed puppy frolicking at her bare heels. I find the scene oddly comforting. The print is complemented by a pink floral chintz bedspread with matching curtains and lampshade. On the dressing table sits a jewellery box which, when opened, strikes up a rendition of *Dance of the Sugar Plum Fairy*, while a pop-up ballerina pirouettes in time to the music. On the bed, wearing a tasselled night cap, its head propped up on a pair of pillows (pink-frilled), is a large acrylic teddy bear, which on closer inspection turns out to be a pyjama case.

My suitcase lies on the floor in front of me, open but unpacked – I've been told not to make myself too at home as my room is only temporary, although I'm unsure what being 'too at home' involves in practice. Mark had been right about there being no spare rooms, at least not of the right kind; staff accommodation at The Mute Swan is segregated, with 'boys'' and 'girls'' rooms being situated at opposite ends of the building, each with separate access, bathroom and toilet. I've been given a girl's room, with a view to relocating to Kevin's former room as soon as he leaves to join the army. I've yet to visit the 'boys'' end of the building, but having spent most of the last day in Kevin's unwashed proximity, the thought of living in his newly vacated space is a prospect that only serves to deepen my gloom. (Rather ominously, I've been told that I am to receive a 'decorating allowance' which will enable me to 'spruce the room up a bit' when I move in.)

It's only when I'm awakened by a persistent gentle tapping at my door that I realise I've fallen asleep.

'Who is it?' I spring to my feet, disorientated. For some reason I'm speaking in a stage whisper.

'Eeez me, Betsie. Opon ze door.' I do as I'm told. Betsie is holding a bottle and a pair of shot glasses, her pneumatic contours swathed in a scarlet velvet kaftan. 'A vilcom drink for our rizing star.' I stand motionless, lamely clinging to the door latch, unsure how to respond. 'Vell, aren't you going to invite me in? Don't vorry, I von't bite you.' Betsie's bosom heaves in time with her words.

'Erm, it's very late,' I say. 'I have to be up for work at nine – '

'Yes, yes. Von quick drink and you vill shlep like a baby. Cannot be all vork and no play, ja? Betsie sidesteps neatly past me and enters the room. 'Sviss schnapps,' she announces, 'ze very best.' Placing the glasses on the dressing table, she uncorks the bottle and pours two generous measures.

Forty-five minutes and three glasses of schnapps later I'm consumed by a balmy glow of wellbeing. Where once they loomed large in my psyche, the troubles of the day have receded to become little more than a distant memory. And despite having just worked a fifteen-hour double shift I'm feeling surprisingly...something. I can't yet put my finger on it.

'You must to understand,' said Betsie, 'Mark is a man on the hedge.' Betsie is embarked on the ambitious project of delivering a character sketch for each member of The Mute Swan's staff, ostensibly for my benefit, although she appears to be relishing her task. So far we haven't got beyond Mark. It promises to be a long night.

'On the edge of what?' I ask. My mouth is beginning to feel numb. I'm conscious not to slur my words.

'On the hedge of a nervous brekdown, zat is vot. Ee'z not coping. He vorks too hard. Zat Gerald vorks him too hard. And zere's vorse...' As she speaks, Betsie leans forward conspiratorially, her breath an eye-watering cocktail of alcohol and cigarettes, with a powerful back-note of garlic. 'You must to be telling no von, but that Tabitha Manning-Smythe is a nymph armagnac. There! I've shed it. Let's speak of it no more.'

'No, let's not,' I agree, nodding solemnly. Perhaps I've missed something during the course of Betsie's monologue, but I have no idea who Tabitha Manning-Smythe is. Though I suspect I'm about to find out.

The Mousse and the Man from the Michelin

'Zat Tabitha is a souhund whore, you know. I vorn you now for your good. She is living in ze next door voom to you, and you are to be caring. Zat voman is a draecks votze bitch. I tell you everysing vun day.' For reasons best known to herself Betsie throws back her head and laughs. Although it translates as more of a groaning sound, like a dowager being lowered into a hot bath. 'But enough said alveady. Instead von last drink for our little rizing star, ja?' Betsie raises the bottle of schnapps entreatingly.

'Well, maybe just one more. What did you say this stuff is called? It goes down very easily.'

'Pear schnapps, ze very best,' said Betsie, lighting the most recent in an unbroken chain of cigarettes, 'made in my home village in Svitzerland. It killed my father. He died ze most horrible death.'

'Killed?' I raise my glass of schnapps to the light as if somehow it might reveal its death-inducing properties.

'Killed as a dodo.'

'Pear schnapps killed your father? No, that's terrible. He drank himself to death?'

'It vos right zare before my eyes. I vos a child of eight years. Papa vos cutting ze grass in our garden vis a lawn cutter, brrrrm, brrrrm, and he gets sirsty, so he goes down into ze cellar for a drink of schnapps. It is a bright and a sunny day and ven he enters ze cellar he is blind in the darkness. He picks up ze bottle of schnapps, places it to his lips and drinks. But, and zis is ze dreadful part, it vosn't schnapps in ze bottle. In his blindedness, Papa has picked up ze vong bottle. Kaput!'

'What was in the bottle?'

'Vos terrible. He coms from the cellar op again into ze garden. His mouth is foaming like a crazy dog, and he is spinning around and around, screaming like a crazy cat. And it gets vorse.' Betsie pauses for dramatic effect, her face contorted, apparently in an imitation of her father's dying rictus. 'Zen blood comes running out from his mouth and out from his nose. Ven I see him, I cry, "Papa! Papa! Votever is ze matter?" But Papa cannot to speak. He just volls his eyes around und makes ein fearful googling sound. He's falling to his knees...clawing at hiz throat. I ran to fetch Mama, and ven ve return Papa vos dead. Still on his knees. Killed as a stone. Vos terrible. Mama never recovered.'

Betsie falls silent. The only sound is of my alarm clock, ticking on the dressing table. Outside in the distance a fox barks. Finally I can bear the weight of the silence no longer. 'I'm so sorry,' I say, 'no child should ever have to go through that.' I imagine the same fate befalling my own fa-

The Mousse and the Man from the Michelin

ther, but, finding myself warming to the idea, quickly dismiss the thought from my mind.

'Oh, ve learn to live viz our pains.' Betsie empties the final dregs of the schnapps into our glasses. Her face is flushed and glistening with beads of perspiration.

'You never told me what was in the bottle.'

'Didn't I? Oh, it vos veed killer,' says Betsie, matter of factly. 'Deadly veed killer...I leave now. I feel blötterli blau.' Betsie drains her glass and rises unsteadily to her feet. 'And vemember, you must beehive ven you is living op ze girlz' end.'

'Beehive?'

'Yes, beehive. You must to beehive yourself. Not to be naughty and try to be playing vis de girls, eh? Vogle! Vogle!'

'No, no, of course not.' I feel myself blush with embarrassment.

'And no playing viz your little glied ven you're in the bed this night.' Betsie sways as she speaks. 'If you need anysing you vill find me on ze sird room on ze landing. Anysing at all. But mind zerefore you do not to go knocking on zat futzgsicht bitch Tabitha's door. She vill veck your life, you must to understand.'

Kent Austin

'Thanks for the advice. I'll bear it in mind.' I'm having trouble focusing on Betsie's face. None of her features will remain still.

When Betsie has left I fall back heavily onto the bed and close my eyes. Very slowly at first, the room begins to revolve.

I was woken the next morning by an aggressive hammering on my door.

'Kent, you awake? Come on, it's nine thirty. You in there, Kent?' It was Mark. The hammering continued. As I raised my head from the pillow I became simultaneously aware of three equally distressing facts. The first was that I had been sleeping fully clothed (these were the same T-shirt and jeans that I'd been working in throughout the previous day); the second was that at some point during the night I'd vomited copiously onto my pillow. One side of my head was caked with congealed sick, and something seemed to be lodged in my left ear.

'Kent, you up yet?' Bang! Bang! Bang!

'Yeah, yeah, I'm awake. Just give me a second.' My head pounded in time with my words.

'I'll expect you downstairs in the kitchen in five minutes.'

The Mousse and the Man from the Michelin

'Yeah, I'll be right down. Overslept...sorry...sorry –' Mark grunted and departed.

My third realisation was that I was suffering from a hangover. It's been said that our first hangover is the worst we'll ever experience. As a hangover virgin I of course had no idea of what to expect; no conception of what creeping horrors the day held in store for me. Hopping briskly out of bed, my first thought was how to prioritise the next five minutes. But, as any practised drinker will confirm, hopping briskly – out of bed, or indeed anywhere else – is incompatible with the demands of a hangover. No sooner had I attained a vertical position than I was struck by an urgent need to vomit. I made it to the washbasin just in time. I retched painfully for a moment or two, but little else happened. Clearly I'd voided the contents of my stomach during the night. Once the spasms had subsided, however, I felt much less nauseous, although my head continued to pound. I was clearly on the mend. I gulped down a large glass of water, held my head under the tap to freshen my fetid hair, pulled on a clean T-shirt and made my way downstairs to the kitchen.

I arrived to find Mark leaning over a table busily writing, cigarette in hand, a large wine glass full of steaming coffee at his elbow. He was poring over a bulging ring-folder, filled with hand-written menus, next to which was an unruly heap of delivery notes, paperwork and assorted dockets.

'You're not getting off to the best start, are you? What happened?' Mark spoke without looking up.

Intuiting that I may be in politically sensitive territory, I resisted telling the truth. 'Sorry, I forgot to set my alarm.'

'Go and find Kevin in the preparation room. He's pheasant plucking. Ask him to show you how it's done. Luckily it doesn't demand much intelligence, or you'd both be up shit creek.'

The preparation room, or 'prep' room, as it was known informally, occupied the ground floor of a medieval flint cottage located at the rear of the garden (said to be so ancient that it is mentioned in the Domesday Book). Upon entering I misjudged the height of the door, which appeared to be designed for midgets, and struck my head on the top of the frame. I groaned with pain.

'You won't do that twice,' said a voice. The speaker emerged from the shadows of the cottage's interior, hand outstretched. 'How do you do. Royston Drax-Boyce, sous chef.' He had the oddest of accents – like a lorry driver from Dartford attempting an impersonation of Noël Coward, and failing badly. 'But you can call me Roy.'

'Oh, I was looking for Kevin, actually,' I said, pawing at

The Mousse and the Man from the Michelin

my head and attempting to recover my composure. I shook Roy's hand. It was damp, sticky and very strong. 'Mark asked me to find him.'

'Oh, he'll still be asleep,' said Roy, matter of factly. 'I haven't had the heart to tell Mark yet. Last time it happened he blew a fuse and got him out of bed with the aid of a bucket of water. And that was three o'clock in the afternoon – on a late shift and still he couldn't get out of bed in time for work. Lazy little shit. The water did the trick, though.' Roy smiled, shaking his head, as if savouring some deeply satisfying memory. On first impressions, he was the opposite of Mark in every way. He was tall – about six-three or four – with a small, pointed head and disproportionately narrow shoulders. By masculine standards, he was endowed with unusually thick thighs and a fulsome bottom. From top to toe, his body resembled a narrow pear. And unlike Mark, he was wearing chef's whites. All things considered, Roy was much closer to my pre-formed notion of how a real chef should look and behave.

The prep room served as a secondary kitchen and storeroom. A row of refrigerators and freezers flanked one wall of the L-shaped room, blocking out most of the small amount of daylight that penetrated through an unseen window behind. Opposite the refrigerators was a multi-tiered, wall-mounted shelf, stacked with sundry dry goods; next to the shelf was a gas stove with oven. Around a corner, in the foot of the 'L', was a recess that housed a sink and a vast, rectangular refectory-sized table. Arrayed on the table was a bewildering variety of game and seafood, most of which I would have been unable to name. The one exception being squid, which I recognised on account of having recently seen the film *20,000 Leagues Under the Sea,* starring Kirk Douglas and a man-eating giant squid. Presuming my ignorance, Roy proceeded to talk me through the produce on the table. It was around this time when the first wave of nausea began to stir in my gut.

'So here we have pheasants,' said Roy. 'The colourful birds are the cocks, and the drab ones hens. Then there are snipe...quail...hare...rabbits – the hare are the ones with the larger feet and ears and, unlike rabbits, their flesh is actually red. It's served with a sauce thickened with its own blood. And here we have woodcock, traditionally served with a liver pate seasoned with its own shit – tastes better than it sounds. Next to the woodcock are partridge – red and grey, the red being the larger of the two breeds. The younger and more succulent birds are distinguished by the shortness of their spur. First class served with braised red cabbage and gratin potatoes, I might add. Are you keeping up?'

'Yes, well, just about, thanks.' I was scribbling frantically in my notepad, but in my fragile state failing to get the

The Mousse and the Man from the Michelin

words down coherently.

'You are keen, I must say. I've never seen a commis chef with a notebook before. And now we come to squid...oysters...scallops...clams...turbot...brill...skate...lobsters...John Dory...sardines...live eels...'

As he spoke, Roy patiently identified each item in turn with the tip of a knife. I found his monologue strangely soothing. Although it did nothing to relieve my growing urge to be sick. It was the sight of a boxful of writhing eels that tipped the balance. Unable to resist a moment longer, I lunged for the sink, an involuntary projectile of vomit arcing before me like a liquid rainbow. Burying my head in the basin I continued to retch, spasm upon violent spasm. I was ejecting mostly water – flecked with the now depleted remains of my previous night's supper which included – somewhat mysteriously, as I had no recollection of eating it – a significant quantity of sweetcorn. As my spasms began slowly to subside, I became aware of a voice...a female voice.

'And this is where your buffet will be prepared prior to serving...Oh my goodness, who on earth are you?'

I raised my head from the basin to be greeted by four faces staring down at me – one of which I recognised as Roy's – each registering a different expression, ranging in degree from bewilderment to anguish.

'Oh, hello, Arabella,' said Roy. 'This is Kent. He's new here. Kent, this is Arabella Golightly.'

Arabella surveyed me suspiciously, while ignoring my outstretched hand. Slim, elegantly dressed, late twenties, honey-blonde hair cut into a bob, an intimidating glint in her green eyes; I intuited she was someone to be taken seriously. 'Are you sure he's alright, Roy? He looks frightfully pallid,' she said, taking a step backwards and placing a cupped hand to her mouth.

'Oh, he's fine,' said Roy, 'just not used to the smell of well-hung game. It often happens with new chefs.'

'Well, if you're sure...' said Arabella doubtfully. She turned her back on me. 'Mr and Mrs Turner, I do apologise for that unfortunate distraction. Anyway, as I was saying, this is our sous chef, Roy. He would be taking charge of preparing your daughter's wedding breakfast. He's a very talented cook. Roy, do meet Mr and Mrs Turner. They're considering holding their daughter's wedding reception here next October. We were just having a tour of the restaurant and I was telling them all about you.'

'All good, I hope?' quipped Roy, grinning enthusiastically.

The Mousse and the Man from the Michelin

The Turners – a nervous couple in their mid sixties, he in a trilby hat and car coat, she in a crimplene twin set – remained pokerfaced.

'Anyway,' said Arabella, cutting short an awkward silence, 'we'll be moving on now. With this she ushered the Turners from the room, flapping her notebook before her like a goat herder with a stick, a frozen smile etched painfully across her face. 'And Roy and Kent, I'll speak with you both later.'

As soon as Arabella had steered her charges safely beyond earshot, Roy turned to me and laughed. 'I wouldn't want to be in your shoes when she gets back. She had a face like a baboon's arse. Just don't let on that you've got a hangover, that's all. It doesn't look good on your first day in the job.'

'Hangover? What makes you think – '

'Oh come on, no use you trying to hide it, you dark horse. Betsie's told me all about your little session last night, and how you couldn't get enough of the hard stuff – leading our woman folk astray with drink, if you please.' Roy assumed an expression of mock outrage.

'Well, it wasn't quite like that – '

'Your secret's safe with me. And don't worry, she hasn't

told Mark...well at least not yet. Although she probably will, she's such a bloody gossip. The thing is, you see...' Roy lowered his voice and tapped the side of his nose conspiratorially, 'I get all the girls, see, don't I, and it pisses Mark off a treat. And the last thing he needs is even more competition from the likes of you. So watch your step, that's all I'm saying.'

'But Betsie's old enough to be my mother...well almost.'

'It would take more than that to put Betsie off. She loves a chase does our Betsie. Besides, age-wise you couldn't be more compatible. You're both in your sexual prime, so it's a marriage made in heaven. I'd go for it. And I'll tell you now for the record, if that Mark gives you any trouble you just come and see me, right? I don't take any shit from him or anyone else around here. Are we clear? Then let's shake on it.' Roy held out his hand. As I made to respond, he evaded my grasp, placed the tip of his thumb on his nose and waggled his fingers in my direction, schoolboy-fashion. 'Anyway, if I can keep a secret, then so can you, if you know what I'm saying. I want to show you something, but mum's the word, okay? Quickly, go and lock the door. You'll be impressed.'

I did as I was asked, while Roy, retreating to the back of the room, opened the lid of a chest freezer and rummaged

The Mousse and the Man from the Michelin

inside. 'Just take a look at these,' said Roy proudly. 'Aren't they beauties?' The top layer of the freezer was stocked with an assortment of pre-packed vegetables and tubs of ice cream. Roy had removed these to uncover a mass of identical cylindrical parcels, made from rolled-up sheets of newspaper. There must have been a hundred or more, each the size of a small cucumber. He carefully removed one of the parcels and, placing it on the refectory table, unrolled it to reveal what appeared to be a dozen or so desiccated penises. 'There, I said you'd be impressed. So what do you think?'

'What are they?' I said, feeling stupid that I should have to ask.

'Lugworm, of course. I dug these with my own hands, down on the beach all hours of the day and night. The next layer down is rag worm. I reckon I've got enough in here to last six months.'

'And people eat these?'

'No, of course not. Would *you* eat one?'

'Then what do you do with them?'

'They're bait, you idiot...fishing bait. I'm an angler. You're obviously not an angler.'

'Wow, so you caught all of the fish on this table yourself?'

'Not as such,' said Roy, seemingly irritated that I'd asked, 'but it's early days. I'm saving up for a boat. I catch cod, mostly, off the beach. But obviously I can't put that on the menu because nobody would order it.'

'Why, doesn't it taste good?'

'No, because it's downmarket, you know, cod and chips and whatever. You can't serve stuff like that in a classy restaurant. I've never even tried it myself. Mind you, I don't eat fish full-stop, can't stand the stuff. For me it's all in the chase. I'm the hunter type, me. I never eat them. It's the same with women.'

'What, you mean you never eat them?' I said, attempting a joke and immediately regretting it.

'Eat what?'

'Er, women?'

Roy looked puzzled. 'Why would I want to eat a woman? No, I mean I enjoy the chase, like with a woman. But once I've had my way with them I pack my bag and move on. That's me all over, won't be pinned down. You know what I mean?' Roy took a cigarette from a packet and tossed it into the air. It described a perfect triple loop before landing neatly in his mouth, tip first. 'Now let's get these pheasants plucked before the day runs away with us. And remember

The Mousse and the Man from the Michelin

you're plucking pheasants, and not fucking peasants.' Sniggering at his joke, Roy looked to me for a response. I had the strong impression he'd made the joke before; possibly many times before. Eager not to cause offence, I laughed with as much enthusiasm as I could summon. I also sensed the creeping onset of another bout of nausea.

Under Roy's expert tutelage I spent the remainder of the morning grappling with the rudiments of food preparation. I learned, among other things, how to fillet and skin a fish – as well as the different techniques employed for preparing both flat and round fish. I learned how to clean and 'de-beard' mussels ready for cooking; how to stun and skin a live eel (a titanic struggle to the death); how to open an oyster using an oyster knife; how to kill a lobster 'instantly' by thrusting a skewer into its brain (A lobster's brain, being extremely small, is not easy to locate, and for a beginner can take several pitiless attempts.); and how to pull the innards intact from the body of a squid.

Extracting innards of one type or another was to form a major part of my daily routine during my formative years as a chef, and it was an activity that required much stuffing of hands up orifices – my least favourite of which was that of the game bird. It is of course the custom to serve most game well-matured, or 'hung'. In the case of birds, this involves hanging them by the neck at room temperature fully intact for anything from two to ten days prior to preparation and cooking, depending on the age and gender of the bird and one's fondness for eating putrid flesh. Grouse in particular is considered at its best when served very well-hung. For many years it was a tradition among chefs to serve it cooked rare and in an advanced state of decomposition ('green and mean', as it was known), although, due to modern food hygiene law, it's a practice that's fallen out of fashion – health and safety gone mad!

My task on this occasion was to pluck, decapitate and eviscerate 12 brace of pheasant and truss them with string ready for roasting. By the time I'd finished removing the birds' feathers – yanking them out in small tufts in such a way as not to damage the skin – the tips of my fingers were aching and red-raw. Yet it was the next part of the process that I found especially taxing (due not least to my hangover in progress). This involved enlarging the bird's anus with the point of a knife to a size where it is able to accommodate the fingers of one hand. The art was to screw one's hand into the bird's organ cavity and remove its innards at one fell swoop, preferably without puncturing its rectum and becoming smeared with excrement, although this frequently did happen. The sensation of grasping a handful of cold, long-dead gizzards with one's naked hand is an experience that defies comparison, (Nowadays one would wear a disposable glove

The Mousse and the Man from the Michelin

to perform such as task, but they'd yet to be invented, and anyway would have been viewed by most chefs of the day as not only unnecessary but downright effeminate.) but it is as nothing when compared to the asphyxiating stench. The trick in overcoming this, according to Roy, was to keep a cigarette on the go at all times. But this presented its own set of problems, principally what to do when you needed to take the cigarette from your mouth between drags, bearing in mind your hands were caked with blood and worse. But, impressively, Roy was able to smoke an entire cigarette to the end without once removing it from his mouth, and he very kindly offered to teach me the technique. By the time I'd finished preparing the 24 pheasants, I'd managed to smoke my way through an almost equal number of cigarettes, each one placed between my lips and lit for me by an ever-helpful Roy, for whom nothing seemed too much trouble. My chest ached heavily and I'd acquired a rasping cough, but it was a price worth paying for having mastered the art of finger-free smoking, and I couldn't help awarding myself a metaphorical pat on the back. I felt sure that with skills such as these I was well on my way to becoming a real chef.

The next day, being a Monday, was my day off. Although on closer inspection of my work rota (a hastily typed sheet that Mark had thrust into my hand the previous evening), I was dismayed to find that Monday mornings were blocked out in red and contained the words, 'FOUR HOURS' CLEANING AND MAINTENANCE'. This involved the chefs having to dismantle, clean and reassemble every item of equipment in the kitchen, commencing at 8am sharp every Monday (no exceptions, despite it being my *day off*). I was not remotely surprised to discover that responsibility for the least popular tasks fell to me (with grudging assistance from Kevin, who applied himself to the job with all the enthusiasm one would expect from someone who has been fired and is working out their notice). These included unblocking the S-bends beneath the sinks with caustic soda, scrubbing the area around the swill bins in the kitchen yard with disinfectant, and applying paint stripper to the burners of the stoves to remove the build-up of carbon. By far the most depressing of my new responsibilities, however, was exterminating vermin (a particular problem because the restaurant was flanked by a chicken farm on one side and a horse stable on the other, which acted as an incubator for all things nauseating and untouchable). My duties included laying poison for rats and mice, hunting for maggot infestations in the ageing kitchen infrastructure and liquidating them with bleach; and, daily before commencing work, eliminating the dense swarm of flies and wasps that had inevitably occupied the kitchen in our absence. This involved closing all doors and windows and emptying half an aerosol of fly

The Mousse and the Man from the Michelin

killer into the air, before returning twenty minutes later to sweep the dead and dying insects – heaving in their hundreds – into a dustpan.

And then there were the cats.

No one had ever formally counted the number of feral cats that inhabited the kitchen garden at The Mute Swan. Estimates ranged from between 15 and 50, depending on whom you believed. But everyone was agreed that a/ they had always been there; b/ there were too many; and c/ they were a health hazard. The question was what to do about them. Aggressive, wormy and overrun with mange, they subsisted on a diet of scraps scavenged from the swill bins, supplemented by the occasional rat or bird. Various solutions had been mooted for controlling the cat population, including shooting, poisoning and drowning, but no one had the stomach for it. Then Gerald had the idea of capturing the cats and taking them to a vet to be painlessly destroyed. This required building a trap – a Heath Robinson device made from a wooden cauliflower crate placed on top of an old refrigerator shelf, onto which was tied a kipper. One end of the crate was propped up by a stick with a length of string attached to its base. The string was then trailed across the garden and in through the kitchen window. My task was to hold vigil at the window until such a time as a cat ventured beneath the crate to take the bait (it seldom took more than a few minutes), when I would pull the string and *voila*! Then all I had to do was transfer the cat to a basket and drive it in my car to the local PDSA dispensary. Except that trying to put a wild cat into a basket is like ... well ... trying to put a wild cat into a basket. It wasn't about to give up without a fight. The cat would emerge from beneath the crate seething with fury, hissing and spitting, a gyrating blur of fur and claws – and, no doubt sensing its imminent demise, urinating copiously. Despite my wearing a heavy jacket and gardening mitts, I was frequently mauled and sprayed with cat piss. I pitied the cats. I pitied myself. After a few weeks in my grisly role, instead of taking my captives to the vet to be destroyed I hit upon the genius compromise of driving them to a nearby wood and setting them free to begin a new life – less genocide; more social cleansing. Oscar Schindler would have been proud of me. It was only much later that I realised the banished cats were finding their way home, as they began reappearing in my trap with worrying regularity. No one else noticed.

I spent the remainder of my day off familiarising myself with my accommodation. My first discovery was that I shared a landing with three women, one of whom I was about to encounter on the stairs as I made my way to my room.

'Who are you?' It was a greeting with which I was now

The Mousse and the Man from the Michelin

familiar. 'You new here? You can help me up with this bloody suitcase, if you want to make yourself useful.'

Tabitha Manning-Smythe – for, based on Betsie's less than flattering description, I could only presume that it was she – stood at the foot of the stairs, perspiring and breathing heavily. Her ample figure – which hovered somewhere between voluptuous and merely outsized – was obscured beneath a loose-fitting floral pattern dress, topped by a lilac velvet jacket and a gargantuan straw hat, woven with silk flowers. 'I'm Kent,' I answered, 'trainee assistant chef. I started yesterday.'

'Oh, so it's you is it? I've heard all about you,' said Tabitha, removing her hat to allow a tangle of flaxen curls to tumble about her shoulders.

'I'm sorry?'

'I hope you're proud of yourself, young man. Not only do you steal Kevin's job from beneath his nose, but I hear you're even plotting to move into his room as well. Talk about taking the biscuit.'

'But I didn't steal – '

'Emphysema.'

'What?'

'You *do know* his mother is dying, don't you?

'No, I – '

'Emphysema. She can't leave the house without oxygen. And she's had her arms and legs amputated because of diabetes and all those cigarettes she smokes. She relies on Kevin's income for her survival.'

'All of them?'

'All of what?'

'Her arms and legs. They were all amputated?'

'Yes, *all* of them.'

'Then how does she – '

'Don't ask – '

'Look, can we just get one thing straight. I don't know where you get your information, but I haven't *stolen* Kevin's job. He was leaving anyway...to join the army – '

'Yes, but his job was safe until you came along, wasn't it, because nobody wanted it? Clever clogs. And do you honestly think Kevin *wanted* to join the army? They'll eat the poor chap alive. I should know. Daddy was a chaplain-general in the Royal Lancers. You wouldn't believe the buggery that goes on in these places.' Tabitha continued to demolish my excuses. I even began to feel guilty. 'Emphy-

The Mousse and the Man from the Michelin

sema, I ask you...Have you any idea what it's like? It's like drowning to death very slowly in your own fluids ... makes me shudder.' Tabitha ushered me into her room before her, suitcase in tow. 'That's it, take it inside and put it down in front of the window. No, not there...Over there...Now open it. You'll find a bottle of champers...buried in my undies. Take it out and pass it here. There's a good boy. Glasses are on the windowsill. Let's get acquainted. Don't worry, the undies *are* clean.'

Wary of women bearing bottles, I was about to make my excuses and leave when we were joined in the room by another woman: pasty-skinned, lank-haired, early thirties, wearing grubby black slacks and a matching T-shirt. She clutched a copy of *The Times,* folded at the crossword page. 'Tabs, how was Paris, darling? Grandpapa well?' The woman in black exchanged air kisses with Tabatha before spreading herself languidly across the sofa and lighting a cheroot. 'And you are?' She appeared to be addressing the ceiling, but I presumed the question was directed at me. She inhaled on her cheroot, blowing a perfectly formed smoke ring which hovered above her head like an outsized halo. 'Henrietta Gough-Calthorpe. Miss,' she continued, extending her hand with such exaggerated aplomb that I was unsure whether I was expected to shake it or kiss it.

'My name's Kent, trainee assistant – '

'Miss, but not for long,' Tabitha interrupted. 'She's engaged to a sea captain, no less. Aren't you, poppet? He says he loves her for her mind. Isn't that just so sw*eeee*t?'

'He keeps hinting,' mumbled Henrietta, who was now immersed in her crossword. 'I'll believe it when it happens.'

'I was just telling Kento here how beastly he was being to Kevin, stealing his job, what with his mumsie, you know, dying and whatnot,' said Tabitha, popping the cork on the champagne and filling three glasses. 'How insensitive can you get, eh? I think a certain someone needs their bottom smacked.' Tabitha cocked her head in my direction.

'It's a dog eat dog world out there, darling. I'm sure Kento here meant Kevin no ill will. And besides, the boy is a blithering moron. Army's the best place for him, I'd say. Might even teach him to get out of bed on time.'

Henrietta spoke without looking up, while scribbling assertively in her crossword with a much-chewed biro. It was her unfailing routine, I was to learn, to complete the *Times* cryptic crossword puzzle in thirty minutes every morning, with or without a hangover. And she really did have a fiancé who was a captain in the Royal Navy. It was his custom to moor his destroyer at nearby Newhaven port and take a taxi to Bovington to engage Henrietta in a steamy overnight tryst before returning to his ship to weigh anchor at dawn. One

The Mousse and the Man from the Michelin

couldn't help but be impressed.

'Yes, but all the same, emphysema...'

'So you're both ... erm ... waitresses then?' I said, intent on changing the subject.

'Waitresses? Good lord no. Did you hear that, darling?' said Tabitha, 'He called us waitresses. How utterly offensive.'

'I'm sorry,' I stammered, 'but I thought that's what you did.'

'You're new here, aren't you?' said Tabitha, glaring at me witheringly.

'Well, I suppose we are, when all is said and done,' mused Henrietta from behind her crossword. 'Genteel bloody waitresses.'

'You speak for yourself, darling. What you absolutely must understand, Kento, is that I'm only helping out here. Gerald and Arabella are close friends of Mummy and Daddy's, and it was the least I could do to offer them a hand to get started with their new hobby. It's a family thingy.'

'That was two bloody years ago,' said Henrietta drolly. 'And you're still here. Funny that. If you really must know the sordid truth, Kento, we're stuck here. This entire set-up is but a protracted rest cure for fallen women of refinement – posh totty with nowhere left to go. Beached, stranded, kaput.'

'Don't listen to her. That so absolutely is not the case,' said Tabitha.

'The only thing we have in common,' continued Henrietta, 'is a gaping hole at the centre of our lives. And don't fool yourself we're all one big happy family. It's strictly us and them, the Golightlys high on the hill with their mansion and pool, while we fester down here in the boondocks with busted heating and a shared bathroom. Any more champers in that bottle, darling, I'm gagging here?'

'Take no notice of her, she's just liverish,' said Tabitha, refilling our glasses, 'because it's a Monday. No, you see, Kento, I think you're confusing us with Betsie. Now, she really *is* a waitress – a career waitress, if you please. That's why she so coveted the post of *manageress*, so called. Who else would want it, I ask you?'

'Not you, perhaps?' said Henrietta.

'At least Henrietta and I have the prospect of our inheritance to comfort us in our dotage, don't we poppet?' said Tabitha, ignoring her companion's barb. 'Betsie, on the other hand, has not a proverbial pot to piss in, and, let's be brutally frank, is past any realistic hope of finding a husband.'

The Mousse and the Man from the Michelin

'Any chance of breaking open that other bottle, darling?' barked Henrietta, suppressing a hiccup. 'This bubbly is going down frightfully well. I'm almost beginning to feel normal again.'

Seizing my opportunity, I mumbled an excuse and returned to my room. Not for the first time since my arrival at The Mute Swan I was feeling ineffectual and hopelessly out of my depth. I'd never so much as met a person with a double-barrelled name, let alone lived with one, and now here I was sharing a roof with two hyphenated heiresses and, for all we had in common, we might have come from different planets. I felt like an explorer who has encountered a potentially hostile tribe; my survival depended on not causing offence. Put a foot wrong, I suspected, and, like the explorer, I could end up in the pot.

Days turned into weeks as I gradually became acquainted with my new environment. (Kevin, meanwhile, had inexplicably stayed on in his role as my 'mentor' – despite his deadline for joining the army having long passed – and, just as annoyingly, he continued to occupy my rightful room.) Sleeping, working and socialising beneath the one roof was not easy, not least because I had to familiarise myself with a whole new code of etiquette and, as an unofficial male in an all female domain, I found myself firmly at the bottom of the pecking order. This included being forbidden from occupying the toilet or bathroom at peak times – which, in practice, meant never. To avoid conflict, I took to performing my ablutions in the early hours of the morning when everyone else was asleep. As well as being treated as a social curio, I was used as a general dogsbody, at the disposal of any 'girl' who might require an errand performing. This included running to the bar for cigarettes or gin, changing light bulbs, killing spiders in the bath and tugging reluctant wellington boots from swollen feet. On top of this, both Tabitha and Betsie made it known independently that should I ever wish to indulge in some discreet, no-holds-barred sex it was there for the taking. All I need do was ask. No pressure. No strings attached. They didn't say it in so many words, of course, but their every mannerism amounted to the same thing. I confess there were occasions when I was tempted, but at the same time I couldn't allow it to happen. Not because I was averse to sexually predatory women of maturing years with a fuller figure and an appetite for younger men – I admit there was a certain perverse allure. No, there was an altogether more practical reason for holding back: each of my would-be seducers never missed an opportunity to remind me darkly that the other was a libidinous whore, and as such I should reject their advances or suffer the consequences. I had no idea what these might be, but the threat seemed real enough. In my darker imaginings castration or eye-gouging

The Mousse and the Man from the Michelin

could not be ruled out. And in the depth of the countryside no one can hear you scream.

Besides, I had a girlfriend.

Her name was Mildred and she was my first love. We'd been dating since we were both 15-years-old, ever since we'd been pupils together in the leavers' class at secondary school. Mildred and I should never have been together. By any measure of compatibility we were ill-matched: I liked reading, Mildred liked watching TV. I liked progressive rock music, Mildred liked easy listening. I drank alcohol, Mildred was virtually teetotal. I enjoyed food, while Mildred ate to avoid malnutrition and without any obvious pleasure. She did, however, have a weakness for sweet, milky tea and garibaldi biscuits, which she consumed daily in alarming quantities. I liked sex, Mildred disliked sex (with me, at any rate), and approached the sexual act with the brisk resignation one might reserve for, say, having a tooth extracted. *'It has to done, so let's get this over with as quickly and as painlessly as possible,'* she might have been saying, as she hopped primly beneath the sheets after extinguishing the light and hoisting her nightdress obligingly to waist level. Mildred's one real pleasure in life, so far as I ever discovered, was riding her pony (an ageing piebald nag that lacked the wind to manage anything faster than a pedestrian trot). This she did with clockwork regularity morning and evening, seven days a week. In all other respects, Mildred appeared to derive as much joy out of being alive as a 17th century Puritan spinster. I wracked my brains on more than one occasion to compile a list of activities that we had in common, but all I could come up with was playing ping-pong, popping one another's less accessible acne spots and sleeping. There was no doubt in my mind that I made Mildred unhappy, not least because she would remind me of the fact, bluntly and with disturbing regularity, and this in turn made *me* unhappy. Under the circumstances, therefore, it seemed only right and proper that we should become engaged to be married. So on Mildred's instigation we went to Samuel's the jeweller and chose a ring. I never paused to question why Mildred should want to marry me (although I suspect the ring played a part – a nine-carat yellow gold engagement band, crafted into a diamond-studded heart and pierced through with a Cupid's arrow in white gold. I was still paying for it on hire purchase when I began working at The Mute Swan, some three years after the event). Still less did I ponder on my own motivations for becoming engaged. With hindsight, I can only suppose I was grateful that someone should have wanted me or, just as likely, I was too emotionally crippled to resist.

Mildred lived in a council house with her parents on the outskirts of Eastbourne. The middle child of seven, she was

The Mousse and the Man from the Michelin

obliged to share a bedroom with three older sisters. Her father cleaned buses for a living at the Southdown Bus Company, and had done so ever since being demobbed from the army in the early 1950s. He wasn't unintelligent but, being unskilled and semi-literate, he lacked the qualifications to do much else. He seemed contented with his lot in life and, on the rare occasions when he wasn't working, he was never happier than when seated in his favourite armchair, contemplating the fish in his tropical aquarium, his pipe in one hand and a glass of home-brewed beer in the other. Mildred's mother supplemented her husband's meagre wage by taking in ironing and working as a part-time child minder. After leaving school Mildred took a job on a production line in a pharmaceutical factory, where she earned just enough to pay her keep and provide livery for her pony. Despite their modest means, however, Mildred's parents regarded themselves a good rung or two higher up the respectability ladder than my own, and as such never missed an opportunity to remind me of how fortunate I was to be engaged to their daughter. I was inclined to agree with them.

CHAPTER 3

As well as integrating socially at The Mute Swan, I had to master my culinary skills, and there was much to learn. This wasn't helped by my beginning from a point of absolute ignorance. Had I come from a different, more middle-class, background I might have found it all less intimidating, but after subsisting on a diet of spam and chips throughout my formative years, my task was akin to learning a foreign language. Everything was strange. Aside from the confusing array of meat, fish and game, which I was already struggling to commit to memory, there were the fruit and vegetables to consider. Forget ocra, salsify, celeriac, haricot vert, mange tout, papayas, mangoes, broccoli, courgettes (and even something called a hairy bringal), all of which were utterly foreign to my eyes; even supposedly run-of-the-mill produce left me puzzled. I'd never so much as *seen* a green pepper or a bulb of garlic, or even a fresh pineapple, let alone tasted one. This was long before such edible exotica had found its way into provincial British shops. Where I came from, a banana was as glamorous as it got.

Most of our produce at The Mute Swan came from just three suppliers. Fruit and vegetables were delivered daily by a lecherous septuagenarian with a heart condition named

Moochie. Moochie's catch phrase, bizarrely, was *'Kids 'n' animals! Love 'em! Kids 'n' animals! Do anything for 'em!'* It was rumoured that Moochie did indeed love kids and animals, and, given the opportunity, was only too happy to do anything for them, and not just in the platonic sense. But for all his faults, Moochie was cheap, which for Mark could compensate for any number of moral failings.

As his wages were linked to the profitability of the kitchen, Mark had over the years perfected an artful system of maximising his income, the mainstay of which was a stubborn refusal to throw anything away – a practice he referred to proudly as 'good housekeeping'. To this end, the menu had evolved to reutilise every last morsel of food. Leftover cooked vegetables were recycled into Spanish omelettes and served as a starter; meat scraps – both cooked and raw – were minced and ground and turned into 'Spiced Beef Pancakes': a fiery chilli stew, rolled up in a pancake and finished under the grill with cheese and béchamel sauce (another bestselling starter and – like most of our so-called starters at the time – a hearty meal in itself). Bones, fish and vegetable scraps became soup or stock; everything else was turned into a curry and served to the staff for supper. The staff ate a lot of curries.

With waste thus minimised Mark turned his attention to saving money on purchases. Moochie's speciality was

The Mousse and the Man from the Michelin

scouring the markets for crates of vegetables that were on their last legs, salvaging what was edible and selling it to Mark, whose guiding principle when selecting vegetables was that they should be as cheap as possible. And, pound for pound, vegetables didn't come any cheaper than celery, which is why it was permanently on the menu. Mark's favoured way with celery was to serve it '*a la provençale*' (for the purposes of our menu, 'provençale' was a catch-all term used to describe anything vaguely tomatoey), which was basically boiled chopped celery mixed with an insipid sauce made from tinned tomatoes. The cooked celery retained a large amount of water which was slowly released into the sauce, rendering it so thin that it lost its viscosity and swamped the diner's plate in a tomato-flavoured gruel.

What couldn't be obtained from Moochie (that is, anything more rarefied than a cauliflower) came from a specialist supplier called Morgan Fresh Foods – essentially a man with a van, a complex network of connections in the London food markets, and the mother of all work ethics. Mr Morgan appeared never to sleep, leaving his house in the early hours of the morning to do the rounds of Covent Garden, Smithfield and Billingsgate long before dawn had broken and any chef had so much as stirred in his bed. (Don't fall for the myth perpetuated by celebrity chefs that they are up at dawn scouring the food markets for ingredients to go on that day's menu. They aren't. They get people like Mr Morgan to do it for them.) Then it was back on the road to do his delivery round of the southeast's premier hotels and restaurants, returning home late evening, only to repeat the same ritual, six days a week, every week. There was nothing Mr Morgan couldn't lay his hands on: foie gras from Strasbourg? No problem! Truffles from Vaucluse? Leave it with me! Salt cod, smoked venison, live lobsters, Whitstable Bay oysters, Loch Fyne salmon, white asparagus, green asparagus, frizzy endive, straight endive? As good as done! A left-handed Swedish masseuse with a penchant for Scrabble? Hmmm ... give me a day! Mr Morgan was far and away the best supplier we ever had. He was also a gentleman and a pleasure to do business with. It was only many years later that I learned he had a son, who was destined to become well known to the British public as a discredited newspaper editor and failed TV presenter. His name was Piers Morgan. That such a fundamentally nice man as Mr Morgan should spawn such a disagreeable offspring is one of life's more banal mysteries.

For more esoteric foodstuffs – everything ranging from tinned snails to leaf gelatine and dried chanterelles – we went to Solomon Houellebecq, a company with an unorthodox method of incentivising chefs to spend their employers' money. Each year around Christmastime, every chef who did business with them would receive an unmarked

The Mousse and the Man from the Michelin

envelope filled with cash (slipped to them covertly by the Solomon Houellebecq delivery man), this being a generous percentage of the sum they'd spent with the company during the previous twelve months. No thank you note, no Christmas card, no remittance advice, just a pleasing wad of banknotes. Innocent times.

More out of sympathy than necessity, we also bought a limited quantity of produce from a market gardener named Sidney, who ran a smallholding in the village. It was our policy to take anything and everything that Sidney grew, in the knowledge that he had little hope of selling his motley selection of slug-infested lettuces and bird-pecked strawberries elsewhere. Although he may not have seen himself as such, Sidney was a progressive, in that, in an age of intensive chemical farming, he employed organic growing methods. Although we suspected his refusal to use synthetic fertilisers and pesticides was driven more by miserliness than by an affinity with the land. Sidney suffered from frequent attacks of epilepsy. It was not uncommon to find him convulsing prostrate among his brassicas, or possibly draped over a hedge on his way home from the pub, foaming at the mouth, eyeballs migrated from view. Villagers knew that should they ever encounter Sidney in such a condition they must immediately send for his wife Doreen who infinitely patient would sit with her husband and hold his hand until he recovered, alternately berating and soothing him according to her mood.

If the sourcing and preparation of food at The Mute Swan were fraught with hazards, then serving it was a shortcut to insanity. The main problem, and there were a few, was that neither the building nor the chefs were in any way equipped to cater on the scale demanded of them. To begin with, the kitchen was the size of a phone box – as assistant chef I was responsible for preparing and serving starters, vegetables, salads and puddings, yet my entire workspace comprised a chopping board perched on top of a drainer at one end of a domestic-sized double sink. Main courses were cooked by the senior chef of the day (alternating between Mark and Roy), who cooked on an ancient six-ringed commercial stove, with temperamental burners and an oven door that required wedging shut with the aid of a drum of cooking oil. Ventilation, such as it existed, was provided by a single grease-encrusted electric fan, embedded in a window to one side of the stove. The remaining space in the kitchen was occupied by two serving tables, a wall-mounted grill, a dishwashing machine (a creaking 1950s dinosaur that performed no identifiable function, aside from belching out stifling quantities of steam) and a struggling refrigerator that acted as a balmy sanctuary for hypothermic bluebottles.

In these conditions we somehow managed to cook and

The Mousse and the Man from the Michelin

serve a full three-course menu for between 60 and 70 diners at a time, all within a three-hour window, and achieved by just two chefs. On the rare occasions when things went according to plan we would survive the onslaught, but all it took was a simple glitch and hell would be un-leached. On one especially bad (though by no means unusual) night, not only did virtually every table in the first sitting arrive late, but the entire second sitting arrived early, meaning that some 50 customers walked through the door at the same time. The result was that the entire restaurant – which was claustrophobic at the best of times – became occupied by a contraflow of squeezed bodies, waddling shoulder to shoulder like so many emperor penguins, one phalanx headed for the dining room, the other struggling in vain to locate a vacant space in one the lounges. The few customers who had found somewhere to sit found were inundated by those left standing, and the needs of all were roundly ignored while the waiting staff grappled ineffectually to impose control. Just as they began to see a semblance of order, their efforts were confounded by a slew of early arrivals from the third sitting.

It was the perfect storm.

Behind the scenes the kitchen was coping no better. Having waited idly without receiving a single order for the best part of an hour, while the chaos front of house was being resolved, we now found ourselves submersed beneath a welter of dockets. Not only this, but two rounds of dockets had arrived simultaneously for each table, one for the first sitting, the other for the second. These were shortly followed by a further round of dockets, belonging to the early arrivals from the third sitting.

Mark was on main courses, with me assisting, and from the outset things did not go his way. Surviving a busy service in The Mute Swan kitchen demanded faultless organisation, intense concentration and split-second physical coordination – none of which was my natural forte. But on a good night Mark was unbeatable. Thirty minutes into service, however, and it was clear that on this occasion he had lost control. I too was fighting a losing battle to keep up with the flow of orders. The best we could do was to manage the crisis as it unfolded, for no matter how fast we cooked we had no realistic prospect of catching up. And we knew from experience that we were about to upset a lot of people. The problems came to a head when a tray of pork fillets cooking beneath the grill burst into flames. In his haste to rescue them, Mark removed the tray too quickly, causing a rivulet of molten pork fat to run the length of his naked forearm. With a yelp of pain, he tossed the tray and its contents into the air, where it struck the ceiling before raining a mixture of searing meat and fat onto his head, which in turn caused him

The Mousse and the Man from the Michelin

to lose his balance and land buttocks-first into an overflowing swill bucket. It should have been funny, yet somehow it wasn't. An embarrassed silence hung over the kitchen as Mark struggled to his feet, shaking, pale-faced, his neck and arms pock-marked with burns, and the seat of his trousers dripping with food debris. He proceeded without a word to lay half a dozen fresh pork fillets onto the tray and replaced it beneath the grill.

'Table six wants to know where their main courses are. They say they've been waiting an hour. They're very angry. Sorry!' Henrietta peered anxiously from the shelter of the dining room door as if half-expecting to receive a missile thrown in her direction, or at least one of Mark's notorious verbal barrages, which was the usual response to any such enquiry. But to everyone's surprise none came – just an unfamiliar silence.

At this time I'd been working with Mark for several months. And while I could hardly claim to know him well, I had nevertheless begun to respect him (his habitual taunts and slights against my character notwithstanding). I'd also witnessed his slow unravelling: from someone who was clearly at the top of his game just weeks earlier, his work had become erratic, while his mood had turned uncharacteristically introverted. Mark was a good chef and dedicated to his job – which in a way worked against him, because he was also his own toughest critic. If he felt he was failing, which was often, he would push himself that bit harder, and now, not that I realised it at the time, he had hit a wall.

It was at this point in the evening that Gerald ambled nonchalantly into the kitchen and helped himself to a generous glass of cooking wine (as was his habit). 'The party on table six have decided to pop out, so need to worry any longer on that one, chaps,' he said, taking a capacious gulp of wine and belching contentedly.

'Whadya mean *pop out*?' Betsie erupted into the kitchen in Gerald's wake, her arms waving like a demented turf bookie. 'They didn't *pop* out, they shtormed out and said they vouldn't be payin' their fuckin' bill, that's what they fuckin' did. And they said they vould never be commink back. They said they vaited an hour and a fuckin' arf for their main course to arrive...and they said their "addock smoky tasted of soap and 'ad glass in it – '

'Did it?' asked Gerald aghast, directing his question at me.

'Did it what?'

'Taste of soap and have glass in it?'

'No, hardly any at all.'

'There, you see, Betso, hardly any at all. It wasn't as

The Mousse and the Man from the Michelin

bad as all that,' soothed Gerald, replenishing his wine glass while picking idly at his teeth with a cocktail stick. 'They'll be back in good time, I'm sure.'

Betsie was not to be so easily placated: 'Zerefore, Gerald, perhaps you vould care to come through to ze bar and deal viz zis draecks votze son of a bitch who is demanding you cancel his bill. He is vun very unappy rabbit.'

'Cancel his bill? What nonsense. Leave him to me, I'll go and have a chat with the fellow now.'

This was another thing I admired about Gerald, his gift for unflappability. While all around him disintegrated into chaos he might have been taking a turn around the garden to admire the roses, such was the coolness of his demeanour. To Gerald's mind, the whole Mute Swan project was no more than an extended dinner party; he was entertaining under his own roof and if his guests failed to appreciate his efforts it was evidently down to their own personal shortcomings and, quite frankly, betrayed a lack of breeding. But, of course, Gerald was no ordinary restaurateur; he was a gentleman restaurateur. Whereas the former is running his restaurant as a business, the latter is doing so merely as an idle distraction. He is a dabbler and, crucially, he must be perceived as such. The alternative is to be accused by one's peers of plying a trade, and for a person of patrician blood such as Gerald this simply wouldn't do. (Gerald claimed quite plausibly to be the bastard lovechild of King Edward VIII – he even wore a signet ring which was said to offer unequivocal evidence of his bloodline – at least to those in the know.) But whereas his forebears' career options would have been strictly confined to land owning, the armed forces or the Church, he was one of a newly liberated breed of privately educated entrepreneur who had entered *trade,* with all its squalid associations, while somehow avoiding being socially ostracised. The trick was not to be seen to be trying too hard, (In practice this meant never actually doing any work – not once had Gerald been seen to deliver a plate or glass to or from a table, nor so much as lift a saucepan in the kitchen. He also made a point of never using 'sir' or 'madam' when addressing his customers.) and yet one must be seen to succeed. It was a fine line to tread. The important thing to understand was that Gerald was fiercely attached to his amateurishness. This was what defined him, the whole point of his having a restaurant; he was following in the grand Victorian tradition of the self-taught, self-financed enthusiast.

But while Gerald may have taken a laissez-faire approach to restaurant management, it did not extend to giving discounts to disgruntled diners. In the event that someone demanded a reduction on their bill, he worked on the axi-

The Mousse and the Man from the Michelin

om that the customer was always wrong, regardless of the strength of their case, and would never hesitate to them tell so. Not once did I see him back down and he unfailingly came away holding the moral high ground, even at the expense of further upsetting the customer. And, my, did they get upset.

It's a truism, but there really are few subjects that human beings take more seriously than their stomachs. While we may be stoically accepting of being kept waiting forty-five minutes at, say, a passport office or a doctor's surgery, a comparable wait for a plate of food can transform an otherwise passive individual into a dangerous psychopath. In the process of upsetting our customers (an area in which we had impressive form), we noticed how they would react to being kept waiting for their food in wildly different ways: some would stew in silence, saving their resentment until it was time to pay their bill, before letting rip with a tirade of abuse. Others would leave their seats and begin prowling the restaurant in search of a member of staff to intimidate. Tired of waiting altogether, some would stalk out in a huff and leave without a word, even before their meal had arrived. While others would form strategic alliances with diners on neighbouring tables and register their dissatisfaction jointly. One especially irate diner even claimed that he wanted to buy the restaurant on the spot, just so that he could enjoy the satisfaction of firing the entire staff: *'Name your price. Go on, name your price. Try me. Look...I'm getting my cheque book out now, see. How much do you want for this piss-poor joke of an establishment...?'* He'd even formed a syndicate of would-be investors, made up of a group of stockbrokers on an adjacent table. When informed politely that the restaurant was not for sale, he refused to back down and had to be frog-marched into the car park by Roy, who enjoyed nothing more than a gratuitous show of strength.

To enable Mark to recover his equilibrium it was thought best that he take a spell of extended rest leave, with Roy standing in to cover his shifts. I missed Mark while he was away, and much more than I would have thought. Despite his fiery temperament, I'd grown to like him and enjoy his company. I'd even got into the habit of dropping by to visit him after work to share a bottle or two of wine. Mark lived alone in a sprawling maisonette that occupied the rear portion of the former village rectory, and it was without a doubt the most minimalistic and avant-garde living space I'd ever seen – in fact it was the *only* minimalistic and avant-garde living space I'd ever seen, which perhaps contributed to my sense of awe: white walls with stripped floorboards; rough plank bookshelves supported on stacks of bricks; a pair of futuristic Habitat bucket armchairs; a hi-fi system, with a record collection housed in old cabbage crates; a writing

The Mousse and the Man from the Michelin

desk (bare, apart from a phone, pen and blotter); a rubber-plant and two outsized Aubrey Beardsley prints on the wall, picked out by spotlights (spotlights!). Apart from this the room was empty. It wasn't so much what Mark *had* in his living room that I found so intriguing it was more what he chose *not* to have. Looking back, I now realise that Mark's taste in interior decor was standard 70s chic, and that his living room had little to differentiate it from a thousand others. But on entering for the first time back in 1971 I'd never seen anything like it. Every living room I'd known until now had been a rough approximation of the last, which in turn was a bit like my grandmother's: a pair of solid half-ton armchairs with matching sofa; an oppressive dark-wood dresser displaying a set of slipware crockery; a Bakelite radio set or, if you were lucky, a monochrome TV with spindly legs; a boarded-over fireplace housing a coal-effect electric fire, above which would be a cheap cardboard print, typically of a weeping female with oddly blue skin. All of which was illuminated by a ceiling lamp that cast a wan circle of light onto a dusty carpet below. And, of course, though it hardly bears mentioning, the all-pervasive odour of moth balls and boiled cabbage. But here was something new – light, space, form, colour... It seems ridiculous now, but I can't overstate the effect all this had on my sensibilities. So far as I was concerned, Mark was an artist, a bohemian, a paragon of taste. And as he held strong opinions on everything from colour coordination and soft furnishings through to interior lighting and the positioning of house plants, this wasn't hard to believe. I hung on his every pronouncement with awe, and from those early conversations I acquired a number of prejudices that have stayed with me to this day, and of which I remain dogmatically proud. These include an aversion to the following items: net curtains and centrally placed ceiling lights, ornaments and knickknacks of every kind, glass-cabinets and patterned wallpaper, bedroom slippers and pyjamas, nylon shirts, sugar in tea, tabloid newspapers and, most emphatically, an insistence that a bathroom should never, ever be painted blue – because blue is a cold colour. Yellow, yes. Blue, never. Was Mark gay? As a subscriber to *House & Garden* magazine and a weakness for stage musicals and pastel fabrics, he should have been. Yet he was resolutely heterosexual. He was, however, undoubtedly in touch with his feminine side.

CHAPTER 4

The atmosphere in the kitchen when Roy was cooking could not have been more different, although, from my point of view, hardly any easier. Roy could be a gifted, if erratic, cook but, unlike Mark, he took a very relaxed – some might say irresponsible – approach to his role. Most worryingly for me, Roy was a compulsive practical joker, and as the new boy in the job I was destined to bear the brunt of his perverse sense of humour. This included having Fairy Liquid squirted into my lager whenever my back was turned – and, as drinking lager in copious quantities daily from noon onwards was integral to life in the kitchen, I was destined to consume more than my share of detergent. To be fair on Roy, he could take a joke as well as the next man. Indeed, one was expected to retaliate with like-for-like. It was a case of *play-up-and-play-the-game*, and the level of fortitude one displayed upon getting caught-out by the opposition was a measure of one's virility. (Pitted against a master practical joker such as Roy, however, my level of success was miserably low.) As a result, many hours and much mental energy were expended trying to outwit each other with ever more elaborate ruses. Some days it was remarkable that we managed to get any work done at all.

Kent Austin

The milder end of Roy's repertoire of practical jokes included wiping the flesh of a freshly cut chilli around the rim of a victim's cup or glass; adding industrial quantities of Tabasco sauce to their food when they weren't looking; hiding things – including half-eaten meals, partially smoked cigarettes, lighters, wallets, car keys, handbags, tampons, false teeth and anything else he could misappropriate through sleight of hand; filling one's work shoes with Bombay duck (aka dried bummalo fish – the most offensive-smelling comestible known to man); scraping the bottom of my pot of béchamel sauce with a metal spoon so that it became contaminated with burnt flecks; offering new members of staff a piece of 'halva' which turned out to be fresh baking yeast (it exploded on contact with saliva and tasted of armpits); attaching raw kippers to the exhaust manifold of cars – Mark once drove his MG Midget around for a week before the stench of rotting fish prompted him to lift the bonnet to investigate. An especially reliable 'joke' – in that it could be repeated indefinitely – was placing a floury handprint prominently on a waitress's buttock, the result being that she would unwittingly become the laughing stock of diners as she went about her work in the restaurant.

If it ever occurred to Roy that most of his jokes simply weren't funny – just cruel – he certainly didn't show it. One of his favourite distractions was to get me into trouble

The Mousse and the Man from the Michelin

with Arabella. And he was very good at it. One particularly fraught evening he instructed me to go through to the restaurant at the peak of service and inform Arabella – who was taking food orders – that the kitchen had 'run out of nil'. Presuming in my innocence that nil was a type of fish (brill, krill...why not nill?), I duly did as I was told. Unfortunately, I had caught Arabella on the wrong day and I was rewarded with a mirthless rebuke for my gullibility. The worst part, for me, was that it reinforced Arabella's steadily growing conviction – since the vomiting episode – that I was borderline dysfunctional and consequently unfit to be trusted with any form of responsibility. But this incident was as nothing when compared to the magnitude of my next indiscretion.

Of all Roy's ruses, for sheer unmitigated cruelty, nothing could match the 'legendary bucket of water over the door trap'. The art was to balance a two-gallon rubber bucket of water on the upper rim of the prep room door with the aim of drowning the first person to enter. Place the bucket over the door at the wrong moment, however, and not only did you risk missing your intended victim, but in all likelihood you would get the wrong person. It was Russian roulette, played with water. As storage space in the main building was at a premium, the prep room was visited routinely throughout service both by chefs and front of house staff, who used it as an overflow repository for everything from champagne to ice cubes. Conveniently for Roy, the prep room door was habitually left ajar (a precondition for bucket balancing). It also opened inwards and, the hinges being stiff and heavy, it took little effort to position a bucket against the inner wall above the doorframe at just the right angle.

The incident in question occurred when – in an ill-contrived attempt to avenge a previous soaking at Roy's hands – I tried to play him at his own game and set a water trap. Success was dependent on a combination of precise timing and economy of effort. The idea was to lure one's intended victim into the prep room at exactly the right moment. This was best achieved by catching them off-guard, such as midway through a busy service, usually with a request that they 'run over to the prep room and fetch x, y or z from the fridge / stove / store cupboard'. This is where economy came into the equation: attempt the trap too often and you lost the element of surprise and it had no chance of succeeding. And even with perfect conditions in place, one could expect nine out of ten attempts to fail, due to the intended victim identifying the trap at the last moment, their fleetness of foot in dodging the deluge, or the bucket falling from the door at the wrong angle, resulting in little more than wet shoes. All of which made scoring a direct hit so much more satisfying when eventually it happened.

I should have known better. As an amateur, I was play-

The Mousse and the Man from the Michelin

ing out of my league. Up until this time, the setting of the 'legendary bucket of water over the door trap' had been the unique preserve of Roy and Mark. It was certainly no place for upstarts like me. My first mistake was to presume that Roy would be taken in by my hopeless acting. My casual request that he 'pop over to the prep room and fetch me a lettuce' was as implausible as it was unconvincing. Roy merely called my bluff and behaved as if he hadn't heard me. My second, and fatal, mistake was not to return to the prep room immediately after my initial failed effort and neutralise my trap. I Instead tried several further and increasingly desperate attempts to coax Roy to take the bait, each as unsuccessful as the last. By the time I'd conceded defeat it was too late.

I would have expected to hear a scream when the bucket of water landed on Arabella's head, but the first I learned of her misfortune was when she appeared at the kitchen door. As a woman who prided herself on her impeccable couture, Arabella should at least have been angry, but she seemed too surprised to register any emotion whatsoever. She simply stood on the doorstep, sodden from head to toe, hair plastered to her ears like so much kelp, makeup streaming down her face, her mouth gulping open and closed like a beached cod. So this was what a direct hit looked like. Under any other circumstances I might even have allowed myself a moment of pride.

Another of Roy's vices was gambling. Roy was a compulsive gambler and he would bet on anything, the more puerile the better – including which chef could produce the greatest number of flammable farts during the course of a day, or who could smuggle the riskiest innuendo into a conversation with a waitress without her noticing – for example, '*You're looking under the weather. I think you should go to bed and get something hot inside you...*' – a practice which also ran the risk of having one's face slapped. Roy loved betting on pub games. As The Mute Swan was closed for weekday lunches, it was customary at lunchtimes for the chefs to frequent the nearby Beachy Head Hotel, a venue fashionable among suicide jumpers, who were well known for taking a final drink in the hotel bar before hurling themselves from the adjacent 600-foot cliff onto the rocks below. At a rate of some 40 jumpers a year, it was, and remains, the most popular suicide hotspot in the country, and as such is a source of considerable local pride. Apart from the occasional solitary depressive – chain smoking and staring pensively into the middle distance, possibly even contemplating that final leap into oblivion – the hotel bar was agreeably empty. It was a particular favourite of Roy's because it hosted a bar-billiard table – a distraction at which he excelled – and, at his instigation, he, Mark and I would play

The Mousse and the Man from the Michelin

'best of threes', with a pound each riding on every game. I of course lost many more games than I ever won, and as a result was permanently in debt on a grand scale. Then there were the poker schools. These happened in the restaurant dining room after service. So addicted were we to poker that we would often play all night long, and it was not uncommon for us to be dealing a final hand to the accompanying strains of the dawn chorus. On one occasion the cleaner arrived at 7am only to find us still engrossed in a six-hour grand slam. She was obliged to dust and vacuum around us, grumbling loudly, while we remained stubbornly seated at our table – unshaven, manic-eyed, surrounded by a litter of bank notes, overflowing ashtrays and drained vodka bottles, each one of us determined not to be the first to break. My poker playing was on a par with my efforts at billiards, and I was soon deeply out of pocket. Some weeks my losses were so heavy they wiped out my entire wage packet and more besides (and there was nothing light-hearted about gambling with Roy and Mark; prompt payment of all debts was expected as a point of honour). However, like so many gamblers before me, I nursed an irrational belief, spurred on by the occasional 'good' week, that if I could only keep on playing, my luck would turn and I would be able to recoup my losses. It never happened. Nor were my money problems helped by my drinking, which had reached a worrying new level. In a matter of months I had changed from being an occasional light drinker into a habitual noon-till-night, seven-day boozer. My bar tab had spiralled to such an extent that Arabella had instructed her bookkeeper to deduct a percentage of my wages at source until I'd cleared the balance which, at the rate I was drinking and on a salary of just £15 a week, was fast becoming an impossibility.

It was reasonable to suppose that Arabella's soaking was not about to pass without consequence. So when Gerald and Arabella summoned me to their office the following morning I was quietly confident that I was about to be sacked, or at the very least press-ganged into the armed forces.

The Golightlys' office was in a converted stable block at the rear of the restaurant car park. I arrived to find Gerald and Arabella seated behind their respective desks, midway through *The Times* and a working breakfast.

'Ah, there you are, Kento, come in and take a pew. Coffee?' said Gerald, wielding a cafetière in my direction. It was typical of Gerald. Even when administering a dismissal, it would seem, he could not help comporting himself with impeccable manners. Although I noted that on this occasion Arabella did not appear to share his good humour, and she glowered at me broodingly from behind her newspaper. 'And do help yourself to an almond croissant, they're fright-

The Mousse and the Man from the Michelin

fully good.

'Anyway, Kento, I'll come straight to the point. We, Arabella and I, that is, were just taking stock of your time here with us, and we were wondering – '

'Look, Gerald, before you continue, can I just say that I know that what happened yesterday has cost me my job, and I accept that it's my own fault.' In anticipation of this moment, I'd been rehearsing my response since the previous night, having concluded that if I had any hope of keeping my job it was not in mounting a defence, but to admit to my crimes and plea for clemency on the grounds of diminished responsibility. The unthinkable alternative was to find myself back on my father's doorstep, humiliated, destitute and once more at his fickle mercy. 'All I would ask of you is that if I'm allowed a second chance, I give you my word that things will change.'

'Cost you your job?' Gerald seemed surprised. 'Good lord, no, not at all. Not you...it's not you. No, you see, Kento, all things considered, Roy has decided it's best that he fall on his own sword, so to speak, fly with the early bird and seek pastures new, or whatever it is people do in these situations...It's all very amicable, of course.

'Roy's leaving? Leaving the restaurant?' My shock at this news was tempered by a deeply pleasurable attack of schadenfreude.

'Er, yes, Roy is indeed leaving the fold...or, in view of us being collectively identified with a swan, perhaps the word *nest* is more appropriate. So yes, Roy is fleeing the nest.'

'Look, Gerald, if this has anything to do with what happened to Arabella then I really must take my share of the responsibility,' I said, with as much sincerity as I could muster.

'Oh good lord, no, Kento, nothing whatsoever to do with the old water over the door jape...all good clean fun, that.'

'Well, actually, now that you mention it –' protested Arabella, but Gerald interrupted her.

'No, it's to do with the worms.'

'Yes,' agreed Arabella, 'frankly, we draw the line at worms. What on earth was the man thinking of?'

'You see, Kento, we've had a visit from the health inspector,' said Gerald, peering at me solemnly over the rim of his spectacles. 'Now the good news is we've been given a clean bill of health, thanks largely to your own efforts in keeping the place shipshape. Yes, flying colours in fact, all bar one rather distressing and potentially litigious detail. The worms.'

The Mousse and the Man from the Michelin

'Worms?' It slowly dawned on me what Gerald was talking about.

'Yes, worms. It would seem that Roy has been hording them secretly in one of the freezers. Obviously you weren't to know...hundreds of the bloody things – '

'If not thousands, added Arabella. 'We think Roy is clearly in need of psychiatric help. What on earth was the man thinking of?'

'Anyway, the inspector took a very dim view of the situation,' continued Gerald. 'It would seem there's a law against storing hazardous organic products alongside foodstuffs intended for human consumption. It took all my powers of rhetoric to convince the chap that we weren't serving them to our customers – the Chinese do, by all accounts, but then one would expect nothing less; they eat anything that moves – including worms, I'm told.

'In fact, if I hadn't happened by on the off-chance and found the inspector fellow rooting around in our freezers, goodness knows how things might have turned out. In all likelihood the restaurant would have been arbitrarily closed down without a by your leave. These people have the powers, you know. He told me as much. And to cap it all, Roy was nowhere to found. Just when I needed him there to cast light on the mystery, it was if the earth had swallowed him up. Turns out he was on the beach – fishing, if you please ... with worms.'

It was true. Roy was seldom to be found when you needed him. It wasn't so much that he was lazy. He just worked to an eccentric routine, aided by an abnormal ability to cope for long periods without sleep. While, following an all-night poker session, Mark and I would head for our beds, in an attempt to catch a few hours of sleep before starting work, Roy would return, semi-inebriated, to the kitchen and begin cooking for the coming evening. He would continue working until around midday, when – freshly sober*ish*, and fuelled by industrial quantities of strong coffee – he would load his fishing tackle into his car and drive to Eastbourne beach for an afternoon's angling. The kitchen in his absence resembled the Marie Celeste, pots simmering on the stove, food cooling beneath tea towels – stocks, sauces, puddings, terrines...anything that needed to be prepared in advance of service. But not a human being in sight. I would often arrive to begin work at 2pm only to discover that I had the kitchen to myself. Returning from his fishing expedition at around 5pm, Roy would then spend a frantic two hours preparing for service. It would be approaching midnight when he finally finished work. His stamina was legendary.

It was then that Gerald dropped his bombshell: 'So, Kento, Arabella and I thought this might be just the moment

The Mousse and the Man from the Michelin

to put you forward as Roy's worthy successor. Obviously, Marko will be on hand to steer you in the right direction.'

'Me? You mean you're giving *me* Roy's job? I'll be sous chef?' I couldn't believe what I was hearing. I'd been in the role of assistant chef for a little over eight months. There were more holes in my culinary knowledge than in Oscar Pistorius' toilet door (or indeed his alibi). Although, as I was fast beginning to learn, it was a move typical of Gerald, who made most decisions based on astrological assumptions and seldom allowed cool logic to interfere with his plans.

'No, not sous chef. We've decided to scrap that title – sounds silly and effeminate, too damn French. No, henceforth you shall be known by the altogether more democratic and Anglo-Saxon appellation of co-head chef. And needless to say a healthy pay rise will be in the offing...and of course a car. We've seen a delightful little MGB GT that we thought would suit you down to the ground, haven't we darlzie-warlzie?' said Gerald, addressing Arabella.

'Simply delightful,' agreed Arabella, although with markedly less enthusiasm than her husband

'You *do want* the job, don't you, Kento?' asked Gerald. 'It's just that you don't seem exactly enamoured at the prospect. It's quite an opportunity, you know.'

'But what about Roy? It's all a bit of a shock. I mean, am

I good enough? Does *Mark* think I'm good enough?'

'No, to be perfectly honest, he doesn't. In fact Marko thinks you aren't up to the job at all. But we do, don't we, darlzie-warlzie?'

'Well, yes...and no –' began Arabella tentatively.

'Yes, yes, of course we do,' said Gerald. 'You'll be up to scratch in no time at all, if I'm any judge. It's a Libran trait. You've the whiff of genius about you, Kento, mark my words.'

'But who will do *my* job?'

'Ah, yes, we've given that some thought, too. It's all taken care of, so no need to worry.'

'We would expect this move to usher in a new sense of purpose and maturity in the kitchen,' added Arabella, determined to make her point, 'because quite frankly under Roy things were going rapidly downhill. We're placing our trust in you. It's a sober responsibility.'

I had the disturbing sensation that I was being handed a poisoned chalice, like being crowned emperor of Rome in the knowledge that one's predecessor has died at the hands of his own lieutenants.

'But who will be assisting me in the kitchen?'

The Mousse and the Man from the Michelin

'Ahem, erm, Kevin,' said Gerald, clicking his neck to one side and loosening his shirt collar with a forefinger.

'Kevin!'

'You *do realise* his mother has emphysema, don't you?'

'I thought he'd signed up to join the army?'

'Oh, I managed to pull a few strings on his behalf with the C.O. at Aldershot ... compassionate grounds and whatnot. Didn't take much persuading, as it happens. Seems they were only taking him to make up the quota.'

'But why Kevin, of all people?'

'Well, in a nutshell, Kento, try as we might we couldn't find anybody else. But, as they say, better the devil you know.'

***

To coincide with our new regime, Gerald had decided to sub-contract the running of the kitchen to his chefs. The plan – a wheeze cooked up by Gerald's accountant – was that Mark and I should become business partners and form a separate limited company called 'Wealden Chef Services' (sadly for Kevin, he was not to be invited to join the partnership). To justify our new self-employed status, all we need do was put a handful of additional cooking jobs through our accounts each year, to demonstrate to the taxman that we were legitimately working for more than one client. By this means Gerald saved a significant sum on National Insurance, while – thanks to a little creative accountancy – Mark and I paid virtually zero income tax. Everyone was happy.

Because we were paid on profitability, and the Mute Swan kitchen was consistently profitable, the upshot was that my income increased tenfold overnight. My live-in status meant that I had no rent or overheads (I'd even been able to escape the 'girls'' end of the building and move into Roy's newly vacated room, with the addition of a self-contained sitting room in the cottage above the preparation room). Add to this my new company car – a midnight blue MGB GT in pristine condition, complete with wire wheels and leather upholstery – and it was a package made in heaven. I had to pinch myself to confirm I wasn't dreaming. I felt rich. I *was* rich, comparatively, and certainly according to my friends, who had begun to view me as some kind of high-flying prodigy. But while I was happy to promote this belief, I knew that I was really just a lucky bastard who happened to be in the right place at the right time – and, most importantly, I was a Libran lucky bastard.

Mark seemed as bemused as I was by the unfolding of events. With some justification, he felt I'd been appointed above my station and that Gerald's new egalitarian plan had

The Mousse and the Man from the Michelin

been forced upon him to diminish his status. He made no secret of his conviction that I wasn't up to the job, and had pressed until the eleventh hour for Gerald to employ an outsider as Roy's replacement – a chef who, like himself, had been college-trained and held a City & Guilds qualification in catering (my lack of formal training being the cornerstone of Mark's objection to my promotion). Perhaps it was something to do with his attachment to inspired amateurism, but Gerald was fiercely resistant to this idea and refused to budge. The job was mine.

Despite Gerald's endorsement, in those early days my lack of college training had left me with me a painful inferiority complex. But I needn't have worried because, not that I knew it at the time, a new breed of chefs was already on course to become tomorrow's stars, and they had one thing in common: they were self-taught and none held a formal qualification in cooking. These included Rick Stein (studied English), Nico Ladenis (studied economics), Raymond Blanc (trained as a waiter), Alastair Little (studied archaeology), Rowley Leigh (studied English), Hugh Fearnley-Whittingstall (studied philosophy and psychology), Heston Blumenthal (former photocopier salesman and debt collector), Ferran Adria (former washer-upper in an Ibiza nightclub) and the granddaddy of them all – the self-professed amateur restaurateur and prototypical gentleman chef –

Keith Floyd. In the process they challenged the traditional catering college / City & Guilds route into the profession, demonstrating that all that was really required to become a successful chef was a love of cooking and an intelligent curiosity about food. It's worth noting that, along with banking and prostitution, cooking is one of the few trades where one can set up in business and be taken seriously without qualifications.

Placing me on my meteoric fast-track up the career ladder was undeniably a gamble, but during my brief time at the restaurant Gerald claimed to have identified in me a gift that apparently set me apart and, as he put it, 'contained the seeds of greatness' (not to mention a whiff of genius). But while Gerald may have been prone to hyperbole, he was no fool. As well as being an astute businessman he was a fearless delegator and he knew what he was doing. And in my own defence – the occasional disaster notwithstanding – my progress since starting in the job had been pretty damn good: from not knowing a cod from a kipper, I'd become a proficient all-round chef – albeit an inconsistent one. But then again most chefs are inconsistent and remain so throughout their careers. There are many qualities that distinguish a mediocre chef from a good chef but, arguably, consistency is the most elemental of them all. Add to this the virtues of dedication, ambition, creativity, leadership, restraint and a

The Mousse and the Man from the Michelin

modicum of insanity, and you might, just might, arrive at the makings of a *great* chef. Did I really possess the seeds of greatness? Whatever the truth of the matter, I was happy to believe the hype.

As too, oddly enough, was Mildred.

No question about it, Mildred was exceedingly happy with events, and understandably so – her erstwhile failure of a fiancé had unpredictably and quite inadvertently made something of his life. The change in Mildred's mood was dramatic. She told me she was proud of me and that she'd always believed in me, that I'd make a wonderful chef, a devoted husband, a doting father... She even told me she loved me. She also brought forward the date of our wedding. Now that I had a proper job, she declared, we could afford to get married right away. But to Mildred's surprise (and indeed to my own surprise) I resisted. Perhaps I'd acquired a new confidence, given my change of fortune, but, for whatever reason, the idea of becoming a teenage groom had lost its appeal. Mildred was wounded, but she respected my wish to defer our marriage. As a compromise, she took to spending the occasional night with me in my rooms at The Mute Swan. Nights turned into weekends, which in turn became weeks, and before we knew it we were cohabiting. Gerald took a characteristically relaxed view of our arrangement and allowed Mildred to stay on indefinitely. He even gave her a part-time job waitressing in the restaurant in lieu of board and lodging, as well as helping her find a field in the village to accommodate her pony. We wouldn't have predicted it at the time, but we were destined to live this way for the next ten years. And although Mildred continued to wear her engagement ring, we never did marry.

CHAPTER 5

Mark quickly warmed to the idea of our new power-sharing regime, not least because it relieved him of the pressure of managing the kitchen singlehandedly. Between us, we'd also landed an employment package that other chefs could only dream of. Most importantly, how we chose to run the kitchen was left entirely up to us. Gerald, who abhorred being mired in detail, wanted no part in it. Provided that standards and profitability were maintained, he was happy. Rather than work together, Mark and I wisely agreed to divide the week between us. The plan was that I worked Monday, Tuesday and Wednesday; Mark was to take over for Thursday, Friday and Saturday, with each of us taking turns alternately to cover Sunday lunch and dinner. (Yes, you read that correctly, I was a chef with weekends off.) And it got better: while still working 40 hours, this gave each of us three-and-a-half unbroken days off each week. Kevin, on the other hand, had Monday afternoons and Thursdays off, and continued to subsist on a wage of £15 a week, on which he paid his full quota of tax and insurance. I'd like to say that I felt sorry for him, but I'd be lying.

However, my newfound autonomy presented me with a dilemma. Despite us getting off to a rocky start, Mark had proved to be a diligent, well-informed and generally patient teacher, and it was thanks to him, rather than Roy, that I'd acquired the requisite skills to have any hope of working independently. If I was to become a fully-formed chef, I had much more to learn, but now I'd be operating in a vacuum with only myself as master and critic. Without Mark at my shoulder, my development had been effectively nipped in the bud. I had no alternative but to begin teaching myself how to cook. To this end I went out and spent a significant chunk of my first outsized pay cheque on cookery books. There was no particular reasoning behind my choice of reading. I just bought whatever seemed interesting, but several books were to have a big influence on my cooking at this time: *Mediterranean Seafood* by Alan Davidson; *The Four Seasons Cookery Book* by Margaret Costa; *Leaves From Our Tuscan Kitchen* by Michael Waterfield and Janet Ross (first published in 1899); *Mastering the Art of French Cooking* by Julia Child, Simone Beck and Louise Bertholle; and, in particular, Elizabeth David's *French Provincial Cooking.* I also acquired a copy of the original *Larousse Gastronomique*, the illustrious door-stop-sized encyclopaedia of French gastronomy, but found it so sprawling and intimidating that I never once used it (and with its labour-intensive recipes and methods for preparing bush meat – including lion and bear! – it seemed hopelessly at odds with modern cooking), but it

The Mousse and the Man from the Michelin

looked good on the shelf. Immersing myself in these books, it quickly dawned on me that if I was to progress as a chef I needed to adapt my style. The quasi-French-make-it-up-as-you-go-along school of putting things on top of things had to go. It was time for a more authentic approach based on the time-honoured principles of real cooking. I was especially influenced by Elizabeth David's writings on French and Italian cuisine and her insistence on freshness, simplicity and using only quality ingredients. She reserved particular scorn for the second-rate cooking and bogus substitutes for classic dishes and ingredients that passed for good food in British restaurants at the time. It wasn't lost on me that, in almost every respect, she might have been talking about The Mute Swan.

But the will to change was only half the battle. Because most of the dubious practices that had relegated us to the culinary second division were necessitated by the same old problem – which was having too many mouths to feed in too few hours. Our crimes were many. They included cooking, or part-cooking, food in advance to speed-up service; devising menus consisting exclusively of ready-made dishes and sauces that could be kept hot and served directly onto the plate; pre-plating puddings and salads and wrapping them in cling film...In fact any short cut to avoid the nightmare of falling behind. It wasn't that the food we served was *bad*; it was tasty, it was filling, it was nosh, it clearly satisfied a majority of our customers or we wouldn't have been as busy as we were. It just didn't add up to a gastronomic experience. We had access to the finest ingredients in the land and we were failing to do them justice. Though we were reluctant to admit it, *The Good Food Guide* was right: in our desperation to get through service unscathed, utility had taken priority over quality, and it showed. This was in no way a reflection on Mark's talent as a chef. He knew as well as I that we needed to adapt to improve but under pressure, and with ludicrously limited resources, he'd had no option but to cope to the best of his abilities. Indeed, considering that The Mute Swan was still finding its way, and that he himself was just three years out of catering college, Mark's achievement in taking the restaurant so far so soon had been remarkable.

To have any hope of success, we agreed, we needed to review the way we worked. The meat-and-three-vegetable mentality that had dominated our approach to cooking for so long had to go. Out went the ready-made, flour-thickened sauces; out went the pre-cooked and reheated vegetables; out went the 'good housekeeping' principle that had necessitated us utilising every last scrap of produce. From now on our cooking would be informed by a new sensibility, following in the footsteps of the great modern chefs. Our first priority was to get more help in the kitchen. Fired by our

The Mousse and the Man from the Michelin

new resolve, we approached Gerald and insisted that he employ an additional chef with immediate effect. And while we were about it we asked him to throw in a new kitchen.

'Another chef! A new kitchen! Have you any idea how much it would cost?' said Gerald, seemingly aghast that we should even consider such an outrageous demand. 'Absolutely not, out of the question.'

For a man in possession of an extensive property portfolio, a bank account with Coutts and two Rolls Royces, Gerald could be surprisingly frugal. It was never going to be easy, but we dug in our heels. Either we got our extra chef, we told him, or we would limit ourselves to cooking for two sittings rather than three. The choice was his. We were, after all, our own bosses now. With great reluctance, Gerald agreed that he would 'look into it'.

Of course, we should have known better than to think that Gerald would agree to our demand without putting up a fight. He did, however, come up with a novel substitute.

'You know, chaps, I've been giving this business of getting a new chef some serious consideration, and bearing in mind that candidates for the job are thin on the ground at the moment, I've had an idea.' It was the occasion of our monthly strategy meeting, a new initiative conceived by Gerald to keep us all on track, as he put it. Mark and I exchanged glances. We smelled a rat. 'Have you ever heard of something called a microwave oven?' continued Gerald. 'Space-age technology from the USA. Cooks without heat, apparently. It's being hailed as the greatest discovery since fire. Catching on like billyo across the pond, so I hear, but yet to make an impact on our own backward shores, alas.'

No, we shrugged, we'd never heard of a microwave oven. And frankly we weren't interested. We wanted an extra pair of hands.

'Ah, but this is just that,' said Gerald enthusiastically, 'or at least the equivalent of a pair of hands – many pairs of hands, in fact. It does the job of three chefs. Cooks a whole turkey in ten minutes flat, I'm told. Anyway, you'll see when it arrives because I've bought one, at considerable expense, I might add. It's being shipped directly from America. Should take about a month to get here.'

The microwave oven caused quite a stir. Word of its imminent arrival circulated around the village like a virus, and when eventually it was delivered there was a small crowd of spectators gathered in the lane outside the kitchen gate to gape at this object of wonder. Sidney the market gardener and his wife Doreen were there, as well as Moochie the greengrocer and Sid and Nancy from The Twelve Cups (who, taking surreptitious notes, were evidently engaged in

The Mousse and the Man from the Michelin

some impromptu industrial espionage), while Betsie and Henrietta cheered us on from an upstairs window. It took five of us to transport the microwave oven from the delivery truck to the kitchen: Kevin and Gerald at one end; Mark and I at the other, with Tabitha clearing obstacles from our path and firing commands. Unlike the compact, lightweight and infinitely more powerful microwaves which nowadays can be carried out under the arm from any supermarket for less than £30, this unwieldy beast was the size of Elvis Presley's coffin and at least as heavy. With much heaving, grunting and crushing of fingers, the machine was finally installed. Perched incongruously on the kitchen windowsill, it dominated the room like a magpie in a crowded nest. Everything about this machine was alien: with its futuristic flashing control panel and sinister chromium-plated fins it belonged in a science fiction movie rather than a kitchen. Even the brand name – the 'Raytheon Radarange' – was straight out of a Dan Dare adventure. You could just hear it: '*Take cover,*' *yelled Dan, 'it's my evil arch-nemesis the Mekon, and he's armed with a deadly Raytheon Radarange.*'

But right now we were blind to the shortcomings of our new toy, because it was about to revolutionise our lives, and all we could think of was to put it through its paces at once. One of the many benefits of microwave cookery, we'd heard, was that you could cook things directly from frozen because, unlike conventional ovens, microwave ovens cook food from the centre outwards. We thought we'd begin with roasting a joint of meat. The chosen cut for our inaugural microwave cookout was a long-forgotten shoulder of pork, excavated from the deepest permafrost of the meat freezer. Ice-burned and misshapen, tufts of grey-black bristle sprouting from its glacial rind, it looked more like a relic from an archaeological dig than an edible foodstuff.

'It's vital when operating a microwave oven that you protect yourself from radiation,' declared Tabitha authoritatively, as we prepared to begin cooking.

'Says the lady who until today had never so much as heard of a microwave oven,' sniped Henrietta.

'Well that's just where you're wrong, as it happens,' said Tabitha. 'Daddy was stationed at Bikini Atoll in the nineteen fifties when they set off the atom bomb. He saw it all firsthand. Basked in the glow, his men did, brains fried to a crisp and all because they didn't understand the danger of radiation. Had they turned their backs to the blast and worn their radiation caps they wouldn't now be growing two heads and shimmering in the dark.'

'What on earth have atomic bombs to do with microwave ovens?' said Henrietta scornfully.

'Because it's all the same stuff, silly, radioactivity, cath-

The Mousse and the Man from the Michelin

ode particles and whatnot. Daddy says that if radiation leaks out through the oven door it will cook your brain from the inside out. And they're notorious for leaking, apparently. To be frank, Daddy's not happy about me being in the same building as one, says they're Satan's own contraption.' To demonstrate her point, Tabitha had fashioned a number of anti-radiation skullcaps from cooking foil – shaped like a Jewish yarmulke, but with a knot tied at each corner reminiscent of the makeshift handkerchief-sunhats once worn by day trippers to the seaside. 'Here, put these on,' she demanded of the assembled group, 'just in case.'

The curious onlookers from the lane had by now drifted into the kitchen, causing it to become uncomfortably crowded. But on the plus side it made for a sense of occasion. Sadly there weren't enough caps to go around, and those left without protection shrank anxiously to the back of the room. (Preferring to risk brain damage rather than look like an oven-ready turkey, I willingly surrendered my cap to Betsie who proudly secured it in place with a length of ribbon.)

On opening the door of the Raytheon Radarange we were struck by a powerful smell – fishy, cheesy...stale food? Stale food! 'It's been used before,' said Mark incredulously. 'It must be second-hand. I don't fucking believe it.'

All eyes turned accusingly to Gerald. 'Not second-hand

as such,' he said sheepishly. 'Previously used would be a more accurate description, but thoroughly reconditioned, of course, and fully guaranteed. Probably got a bit musty on its way across the Atlantic, but nothing that a drop of bleach won't solve, I'm sure.'

'Right, that does it,' said Tabitha, producing a gargantuan pair of bug-eye sunglasses from her handbag and wedging them on her nose. Along with the foil cap they gave her the appearance of an insect mutant android from a 50s B-movie. 'Obviously a second-hand microwave is going to bleed gamma rays like a leaky sieve. It's probably why they got rid of the thing. It's a bloody death trap.'

'Well surely you wouldn't expect me to buy a brand new one?' said Gerald defensively. 'Have you any idea how much these things cost? You could buy a decent racehorse for the same price.

Evidently concluding that the time for talking was over, Mark sat the joint of pork in a roasting pan and placed it in the cooking chamber of the microwave. 'Five minutes should do the trick,' he said confidently, setting the dial on the control panel. 'I've added a couple of extra minutes to be on the safe side.'

How Mark had arrived at this arbitrary cooking time was a mystery; the machine had come without a manual and

The Mousse and the Man from the Michelin

we were operating completely by guesswork. With due solemnity, Mark closed the door and pressed a button marked 'FULL POWER'. In an instant a miniature electric storm, complete with sound effects and authentic lightning bolts, erupted inside the microwave.

'I suspected as much', said Sidney, amid gasps and shrieks from the assembled onlookers, "tis the devil's own work, flying in the face of nature. You'll put us all in an early grave. Shut the infernal thing down before there's a stampede, or be damned.'

'It's all right, don't panic, it's the pan,' said Mark, hitting the OFF button. 'It's the metal pan. I forgot, it says on the label you shouldn't microwave metal objects.' He took the pork from the cooking chamber and replaced it without the pan.

We looked on in anticipation as the microwave once more sprang noisily to life, an ominous whooshing and buzzing emanating from its bowels. All eyes were fixed on the glass observation panel in the oven door. The air was pregnant with suspense (as well as, by now, a hint of body odour in the crowded kitchen, not to mention an abrupt intensification in the smell of cheesy fish). A minute passed... two...three. No one spoke. At this point our view of the pork joint became obscured by a steady build-up of steam in the cooking chamber. Clearly it was working – so far so good. On the stroke of the fifth minute, the microwave switched itself off with a loud ping. We craned our necks to see in as Mark opened the door, confidently expecting to find a perfectly roasted joint of pork. 'Save me some crackling,' squealed Henrietta. 'I just love the crackling. It's the best bit.'

Henrietta was to be disappointed. Its five minutes in the microwave had left our joint of pork pretty much unchanged, the only difference being that it looked fractionally less frozen and was now swimming in a puddle of pale milky liquid, flecked with sinewy streaks of crimson blood.

'Yuch! I've never seen anything more disgusting,' said Tabitha contemptuously. 'Talk about a damp squib.'

'No, give it a chance, it just needs a bit longer,' said Gerald, endeavouring without success to sound upbeat. 'Try another twenty minutes.'

'I'd make it thirty, if I were you,' said Tabitha. 'Undercooked pig causes tape worms. Daddy once caught one from a boar when he was a missionary in the Congo. Twenty feet long, it was. It was only when he went to the latrines and noticed this horrid thing dangling out from his – '

'Oh, spare us ze details von't you, madam,' interrupted Betsie caustically. 'Zis is our lunch ve are talking about

The Mousse and the Man from the Michelin

here, ja?'

Mark reset the timer for thirty minutes, as an anti-climactic gloom descended upon the kitchen. Our audience of curious villagers began to evaporate – drifting off to go about their day, shaking their heads in disillusionment, the promise of a brave new world as remote as ever – leaving just a handful of hardcore optimists to witness history in the making.

To our relief, some 25 minutes into the cooking cycle we noticed an unmistakable aroma of roasting meat. Worryingly, however, this soon turned into a smell of burning, and a blue carbonic haze began to fill the air, causing our eyes to smart and water.

'It's the Somme,' said Moochie darkly. 'The stench of death, that's what it is. I'd know it anywhere. It's the bloody Somme all over again I tell you. I was there. No man should ever witness such a thing.'

Moochie was not so far from the truth. What we found when we opened the door of the microwave oven resembled a scene from a battlefield. Unlike modern microwaves, the Raytheon Radarange did not feature a revolving turntable to ensure an even distribution of heat, the result being that one small area of the pork joint had borne the concentrated brunt of a zillion microwaves for almost half an hour. A black, chimney-like hole, the diameter of a 10-pence piece, had been burned into its upper left flank, out of which streamed a steady column of smoke. The rest of the meat remained uncooked – wet, slimy and frigid as a corpse. Even Gerald had to concede that it was back to the drawing board.

CHAPTER 6

It was around this time that we began to attract the attention of the national press. It started with a handful of short features in the broadsheet Sunday supplements – in the main anodyne, uncritical pieces, but they at least made a change from being savaged by the guides.

The big breakthrough came when Gerald received a call from the BBC. They wanted to feature The Mute Swan in a pilot episode for a new television programme called *Success Story,* a weekly prime-time lifestyle series that showcased successful entrepreneurial ventures. The good news was that the producers had insisted on filming the programme over a Monday and Tuesday, meaning in effect that it would be as much about *me* as The Mute Swan as a whole, because of course it was on these days that I managed the kitchen. My fantasy not so many years earlier of following in the footsteps of Fanny Craddock was, it seemed, about to be fulfilled. I was to become a television personality. To have called me smug would be understating it.

A week before the scheduled recording date, I was with Gerald in the restaurant bar, enjoying a glass of wine after service, when, upon paying his bill, a customer enquired whether he could reserve a table for the following Tuesday. This was the very same day when the BBC would be filming in the restaurant. As expected, we were fully booked, and it was only as a cursory politeness to the customer that Gerald bothered to check in the reservations diary. 'Ah, as I thought, not a single table remaining,' he said breezily, snapping the diary closed with an air of finality. 'Sorry. Is there anything else I can do for you?'

'Oh dear,' said the man, visibly disheartened. 'You're definitely full?'

'Absolutely chock–a, I'm afraid.'

'That *is* a shame. We've had an excellent meal here this evening and I was looking forward to bringing a dear friend of ours to show him what all the fuss is about. It would have been our only opportunity, sadly. So there's nothing you can do?'

Gerald gave the man one of those wooden smiles, favoured by officials and bureaucrats the world over, that says something along the lines of, *I'm very sorry, but I don't make the rules here and there is nothing I can do to change them, and, frankly, even if I could, I wouldn't, at least not for an insignificant schmuck like you.*

'Oh, well,' said the man resignedly, 'can't be helped, I suppose. It's a great pity because we know that Clement

The Mousse and the Man from the Michelin

would have just loved it here.'

'Clement?'

'Yes, Clement...Clement Freud. A dear, dear friend, godfather to our daughter. He would have loved it here.'

Clement Freud: grandson of Sigmund, brother of Lucian, father of Emma, uncle of Esther and Bella; member of parliament, university rector, satirist, wit, author, journalist, raconteur, gambler, restaurateur, TV personality, knight of the realm and all round polymath and *bon viveur*. But perhaps best known to the man in the street as the face of Chunky Meat dog food, in the TV ad in which he co-starred with a deadpan bloodhound lookalike named Henry. He was also – in the strictest sense of the term – one the country's first celebrity chefs, as well as being a highly influential food writer and restaurant critic.

Only one thing impressed Gerald more than wealth, and that was status. He was, after all, on the peripheries of a set that routinely socialised with the royals; some of his friends even knew the Queen and Prince Philip personally. But for Gerald there was a problem. Most of his male circle had attended premier league public schools – Eton, Harrow, Rugby, Westminster, Charterhouse, Gordonstoun... (Clement Freud himself was educated at Darlington Hall and St Pauls.) In the main, they had then 'come up' to one of the Oxbridge colleges to graduate. It went without saying; it was the done-thing, a rite of passage bestowed by entitlement. Gerald, by contrast, had attended a minor public school of little note and had somehow missed going to university altogether, due, he claimed, to his parents having suffered at this time in his life from 'one or two little hiccups with their share portfolio'. It was an irregularity which, by his own admission, had left him with an odd kind of inferiority complex: he was posh but, on one level at least, not posh enough. Perhaps it was this perceived lack of status that resulted in him being in thrall to those who, in his view, possessed it. Whatever the reason, the mere mention of Clement Freud's name was enough to transform him instantly into a grovelling sycophant. Gerald's volte-face was as comical as it was unconvincing, as he reopened the reservations diary and, with furrowed brow, ran a finger down the page.

'Hmm, ah, now let me see. I'll just have another quick look to see if there isn't a table I've missed... Oh, yes, look, now I'm sure if we do a bit of juggling... What sort of time did you have in mind?'

'Nine o'clock will do nicely,' said the man, a new tone of authority having entered his voice, 'party of eight.'

'Eight, you say? That's quite a tall order,' said Gerald,

The Mousse and the Man from the Michelin

stroking his chin fretfully. 'Couldn't make it for four people, at seven o'clock, could you?'

'Eight it has to be, at nine o'clock, or nothing at all, I'm afraid, old boy.'

'Right you are, eight people it is then, arriving at nine,' said Gerald submissively, while avoiding my own beseeching eye. 'And I look forward to welcoming Mr Freud to our restaurant.'

'But where the hell are we going to put them?' I said to Gerald after the man had left.' Eight extra diners in a fully-booked restaurant? We'll never cope.'

'It's alright, I've already thought it through,' said Gerald. 'I'm going to phone the party that's reserved the table at that time and cancel them...tell them there's been an emergency...death in the family, chimney fire, salmonella outbreak...I'll think of something to put them off.'

'Do you really think that's fair?'

'No, not in the least, but unless you can think of a better solution, I have no qualms.'

I understood Gerald's dilemma. It was too good an opportunity to pass over: the BBC together with the nation's foremost gastronome and food critic coincidentally in the restaurant at the same time. It was going to be a media sensation.

'You do realise it needs to be a knockout menu on Tuesday, don't you, Kento?' said Gerald. 'If we get this right, it could be just the kind of publicity that bags us our first Michelin star, especially if Freud gives us a good review into the bargain. But I know I can rely on you.'

But could Gerald rely on me? I had less than a week left to prepare for the big night, and I was feeling the strain. The BBC's plan was to film the chefs working in the kitchen throughout Monday afternoon and evening. They would then shift the action to the dining room for the Tuesday shoot. The programme would culminate with the presenter dining at the restaurant, accompanied by Gerald and Arabella – cheek by jowl with an unwitting Clement Freud who, it was planned, would be cunningly positioned on an adjacent table, making him impossible for the television cameras to miss.

I agonised over my menu, lay awake nights wrestling with it, rising at all hours to pore over cookery books, pacing the room chain smoking, breaking out into mysterious rashes. But no sooner had I settled on a menu in my mind, than I was off on another trajectory. I spent hours on the telephone, ordering ingredients, cancelling them, reordering and re-cancelling. I drove my suppliers to distraction with

The Mousse and the Man from the Michelin

my indecisiveness.

Finally, after countless dead ends, I arrived at the definitive menu – suitably whimsical, I felt, without appearing to be trying too hard; modern, yet demonstrating that my cooking was rooted in a solid classical tradition. This was the menu, at least as I remember it, and not a stick of celery in sight:

STARTERS

Gazpacho

Croustade of Quail Eggs

Warm Salad of Scallops and Bacon

Spinach Soufflé, Anchovy Hollandaise

Devilled Squid Stew

Brandade of Salt Cod

Dublin Bay Prawns and Mussels, Tagliatelle

Terrine of Game, Onion Marmalade

MAINS

Fillet of Turbot, Leaks, Beurre Blanc

Feuilletés of Lobster

Rack of lamb, Cumberland Sauce

Kent Austin

Cassoulet

Pan-fried Breast of Duckling, Pink Peppercorns, Madeira Sauce

Filet of Beef Wellington

Roast Grouse with all the Trimmings

Sauté of pigeon, Chanterelles, Red Wine Jus

PUDDINGS

Chocolate Marquise

Baked Cheesecake, Compote of Raspberries

Shortbread, Caramelised Pears

Summer Pudding

Sticky Toffee Pudding

Apricot Vacherin

Crème Brûlée

Brown Bread Ice Cream

Passion Fruit Sorbet

***

Cheese Board

***

The Mousse and the Man from the Michelin

Coffee and Petits Fours

Is it a good menu? It's dated by today's standards, perhaps, but it was pretty damn good for its time, and easily the most ambitious menu I'd ever attempted. It was also anchored in reality, in that every dish had been practised and perfected over time (many of them, to be fair, by Mark, who had taken to our modernisation project like a man possessed). I even had the opportunity to give the entire menu a trial run the preceding Sunday. It operated like clockwork. Following weeks of anxiety, for the first time I began to feel a semblance of confidence.

Monday arrived. It had been arranged that the combined staff would join the film crew for an early buffet lunch in the restaurant. This would allow us to get to know each other and 'bond' with the presenter and film crew prior to filming. The presenter's name was Crispin Sutherland. When he wasn't hosting *Success Story*, Mr Sutherland hosted a nightly BBC TV news programme called *South Today* and, we were told, was 'one of the best-known faces in the south of England' – although it seemed his fame had yet to extend to the wilds of Bovington, because when Mr Sutherland made his grand entrance not one of us recognised him. This could perhaps be excused on account of us not possessing a television set, although it didn't exactly get us off on the right foot. But Mr Sutherland brushed aside the unaccustomed shock of being greeted by so many blank expressions with a self-effacing smile.

There was another problem. Having engaged Mr Sutherland in conversation for half an hour, it became clear to me that – seasoned professional though he was – his expertise did not extend to food. Indeed he appeared to have no interest in cooking whatsoever. Try as I might, all attempts to steer our conversation onto the subject of my ground-breaking new menu were politely but firmly rebuffed. He did, however, take an ardent interest in Arabella and Tabitha, and regaled them at every opportunity with risqué and interminable anecdotes from his life in broadcasting. I gave up trying to impress Mr Sutherland and instead concentrated on the wine – to mark the importance of the occasion, Gerald had broken open several bottles of his best Sancerre, preceded by a jeroboam of champagne, and I was doing my damnedest to drink more than my fair share before it was all gone. As indeed was Mark – who, unable to resist the allure of fame, had volunteered his services for the duration of filming, even if it meant sacrificing his days off – as well as, worryingly, Kevin, who was noted for a total inability to hold his drink.

With lunch over, Mark, Kevin and I set about work, more than a little drunk and definitely in no condition to be let loose in front of a TV camera. We were accompanied

The Mousse and the Man from the Michelin

in the kitchen by the director, the camera and sound crew, and about six truckloads of lights and equipment. The director's name was Don Mote, a highly strung man in his late twenties with a penchant for flamboyant hand gestures and implausibly tight jeans. He seemed as concerned as I was about his presenter's indifference to my menu, and asked for a copy to be sent to the dining room with instructions to Crispin Sutherland – who, with Arabella and Tabitha hanging on his every word, remained in full rhetorical flow – that it should be read.

To put us at our ease, Don told us to go about our work as normal. They would set the cameras rolling, he said, but only to get the angles and lighting right. They wouldn't be filming proper. 'Just relax and forget that we're here,' he told us – an instruction that was wholly unworkable due to the floor being strewn with several miles of cable, as well as two strategically placed lighting rigs, one at either end of the kitchen. The kitchen ventilation system (though 'system' is perhaps too grandiose a term for a single crotchety extractor fan) struggled at the best of times, but now with the additional heat generated by the lights, the kitchen quickly became a sauna. My first task in front of the camera was to assemble an almond roulade. This involved spreading a freshly cooled sheet of almond sponge with whipped cream and booze-soaked apricots and rolling it into a cylinder –

a kind of posh Swiss roll. At high temperatures, however, whipped cream loses its stability, and as I spread the cream onto the sponge it began instantly to liquefy beneath the glare of the lights, swamping the entire confection.

'Is it supposed to do that?' asked Don, puzzled. He had been watching with interest at my shoulder while at the same time fiddling with some sort of meter. As he spoke, the sound man positioned a microphone boom above my head – one of those with a furry appendage at the end that resembles a badger.

'No it isn't,' chirped an inebriated voice from somewhere behind me. 'He's messed it up!' I turned, aghast. It was Kevin.

'Did you get that?' said Don, addressing the cameraman who, I realised to my dismay, was pointing his camera in my direction.

'Don't think I got a clear shot,' said the cameraman. 'Boom was in the way. I'd like a retake.'

'Could you just do that again, Kent?' said Don.

'Do what again?'

'That look you gave your, erm, colleague there?'

'What look?'

The Mousse and the Man from the Michelin

'You know, that *if looks could kill* look that you just gave him. Says it all. Things don't go according to plan...bit of internal rivalry...stress of the moment...could turn nasty...bit unpredictable...blah blah blah. Love it. Reality, fly-on-the-wall, it's the future of TV, mark my words. So just once more then for the camera, in your own time, turn slowly around aaaaaaand *filthylook* –'

'You aren't filming, are you?' I asked suspiciously. 'You said you wouldn't be filming yet.'

'We aren't filming,' said Don. 'Not as such. Besides it all gets edited.'

I decided to postpone any further pastry work until the film crew had left and the kitchen had cooled. I instead moved on to meat and fish preparation, beginning with a demonstration of how to cook and dress a live lobster. All went well, but to my annoyance midway through filming Don ordered the cameraman to stop.

'What's the problem?' I asked.

'No problem,' said Don, 'at least not on my part. But obviously it's too gruesome for pre–watershed screening. Not that we were actually *filming*, you understand.'

'Gruesome?'

'Well, you know, torturing live creatures, skewering

their brains, boiling them while they're kicking and thrashing...smashing their heads open with a hammer. It's not exactly family viewing, is it? This programme goes out before nine o'clock. All it takes is for one nervous child to get upset, parents complain to the Beeb and then yours truly takes the rap, blah blah blah. It's happened before. I once filmed a farmer shooting a rat for a countryside documentary. Put a kid in therapy for a year, it did. Almost cost me my job. But don't worry I'm sure we'll get plenty of other good stuff.'

'What about butchery?' I asked.

'What about butchery?'

'You know, is it likely to put a child into therapy?'

Don considered my question. 'No, butchery won't be a problem.'

'You're sure? Because I'm about to butcher a lamb. I wouldn't want to get you into trouble with the censors.'

'Ah, but there's an essential difference here,' said Don, impervious to my sarcasm. 'Firstly it doesn't look like a lamb, and secondly it's already dead and as such doesn't carry the same emotional resonance, like, you know, ahhh, *baby–cuddly–lamb* blah blah blah. Now if you said you were *slaughtering* a lamb live on TV, of course that would be another matter –'

The Mousse and the Man from the Michelin

It was at this point that the residual effects of my lunchtime drinking were to take a bloody and unexpected turn.

My plan had been to fillet a side of lamb and so demonstrate my expertise as a butcher. I'd mentally rehearsed my routine, which was to commence with an extravagant display of knife sharpening. The art of knife sharpening, it's important to understand, is one of those totemic skills upon which all chefs are judged by their peers, and the faster and more flamboyantly it is performed is considered to be in direct ratio to the size of one's penis. It is, however, ill-advised to show off with a potentially lethal weapon while drunk. Nor did it help that I am terminally cack-handed and had never properly mastered the technique of using a sharpening-steel. As a result, on my third or fourth downward stroke I badly misjudged the angle, causing the blade of the knife to glance off the hilt of the steel and slice liberally into the top of my thumb. A fountain of blood spurted from the wound.

'Cut!' yelled Don.

'Cut? But you aren't filming,' I said accusingly, nursing my throbbing thumb in the folds of a tea towel.

'We *aren't* filming. I meant cut, you know, as in cut your thumb,' said Don. But his smirk suggested otherwise.

The cut was deep and it was impossible to stem the bleeding without applying continuous pressure to the wound. I was left with no alternative but to allow Mark to stand in and butcher the lamb on my behalf, a task which he performed with such textbook dexterity that Don even forgot to pretend that he wasn't filming: 'That one's in the can then, my darlings. Brilliant, pure craftsmanship, simply love it.'

With the addition of a few staged motion shots, which involved the chefs moving purposefully around the kitchen pretending to be busy, the film crew seemed satisfied they had enough footage for their needs. The remainder of the filming was to take place in the restaurant the following evening with Crispin Sutherland – whom I'd been hoping would at least make an appearance in the kitchen to interview me about the brilliance of my menu, but I was informed this wasn't going to happen. I was disappointed, but I had other things on my mind, the most pressing of which was to find out what had happened to Kevin. His task for the day, as usual, had been to prepare the vegetables and salads ready for service, but at some point during filming he had disappeared, without having peeled as much as a single carrot. Mark and I discovered him in his room, where he lay in a drunken stupor, face down on his bed, still clothed in his chef's whites.

'I don't fucking believe it, I really don't, today of all days,' said Mark. 'Leave it to me. I know just how to deal

The Mousse and the Man from the Michelin

with this. It wouldn't be the first time.' Mark disappeared into the adjacent bathroom, returning moments later with a bucket brimming with cold water which he proceeded at a slow trickle to pour over Kevin's head. 'Get up, you lazy little malingerer!'

'What the fuck!' shrilled Kevin. 'What's going on?' The shock of the cold water catapulted him into an upright position, causing him to crack his head sharply against a shelf above the bed.

'Want more, do you?' chuckled Mark, clearly enjoying himself. 'If not, then get out of bed now and get back to work.'

I too found myself submitting to a frisson of sadistic pleasure at witnessing Kevin's discomfort. It was pay-back time, I told myself, for every snide and underhand remark he'd ever made at my expense.

It was possibly more of a reflex action than a premeditated assault but, without warning, Kevin kicked a leg into the air, catching Mark squarely beneath the chin with the toe of his shoe. With a yelp of pain, Mark raised his hands to his jaw, in the process discharging the full content of the bucket over Kevin's bed. Instantly a fetid stench filled the air. It was as if an accumulation of long-dormant bodily detritus had been released in vaporous form from Kevin's bedding, raised from the dead by contact with water.

'He attacked me,' said Mark incredulously. 'Did you see that? He fucking attacked me.'

'Get away from me,' wailed an anguished Kevin. 'You're victimising me. I'm sick and you're fucking victimising me.'

'He fucking well attacked me,' said Mark again, nursing his injured chin.

It was then that Kevin did something quite unexpected: he slithered across the bed and – with a departing cry of 'Death or glory!' – allowed his flaccid body to fall like a rag doll from the open window (all windows in this ancient building being at knee level) to the road below, leaving Mark and I gaping at each other in stunned disbelief.

'Shit,' said Mark, turning pale. 'We've killed him.'

'*We've* killed him?' I said defensively. 'What do you mean *we've* killed him? I didn't lay a finger on him.

'Nor did I, never touched him.'

'But it was you who tortured him.'

'Tortured? I wasn't torturing him...not exactly. It's standard practice in the trade, cruel to be kind, you know, for their own benefit. It works.'

The Mousse and the Man from the Michelin

'I can see it works.'

'And besides you're an accessory after the fact, because you failed to stop me.'

'How was I to stop you?'

'You're in charge here. It's my day off. All you had to do was say.'

'Oh, yeah, as if you were about to take any notice.'

'Besides, you were relishing every moment of it. I could see it in your eyes. Like it or not, you're an accomplice. If I go down for this I'm taking you with me.'

'That's blatantly unfair.'

'Tell that to the judge.'

Just then a voice called from the foot of the stairs: 'Excuse me from interrupzing, boyz, but I sink I just saw Kevin fall pasht ze vindow.'

'Yes, we know.'

'OK, vell just so long as you are avare.'

'Don't worry, Betsie, we're onto it. But thanks anyway.'

'Bitteschön. You're velcome.'

We had at best expected to discover Kevin lying injured, or at worst crushed to death by a passing truck. Yet when we arrived in the road below there was no sign of him. Was this a good or a bad thing? On a positive note, we could at least assume that he was well enough to walk. But he'd plunged a good three metres, head-first at that. What if he'd staggered off injured or concussed, perhaps even to suffer a lingering death in some remote thicket or hedgerow? Our fears were compounded by the discovery of a quantity of fresh blood on the tarmac beneath Kevin's window (The Mute Swan abutted directly onto the main road and there was no proper footpath), together with a tell-tale trail of bloody droplets leading away from the scene. Sleuth-like, we followed our macabre trail into the lane at the side of the building to where it abruptly ended at the foot of Sidney and Doreen's garden wall. We were debating what to do next when we were startled by a commotion from above our heads.

'Arrrrrrrrrrrhhhhheeeeggg!'

Kevin's battle cry – as one could only suppose this was how he intended his mangled scream to be interpreted – was cut cruelly short. His intention, it seemed, had been to take us by surprise in an audacious Zorro-style aerial attack. But in launching himself from the roof of Sidney and Doreen's potting shed, he had badly mistimed his leap. Mark and I turned around in time to see him hit the ground belly first. You might have thought that two full-frontal impacts in the space of five minutes would prove too much for Kevin's

The Mousse and the Man from the Michelin

constitution, but not a bit of it. Perhaps it was the anesthetising effect of the alcohol in his system, but he was immediately up on his feet, fists clenched and coming for us. Face smashed, knees and elbows lacerated, chef's whites hanging from his limbs in tatters, he looked as if he should ideally be dead. It was a scene from a zombie movie, and – as we were now very clearly dealing with a deranged mind – a case of kill or be killed. Kevin lunged in my direction, arms flailing. Fortunately I was both broader and heavier than my assailant, and as our bodies locked in combat it became obvious that I had the upper hand. Holding Kevin's neck in a head-lock, I grappled him to the ground, while Mark placed a well-aimed kick at his solar plexus.

'What are you doing, you oafs? Leave the poor boy alone. Don't you know his mother has emphysema?' Tabitha leaned from her bedroom window overlooking the lane, wagging an accusatory finger.

'Keep out of this, Tabitha,' said Mark. 'You've no idea what happened. We're dealing with a psychopath and we're restraining him for his own good.'

'I jolly well will not keep out of it. Psychopath my hat! I saw you kicking him, you bullies. Not content with humiliating him, you now want to kill the poor boy. Pick on someone normal.'

'He hit me first,' said Mark sullenly.'

'*Oh, he hit me first...he started it,*' mimicked Tabitha. 'What nonsense. You know as well as I that Kevin couldn't hit a pig's bottom with a broom. He's perfectly harmless.'

Mark and I remained draped prostrate over Kevin's now limp body, while beginning to feel more than a little ridiculous. We were just pondering on a course of action when a car turned into the lane. It was Don Mote with the film crew.

'Oh sweet serendipity,' squealed Don, jumping from the car, 'reality TV at its most trenchant. Just hold that position while we set the camera rolling. Don't move. Love it! Simply love it!'

The following morning I began work early. Thankfully today we would be spared the distraction of a film crew in the kitchen. To my dismay, however, my wounded thumb continued to bleed sporadically. I should really have gone to the hospital to have the cut stitched, but I was intent on staying in the kitchen for fear that in my absence I would once again be sidelined by Mark. Midway through the morning, Gerald arrived with a note from Don Mote to say that Crispin Sutherland had read my menu 'with interest', but unfortunately nothing was to his taste. Would I mind ordering in a melon for him as a starter? And for the main course could he request a plain fillet steak, cooked well-done?

The Mousse and the Man from the Michelin

Would I mind?

You would need to be a chef to appreciate the significance of such an insult; it strikes at the very heart of one's honour as an artist. It would be like asking Vladimir Ashkenazy to play the Beer Barrel Polka, or Mark Rothko to give a lick of paint to the outhouse.

'Yes, I bloody well would mind,' I said. 'How could any sane person have an aversion to an entire menu?'

'Quite right, couldn't sympathise more, Kento,' said Gerald. 'I suspected the fellow was a charlatan the instant I met him. Weak handshake, always a giveaway, and I'm damned sure he's got his sights set on Arabella...But under the circumstances we can hardly deny him his whims.'

Having written-off Crispin Sutherland as a lost cause, I consoled myself with the prospect that, as a fellow professional, at least Clement Freud would appreciate my efforts, so for the remainder of the day I concentrated on fine-tuning my stellar menu while trying to put the events of the previous day out of my mind. When seven o'clock arrived all the elements were in place for a pain-free service. Every last detail had been considered: quail eggs sat ready to be loaded into wafer-thin pastry tarts – crisp, delicate and lined with a base of fragrant mushroom *duxelle*; the hollandaise sauce rested gently in its *bain marie*, rich and gelatinous; in the refrigerators sat tubs and bowls laden with stocks and essences; meat and game neatly butchered; fish, skinned and filleted and buried in a box of ice to maintain peak freshness; baking sheets laden with pastries and a variety of homemade breads...and, though it pained me, Crispin Sutherland's melon and steak, sliced and ready to go. The atmosphere was tense, but confident. To be on the safe side, all three chefs were in the kitchen: Kevin (bandaged, dosed with painkillers and duly contrite) on cold starters, salads and vegetables; Mark on hot starters and puddings; me on main courses. And although I'd been unwilling to relinquish any more limelight to Mark than was necessary, I found his presence reassuring.

The evening got off to a promising start: every table in the first sitting arrived more or less on time, which meant no bottlenecks in the second sitting. The filming in the restaurant, we were assured by the waitresses, was in full swing and going well. But we had a problem: nine o'clock had been and gone and the Freud party had yet to show. Fifteen, thirty, forty-five minutes passed...Every stroke of the clock brought us a fraction closer to the truth. Of course, there might have been a perfectly legitimate reason for the Freud party not arriving that night, but both Gerald and I knew in our hearts that we'd been stung, the subjects of a cruel hoax. It seemed so obvious now: there had of course never been

The Mousse and the Man from the Michelin

a Freud party. In all likelihood, the customer who'd made the booking had never met Clement Freud. We were being punished for our hubris, and we'd fallen for it – hats off to the man for pulling it off with such aplomb.

CHAPTER 7

Tabitha, meanwhile, had announced that she was seeking spiritual enlightenment (it's what people did in the 70s). This involved her spending two days a week at a house somewhere in Crouch End, where she would take part in something called an encounter group.

'Encountering is all the thing in London now – *sooo* right on, and fab for cleansing the karma,' declared Tabitha. 'You really should try it.'

This was the worrying part. None of us was especially interested in Tabitha's divine quest. But this did nothing to deter her from sharing her newfound insights with anyone who was prepared to listen, as well as those of us who weren't. Even more worryingly, she had decided that an 'encounter' was just the thing that was needed to heal the growing rift in the kitchen among the chefs.

'All this negativity is so obviously bad for your karmas,' announced Tabitha when she suggested the idea (in fact it was less a suggestion and more a command), especially as it now appears to have lapsed into physical violence. It's all the fault of the ego, you know. Tame the self and harmony will surely follow... that's from the *Bhagavad Gita,* verse six hundred and twelve. Look it up.'

Immune to our objections, Tabitha informed us that she had scheduled our encounter to take place the following Monday, and that Mark, Kevin and I should report to her room at 6 am sharp.

'Six o'clock!' we complained, but that's way too early. 'Can't we make it later?'

'Certainly not. Mornings are best for doing group work, as our vibrations are more in tune. Besides, I've a busy day, and I'm arranging this for you at considerable personal inconvenience. The least you can do for me is to make an effort.'

Terrified of oversleeping and risking Tabitha's ire, instead of going to bed on the Sunday before our encounter group, we played poker throughout the night. It had seemed like a good idea at the time, especially as Kevin had borne the brunt of the losses. But when we arrived at Tabitha's room the following morning we were tired, fractious and hung over. None of us had any idea of what to expect, as Tabitha had neglected to tell us. We were, however, united by a collective lack of enthusiasm.

Our first shock was to discover that Tabitha's room had been transformed beyond recognition, beginning with a sign on the door, upon which was written the word 'Sam-

The Mousse and the Man from the Michelin

bodhi' (which is Sanskrit, Tabitha helpfully informed us, for 'know all'). On entering we found ourselves groping in semi-darkness, at least until our eyes became accustomed to the gloom. Despite it being daylight outside, the curtains were closed. The only source of light was a pool of candles set on a low table in the centre of the room. The air was heavy with the fug of burning incense; a record of sitar music droned softly on the gramophone. Lining one wall was a gaudy array of Indian silks, in the centre of which was an autographed framed photo of a doe-eyed man in an orange kaftan, smiling serenely from behind a vast beard. Seated cross-legged on a cushion in a corner of the room was a second doe-eyed man. He too wore an orange kaftan and smiled serenely from behind a vast beard. (I found myself unable to take my eyes off what appeared to be the remains of a digestive biscuit which had lodged itself in the beard's lower left quadrant, clearly beyond its wearer's field of vision.)

'Who's the geezer with the beard?' said Kevin, pointing at the photograph.

'He is not a geezer,' replied Tabitha indignantly. 'How dare you be so disrespectful? That is His Holiness Bhagwan Shree Rajneesh, my guru. He's attained full enlightenment, I'll have you know. It's an extremely rare state.'

'What's enlightenment?' I asked.

'How should I know?' said Tabitha.

'So you don't know?'

'Well obviously I can't tell you what enlightenment is because it's, you know, an abstract thingy... Gnostic knowledge and whatnot. It's impossible to know what it is until one has actually found it, but it's all about, you know, feeling blissful and suchlike.'

'Can I get some coffee?' said Mark. 'I really need a fag and some coffee.'

'You may do neither,' said Tabitha, 'it will interfere with the vibe, just the same as alcohol does. I personally now drink raw vegetable juice in place of alcohol.'

'Really, since when?' said Mark.

'And I'd advise you to do the same, if you're serious about change.'

'Give up alcohol?' said Mark aghast. 'I'd never cope.'

'Nonsense, you'll be on a vitamin C high in no time at all.'

'But if you don't know what enlightenment is, then how would you know if you've found it?' I persisted, determined to get the bottom of the conundrum. 'I mean, how did Bag...

The Mousse and the Man from the Michelin

er....your guru get enlightened?'

'I'm not about to be cross-examined on this issue,' said Tabitha. 'Besides, Bhagwan says that the very act of questioning by a process of logic is a Western aberration. But if you really must know, in Bhagwan's case, enlightenment happened purely by accident. When His Holiness was just nine years old he fell out of a tree when he was playing with his chums. He landed on his head and knocked himself unconscious. And when he regained consciousness he knew all there was to know about love, life, God, death and the truth, and he's never looked back. Before the bump on the head he was just a normal child.

'You know, that's really weird that, coz the same thing happened to me,' said Kevin. 'Knocked out cold, I was.'

'Are you trying to be funny, Kevin?' said Tabitha, 'because if so you can stop it now. How could you possibly compare yourself with His Holiness?'

'I'm not being funny, I'm being serious. I landed on my head. My mum says I've not been the same since.'

'It would explain a lot,' said Mark.

'What's an ashram?' asked Kevin.

'It's a bit like, you know, a hermitage, but with better amenities.'

'What's a hermitage?'

'It's a place of asylum.'

'Aren't asylums where they put mad people?' asked Kevin suspiciously.

'Kevin, you are trying my patience,' said Tabitha. 'Well then, what are you waiting for? Don't just stand there all of you, take off your shoes and place them in the corridor outside then come back in and sit cross-legged in a circle on the floor. Quick! Quick!'

We dutifully did as we were told.

'I've put together an agenda for the day,' said Tabitha brightly when we were seated, 'but as this is an encounter *group*, and as such a collective enterprise, please feel free to add your own thoughts.'

Kevin cleared his throat in preparation to speak. 'Yeah, well. I was thinking – '

'But first I want to introduce you to Swami Chaitamya Yogendra,' continued Tabitha, beaming benevolently in the direction of the bearded man in the orange kaftan, 'but you can address him as Swami Yogi. He's here to facilitate our day and guide us through our encounter.' Tabitha emphasised the word 'encounter' with an air quote wiggle of the finger tips. 'He's frightfully good, aren't you, poppet? He's

The Mousse and the Man from the Michelin

even been to Bhagwan's ashram in Poona to learn from His Holiness himself.'

'Peace and love peace and love,' said Swami Yogi. As he spoke he gave a little modest half-bow and raised his hands in a gesture of supplication. In dramatic contrast to the guru in the photograph, Swami Yogi was albino in appearance. His translucent, freckly skin was rendered doubly striking by a ginger beard and shock of orange hair that coordinated perfectly with his kaftan.

'But first, some housekeeping,' said Tabitha. 'Swami Yogi has selflessly given up his time to be with us today, but sadly, due to the materialistic nature of the world in which we live, it all costs money. So to cover his very modest expenses we've applied a small voluntary contribution of ten pounds each.'

At this point, Swami Yogi reached into an orange cotton shoulder bag and handed each of us a business card. The top side of the card was emblazoned with a circular symbol that resembled a black tadpole performing *soixante-neuf* with a white tadpole while rotating in a tumble dryer. On the flip side of the card was printed:

'Crouch End Zenterprises'

Swami Chaitamya Yogendra (formerly Duncan Marshall)

Kent Austin

Crouch End Ashram, Crouch End, London, N8

Encountering | Chakra cleansing | Soul work | Purification

Telephone 01 76651

I know Crouch End isn't like having Chelsea or Mayfair or somewhere,' he said apologetically, 'but the early adopter sannyasins arrived back from India first and got the wealthier boroughs sewn up. I got left with Crouch End, but they say it's up and coming.

'You mean we have to pay?' I asked.

'No one said anything about us having to pay,' said Mark. 'It's not as if we asked to be here.'

'We all pay in the end,' said Swami Yogi portentously, 'through our karma. You can't escape your karma.'

'Swami Yogi has renounced his former identity and all his worldly possessions so that he may help people like you,' said Tabitha. 'He's even given away his extensive record collection, and he's driven all the way from Crouch End this morning in the rain and on a dangerous motorcycle with defective brakes, and yet you would deny him the crumbs from your table?'

'Help people like who?' I asked.

'People like you, of course! People in thrall to the world

The Mousse and the Man from the Michelin

of dull materialism. Now pay up, and we'll hear no more of it.'

With any remaining fight knocked out of us, Mark and I begrudgingly handed over our ten-pound notes.

'Yeah, well, if it's a voluntary contribution, I think I'll give it a miss, if you don't mind,' said Kevin.

'I most certainly *do* mind. It's only voluntary up to a point,' said Tabitha, 'such as for the poor and whatnot.'

'Yeah, well. I am poor, see, 'cause them two cleaned me out at cards last night. A whole week's wages.' Mark and I shifted uncomfortably as Kevin, no doubt confident that he could rely on Tabitha's enduring sympathy, pointed an accusing finger in our direction.

Tabitha took the bait: 'How utterly disgraceful, but frankly I'm not surprised. It's just the latest in a catalogue of abuses this poor boy has had to suffer at your brutish hands.'

'Hey, now hang on a moment,' said Mark. 'He chose to play poker with us. It's not as though we forced him. It's not our fault if he lost.'

'It most jolly well is. You could have predicted that someone like Kevin would lack the mental faculties to excel at a game of skill such as poker.'

'Yeah,' said Kevin, nodding vigorously in agreement.

'So pay up now, the two of you. Five pounds each for Kevin's contribution to Swami Yogi. No buts.'

Mark and I searched through our pockets and raised a further ten pounds in one-pound notes.

'Thank you, boys, much appreciated,' said Tabitha, tucking the bank notes into her cleavage, while seemingly aglow with the righteousness of her calling. 'And this brings us neatly to the business in hand. Now, as we all know, we're here today for a reason. Kevin, of course, has acknowledged that he needs help with his anger issues.'

'Have I?' said Kevin, looking mildly surprised.

'Not in so many words, but it shows in the eyes,' said Tabitha.

'It definitely shows in the eyes,' confirmed Swami Yogi, nodding sagely.

'What does?' said Kevin.

'Your self-loathing.'

'But I don't loath myself...do I?' Kevin looked around the room, as if seeking affirmation of his self-worth.

'Frankly, Kevin, I find that very hard to believe,' said Tabitha.

The Mousse and the Man from the Michelin

'So do I,' said Mark, seeming for the first time to warm to the occasion.

'Me too,' I said.

'Very often people hate themselves without realising it. It's so deeply repressed,' said Swami Yogi. 'I know I used to hate *my*self, at least until I followed the light, because we're all basically full of shit.' Swami Yogi stared unblinkingly in my direction, his eyes moist with empathy.

'Bhagwan says it's the default position of the human race,' said Tabitha. 'Until we are cleansed we embody the very essence of dull materialism.'

'Yeah,' said Kevin, 'but if we're all full of shit like, you know, Swami Yoga sez we are – '

'Yo*gi*,' corrected Swami Yogi. '*Gi*, not *ga*.'

' – like Swami Yo*gi* sez we are,' continued Kevin, 'then you an' him must be full of shit as well. So what gives you the right, like, to tell us that we're full of shit?'

'He has a point, Tabitha,' I said.

'And what about them two,' said Kevin, pointing at Mark and me. 'Don't *they* hate themselves?'

'Not as much as we hate you,' said Mark. 'Besides, this isn't about us. It's about you. You're the one with the problems. That's why we're here.'

'Well, that isn't *entirely* true,' began Tabitha. 'I mean there are wider issues to consider – '

'What bleedin' problems?' said Kevin.

'That's it, just run with your feelings. Let it all out,' said Swami Yogi. 'Now we're getting somewhere. It's all happening as it should. This is healing stuff.'

'Your *bleeding* sleeping problem, for a start,' said Mark.

'That's it, keep it coming,' enthused Swami Yogi.

'Kevin sleeps so much because he's depressed, so I don't think he can be held directly responsible,' said Tabitha. 'And at the bottom of it all is a deep spiritual malaise, a bottomless pit of unhappiness, isn't that right, poppet?'

'Yeah, well, I wouldn't say bottomless, exactly, but deep for sure,' said Kevin, clearly warming to his victimhood.

'That's bollocks and you know it,' said Mark. 'You're just lazy.'

'Actually, I think someone's more than a little bit unhappy them*selves*, perhaps even projecting their own deep-seated insecurity onto others in the room?' said Tabitha, fixing Mark with her trade mark head-to-one-side-condescending-half-smile, that was simultaneously intimidating and infuri-

The Mousse and the Man from the Michelin

ating. 'Bhagwan calls it transference. Perhaps, Mark, there's something you'd like to share with the group?'

'Fuck off, Tabitha! I've had it up to here with you,' said Mark. 'And I don't give a toss what Bagwash calls it.'

'That's it. Let it all out,' urged Swami Yogi. 'It's why we're here.'

'Yeah, well, but I'm not really a morning person, am I?' said Kevin, his voice breaking into a self-pitying whine.

'Not a morning person? You're not an afternoon person,' snorted Mark. 'I've lost count of the number of times I've had to kick you out of bed at four o'clock.'

'That's it, let it all –'

'And you can shut up as well,' said Mark, glaring crossly at Swami Yogi. 'You do realise no one's taking a blind bit of notice of anything you're saying? Is this what we get for our ten pounds?'

Swami Yogi, his air of blissful equilibrium having apparently deserted him, seemed at a loss for an answer, and an awkward silence descended upon our encounter group. Just when I'd convinced myself that he'd fallen asleep or entered a sulk, Swami Yogi came back to life: 'Well, you do get one of these, too, of course,' he said, reaching into his bag to produce three small cameo photographs of Bhagwan

Shree Rajneesh, each housed in Perspex and threaded onto a wooden bead necklace. 'Peace and love peace and love.'

'Well, I think that will do us for one day,' said Tabitha. 'I believe we've made some very real progress with your group healing, don't you?'

'Yeah, well, I was going to say – 'began Kevin.

'So all that's left now is to consummate things with a group hug,' continued Tabitha.

'A group what?'

It began in the 70s. Since then British society has undergone a progressive erosion of physical etiquette. Once upon a time we had a physical response to cover every conceivable occasion. It came in two forms: the peck on the cheek and the standard handshake. And everybody knew exactly where and when each form was applied without any risk of confusion. If a man, the peck on the cheek was reserved for female family members and close friends of the opposite sex. Everyone else received a handshake. If a woman, the peck on the cheek was reserved for male and female family members and close friends of both sexes. Everyone else received a handshake. Whatever became of the standard handshake? Brusque and reassuringly formal, it has much to recommend it, especially as it is performed at a full arm's length, thus creating a healthy distance between

The Mousse and the Man from the Michelin

the respective shakers. As a means of non-verbal communication (whether firm, weak, damp, diffident or assertive) the standard handshake has yet to be improved upon. Yet it has become an endangered species, made redundant by the infernal hug. What is this compulsion to get physical? To savour one's neighbour's sweat, to feel their stubble upon one's cheek, to fondle the alien folds of their flesh, perhaps even catch a whiff of that morning's fried breakfast on their breath or the tell-tale scent of an earlier sexual encounter lurking in their bodily hair. Why has it, in recent times, grown so universally fashionable, spanning class and sexual divides, to become the default response to every social interaction? Whenever such an obligation presents itself there's a part of me that recoils in horror, and to this day I remain suspicious of any situation that entails gratuitous physical contact. '*Sorry,*' I should say, '*but this just isn't for me. I'm just too staid, too English, too terminally self-conscious, to engage in this kind of stuff. Yes, I may be repressed, but I'm happy with it. And, yes, you may well think I'm a prig, but I don't care. Please allow me to wallow in my hang-ups at peace. Allow me the dignity and good grace to opt out from your physical affectations forever.*'

But of course I say nothing of the sort. Instead I experience a dutiful need to cooperate without protest, so as not to cause offence and embarrassment, which, paradoxically, is every bit a symptom of my repressed English character as not wishing to indulge in physical contact in the first place. Yes, the hugging, squeezing and general back-slapping that is now so much a part of our social fabric owes its origins to the emancipated 70s, and as a surviving representative of that generation, I apologise unreservedly.

'A group what?' I asked.

'A group hug,' repeated Tabitha, smiling sweetly.

'Must we?' I said.

'You'll find it most beneficial. Come along, gather round, drop all those pesky male inhibitions and let it all hang out. I guarantee the negative vibes will just melt away. This is the cathartic phase of our encounter. Feel the joy. Feel the peace.'

The group hug involved each of us draping an arm across our immediate neighbour's shoulder and forming a kind of circular kneeling scrum. In the process I found myself sandwiched between Kevin on the one side and Swami Yogi on the other. The former smelled vaguely of cheese and wet dog, the latter a sickly blend of patchouli oil and wholemeal biscuits. The whole affair was made doubly agonising by the fact that no one seemed to know when to stop hugging. As a result we just hung there in suspended limbo, listening to the rasp of one another's breath and the intermittent

The Mousse and the Man from the Michelin

grumblings of our collective digestive systems, linear time as we once knew it teetering on the edge of a black hole. 'Ahhhh...Ummm...' intoned Tabitha. 'Breathe in...Breathe out...Feel the joy...Feel the peace.'

I breathed in. I breathed out. I couldn't recall a time when I'd felt less joyful or less at peace.

CHAPTER 8

It was with a cold dread that I looked forward to the screening of *Success Story*. When it was broadcast some two months after filming, my fears were confirmed. Watching the opening minutes of the film, it quickly became clear that the 'success' element of *Success Story* had nothing to do with *my* success, or otherwise, and everything to do with the success of the Golightlys. The final programme had been edited to reflect this, and with the exception of a few action shots of me at work in the kitchen, both I and my landmark menu failed to get a mention. There was, however, no shortage of shots of Gerald and Arabella chatting animatedly over dinner with Crispin Sutherland. I was hoping that he might at least throw in a well-timed compliment about the food, which, to his credit, he did. However, it wasn't quite what I'd had in mind.

'While mine host has settled upon a superb summer soup, I've opted for this mouth-watering and oh-so moreish minted melon,' lilted Crispin Sutherland, rubbing his hands together unctuously for the benefit of the camera. 'Mmmmm... an *apt* appetiser in anticipation of the arrival of an altogether amazing *Ab*erdeen *An*gus steak... Who says a BBC presenter has to survive on sandwiches alone?'

Kent Austin

With his clipped vowels and sing-song delivery, Crispin Sutherland seemed to belong in a different era. Listening to him was like being sucked through a wormhole to the 1950s and the world of the Pathé newsreel. BBC was pronounced Beer-Beer-Seer. To my ear at least, it sounded ridiculous and completely out of step with the times. I could hardly bring myself to continue watching, but I was unable to take my eyes off the empty table in the background, at which in an ideal world Clement Freud would have been seen dining in full view of the camera.

'Oh, that was marvellous. Crispin is good, isn't he?' oozed Tabitha, after the programme had ended.

In the absence of a television, and with the video recorder yet to be invented, the restaurant staff had been invited to watch the programme at Gerald and Arabella's house. Hunched glumly in front of the TV set, Gerald and Mark looked almost as offended as I was. The females, however, were unanimous in their approval, even to the point of being dewy eyed. For reasons I would have been unable to explain, this added immensely to my annoyance.

'Good? You can't be serious! The man is a total prick,' I said.

'Couldn't agree more,' said Gerald, 'an imposter of the first water.'

The Mousse and the Man from the Michelin

'And why does he have to speak in that ridiculous sing-song voice?' I said.

'Ridiculous? Not at all, Kento. It's how educated people speak,' said Tabitha. 'Received pronunciation. It's perfectly normal. Are you suggesting the way *I* speak is ridiculous? I'd be careful if I were you.'

'Well, there must be lots of educated people who don't speak like that. What about David Bailey? He doesn't speak like that, nor does John Lennon, and they're both educated. And why does he have to keep rhyming his bloody words?'

'It's called assonance and alliteration, Kento,' groaned Henrietta, rolling her eyes. 'It's the done thing if you're presenting, and a real art I might add, especially to do it off the cuff the way Crispin does. The mark of a true professional.'

'Well I still think it sounds stupid.'

'And anyway, it depends on what you call educated,' continued Tabitha. 'As for David Bailey and John Lennon,' 'the one sounds like an East End spiv and the other speaks with an incomprehensible Liverpudlian brogue. Charming though it may be, could you honestly imagine someone with a regional accent presenting a programme on the BBC? It would be unthinkable, and quite rightly so. There is such a thing as standards, and if any place should be the preserve of the Queen's English surely it's our national broadcasting network. Besides, I think someone's just a teensy-weensy bit jealous of Mr Sutherland's charisma, don't you, Kento? You've never taken to him, if we're honest?' Tabitha fixed me with her trademark patronising glare.

'But what kind of message does this send out about my cooking, him droning on about steak and melon like that?'

'Ah, so now at last we get to the nub of the matter. But the programme isn't about your cooking, silly. Why does everything have to be about you all the time? It's about how wonderfully successful Gerald and Arabella have been with their little hobby and all the opportunities they've created for their staff and whatnot. Isn't that right, Gerald?'

'Oh, don't be ridiculous, Tabso,' laughed Gerald modestly, giving a dismissive wave of the hand. 'It's about all of us equally. We're one big family here.'

'Not that I count myself as a member of the staff, you understand,' continued Tabitha, 'because of course I'm only here to help out as a friend, but I really think it's, you know, marvellous for all of you who've worked so hard. So let's raise our glasses to Gerald and Arabella and drink to their continued success.'

While people groped half-heartedly to fill their glasses for the toast, I left the room, with what little hope I'd been nurturing of saving face finally dashed. My one consolation

The Mousse and the Man from the Michelin

was that the brutality of the final edit had meant that any scenes in the film of a potentially humiliating nature that Don Mote might have been plotting to include had been cut. I took comfort also in the discovery some weeks later that we'd given birth to a turkey because, according to the programme producers, *Success Story* was deemed to be so bad that it failed to make it past the pilot stage, and any plans for a series were quietly shelved.

But whilst my own short-lived career as a TV personality may have lain in tatters, the appeal of The Mute Swan among celebrity diners remained unstoppable. During one particularly star-studded, but not untypical, weekend in the late 1970s we played host to actors Alan Bates and Vanessa Redgrave; the writer and presenter Bernard Levin; the future London mayor Ken Livingstone; the rock band America (the whole band – for some reason they liked to dine en-masse), musicians John and Beverly Martin; actor Bob Hoskins; 'fifth Beatle' and Beatles record producer George Martin; Booker Prize-winning writer Beryl Bainbridge; Roger Daltrey of The Who; and former Labour Party leader Lord George-Brown (many of whom were regular customers).

I'm dropping names here. But it's central to my tale, because the fact was we'd become a little star-struck – the very idea that so many important and successful people (at least that's how we viewed them) had made a conscious decision to book a table at our humble rural eatery had gone to our heads. However, we were not easy to impress. As in all exclusive restaurants, customers – including (or especially) celebrities – were upon arrival subjected by staff to a covert appraisal of their worthiness to be catered for, and if they failed to come up to scratch they were, often on the flimsiest of grounds, arbitrarily condemned to the second tier. (That I, a former impoverished barrow boy from the provinces, should be party to such misplaced snobbery did not at the time present an irony.) This didn't necessarily mean we treated one customer any differently from another – at least on face value – but if it came to a toss-up between who got the best table or the choicest cut of meat, they were destined to lose out. For the unsuspecting diner, it was a minefield strewn with socially compromising trip wires. Giveaway signs included arriving in a car with a personalised number plate; ordering a gin and tonic as an aperitif; drinking beer with one's meal; drinking rosé wine with one's meal; referring to lunch as dinner; referring to dinner as dinner (the proper term, of course, being supper); asking for mint sauce, ketchup or any other form of proprietary sauce; clearing and stacking one's empty plates in an effort to assist the waiting staff; talking about greens instead of vegetables; requesting that the head be removed from one's trout; seasoning

The Mousse and the Man from the Michelin

food without first having tasted it; smoking a pipe; asking the whereabouts of the toilet (only loo or lavatory will do); calling a sofa a settee; calling a napkin a serviette; saying cheers instead of your good health; if a man, wearing any form of jewellery other than a wedding band or signet ring; if a woman, wearing strong perfume or faux fur; asking for a plain steak, well-done; and, perhaps the most heinous crime of all, sending a perfectly cooked piece of beef back to the kitchen to have it cooked 'properly'.

As did the popular comedy double act Little and Large. (Although it may equally have been the popular comedy double act Cannon and Ball – we never did quite get to the bottom of it.)

Comedians Syd Little and Eddie Large (or was it Tommy Cannon and Bobby Ball?) had reserved a table with their wives for Sunday lunch, each couple arriving separately in their own prestige black saloon – a Mercedes and a BMW respectively (and, in case you were wondering, yes, they did have personalised number plates). All went unremarkably until the main courses were served. The four had ordered roast rib of beef. Like all good restaurants, unless otherwise stipulated, we served our beef rare. Though Syd and Eddie (or Tommy and Bobby) and their wives preferred their beef well done, so they sent it back to the kitchen. With much voluble cursing I blasted the beef beneath a hot grill and sent it back to the table. But I hadn't seen the last of it, because moments later all four plates were returned to the kitchen for a second time.

'Zey shay zere beef is still uncooked,' said Betsie. 'Pleaze to cook it vell done. Zey shay zey are very dishappointed.'

'But it *is* well done,' I protested.

'Oh nein, es ist nicht. I sink I see a liddle biddle pink blod here,' said Betsie, placing her nose up close to a slice of beef and prodding it with a finger.

'But barely. I mean, surely they don't want it completely cremated?'

'I don't know. Warten ein moment, I vill go and ashk zem.'

'Yesh zay do,' said Betsie, returning from the dining room a moment later. 'Zay shay they vont it cooked as if it has been nailed to a tree in a bush fire.'

'Nailed to a what?'

'Ein tree in ein bush fire. Zat is vot zay shed. I know not vot it meanz.'

'Now that is one very good reason why we should never cater for comedians,' said Gerald, who, alerted to my pre-

The Mousse and the Man from the Michelin

dicament, had appeared in the kitchen and was minutely inspecting the returned plates of beef. 'There really is no place for such end-of-the-pier pointlessness when discussing something as serious as good food.'

'Anyway, that would mean they want their beef cooked rare – very rare, in fact,' said Tabitha.

'Surely the opposite?' said Gerald.

'Not at all. Obviously clever clogs Morecambe and Wise out there have never seen a bush fire. Daddy has. He almost lost his life in one when he was stationed as a missionary in the veldt. The flames travel at speeds faster than a running gazelle. It would therefore follow that any piece of steak nailed to a tree under such conditions would receive only the most rudimentary grilling before the fire had passed on. Hence the steak would remain rare.'

'That is a very good point, Tabso,' said Gerald, stroking his chin thoughtfully. 'I hadn't thought of it like that. Although I suppose it would depend on the speed of the wind, which could act as a kind of variable. But I shall go and inform them of the error in their logic right away. Actually, I'm sure they'll find it amusing, being comedians. Did you say it was Morecambe and Wise? Arabella likes Morecambe and Wise. I'll ask them for their autographs while I'm at it. She'll be cock-a-hoop.'

'Zay are mosht definitely *not* Morecambe und Vise,' announced Betsie, after Gerald had left. 'Even I vould recognishe Morecambe und Vise. Henrietta took ze booking. She sinks zey are ze people called die Little und die Large or may be even die Cannon und die Ball.'

'What, you mean she doesn't know?' said Tabitha. 'Surely she must have asked for a name when they reserved the table?'

'She shays she doesn't know. She shays die von vears glasses und die ozer doesn't. Zat is all.'

'Ah, so I was right then, said Tabitha triumphantly. 'It *is* Morecambe and Wise. They've obviously booked under a pseudonym.'

'I made your point about the bush fire, Tabso,' said Gerald breezily when he returned from the dining room. 'They didn't find it funny for some reason. So much for them being comedians. Plainly there's no accounting for taste. Oh, and by the way, they say they *aren't* Morecambe and Wise, so I told them not to bother with the autographs.'

I returned the roast beef to the comedians for a third time, having given it a further extended blast beneath the grill. So well done was this beef by now that it was begging for mercy, and by any standards ruined. Undeterred, the comedians sent it back, complaining that it still contained

The Mousse and the Man from the Michelin

traces of blood.

A word of advice from an insider for those who like their meat well done: never, ever send back a piece of rare meat to a chef to have it cooked well done without at the very least expecting it to be wiped around his scrotal sack before it is returned to you on your plate. As for the consequences of sending it back three times...I'll allow you to use your imagination. And if you're reading this, Little and Large (Cannon and Ball), and if you dined at The Mute Swan sometime in the late 1970s, and if you recall feeling a little queasy after your meal, it was with good reason. Enough said.

There's a postscript to this story, because, as fate would have it, just weeks later the real Eric Morecambe booked a table for Sunday lunch. Under normal circumstances I seldom came into contact with our customers (unlike so many chefs, who insist on swanning around the dining room from table to table fishing for compliments). But on this occasion I quite literally bumped into the great man as he came out of the gents' washroom. So shocked was I that, for reasons which now escape me, I turned and fled in the direction of the kitchen with, bizarrely, Eric Morecambe following in hot pursuit. He caught up with me at the kitchen door. 'Eh, don't run away, lad, I only wanna shake your hand. I won't eat you. That was a great meal, so be sure you have yourself a drink on me and stick it on the bill.' And with that he took me in both arms and gave me a bear hug. There is no particular point or moral to this aside. Although it's worth noting that Eric Morecambe preferred his beef served *rare*. Read into it what you will.

It was at the tail end of the 70s that we began to experience the occasional quiet weekday night – something that was previously unthinkable. Weekends remained busy, but even here demand was falling off. Where once we were fully-booked six weeks in advance, it was now possible to reserve a table at a mere fortnight's notice. Initially we dismissed it as an irrelevant blip, but a pattern was developing. Why the slow down? First, we no longer had the field to ourselves. Until now, competition had been restricted to wayside inns of the Beefeater-Harvester variety and a handful of mediocre old-school establishments, staffed by hand-wringing waiters in bow-ties and egg-stained waistcoats. But now new restaurants were opening up all around us, serious, modern restaurants with ambitious, talented chefs who were determined to make their mark. One such restaurant in nearby Lewes received a glowing review in *The Good Food Guide,* placing our own predictably lacklustre entry into shameful perspective, and – horror of horrors – it was even rumoured they were being groomed by Michelin to receive their first star.

Second, we hadn't reckoned on the state of the econ-

The Mousse and the Man from the Michelin

omy. The winter of 1978-79 was to go down in history as the Winter of Discontent. The country was in the grip of a crisis the like of which had not been seen since the Great Depression: bitter disputes between the government and the trade unions resulted in energy and fuel shortages; oil prices soared. Much of the nation's labour force was reduced to working a three-day week. The government attempted to impose a wage freeze, while workers demanded ever-larger pay rises. Multiple strikes were made worse by intransigent trade unionists and incompetent management; picket lines blockaded hospitals, refusing admittance to all but emergency cases; a wildcat stoppage by gravediggers left the dead unburied; while striking refuse collectors allowed mountains of uncollected rubbish to accumulate in the streets. We also had to contend with galloping inflation – which at its height reached an eye-watering 30 percent. The weekly rent for a house doubled to more than £20. Meanwhile the average daily wage for an unskilled worker had stalled at around £8, and a full-time, fully trained middle-manager could expect to earn about £240 a month. The stock market plummeted and – clearly in an effort to sabotage what little confidence remained in his leadership, not to say national pride – Labour Prime Minister James Callaghan announced that had he been a young man he would have left the country never to return. Unsurprisingly, it would be a matter of months before his government's impotence in dealing with the strikes contributed towards a landslide victory for Margaret Thatcher, in the 1979 general election.

As if to mirror the national mood, in January of that year, a blast of freezing air arrived from the Arctic. It was the coldest winter in two hundred years, bringing blizzards and deep snow to add to people's misery. This coincided neatly with the power cuts. Timed by militant electricity workers to cause maximum disruption, the entire country would be blacked out on cue, and it could be several hours at a stretch before power was restored. In the kitchen, we were frequently reduced to cooking for a busy restaurant by candlelight. Fortunately we cooked on gas, but the ventilation system went down along with the lights. During one especially prolonged power cut, the build-up of heat in the kitchen was so intense that the phalanx of candles on which we were relying for light simply melted before our eyes and drowned in their own wax, plunging us into darkness.

And all while customer numbers continued to dwindle. We feared for our survival. Our glory days, it seemed, were over.

PART TWO

THE 1980s – THE MOUSSE

'Me? My character is still forming, and at this moment I'm in the middle of a revolution with myself. I still haven't truly found myself as a cook and this shows in my food. I'm beginning to blossom; the tagliatelle is the first perfect flower. There will be others.'

From *White Heat* (1989) by Marco Pierre White, chef-proprietor, Harveys, London (1 Michelin star)

CHAPTER 9

The year is 1980. Somehow a decade has passed since I arrived at The Mute Swan with a suitcase under my arm and a half-hearted plan to become a chef. Much has changed. Mark has left for another town to open his own restaurant. Henrietta has finally married her sea captain and is busy raising a family somewhere near Portsmouth. Betsie remains and is now indistinguishable from the fixtures and fittings. As too does Tabitha, who, despite the strictly temporary nature of her employment, continues to help out, her capacity for charity seemingly knowing no bounds. Kevin – who had long abandoned any hope of promotion – has finally, and to his infinite shock, graduated to the newly-reinstated role of sous chef and, with Mark gone, is now entrusted with managing the kitchen on my day off. My democratic power-sharing arrangement with Mark having ended with his departure, I am now sole head chef, with exclusive responsibility for the kitchen, and with Kevin reporting to me as my second in command. And we've just published our third cookery book – *The Secret Sauce Book of the Mute Swan* – a sequel to *The Secrets of the Mute Swan* and *The Deeper Secrets of the Mute Swan* – available at all good book shops and selling well.

Kent Austin

Life in many respects could be worse.

We'd even survived the recession of '79, because, despite fearing for our survival, we'd failed to account for Gerald's ingenuity in the face of adversity. Our weekday business had indeed suffered, but, severe as it was, the recession had not proved deep enough to affect our weekend trade. True, we no longer enjoyed the luxury of a fully-booked restaurant six weeks in advance. At weekends, however, we continued to turn away at least as many customers as we fed. It was this variance that Gerald set out to exploit. His plan involved knocking through the rooms that served as staff accommodation above the restaurant and converting them into a suite of four luxury private dining rooms. I'd vacated my own rooms a year earlier and moved with Mildred into a cottage in the village, and now, in the name of progress, Betsie, Tabitha and Kevin were obliged reluctantly to do the same. By this means we could effectively double our weekend customer numbers.

Six months later, and with the new dining rooms up and running and doing a brisk business, Gerald's plan was working like a dream; we were recouping our lost revenue and more. However, success came with its own set of problems. Because if the kitchen had struggled to cope before, it was as nothing when compared to cooking for up to one hundred diners in a three-hour window. We circumvented disaster by

The Mousse and the Man from the Michelin

employing an ever-growing brigade of junior chefs. I use the term 'chef' here loosely, because, apart from Kevin and me, our kitchen team comprised entirely of lowly-paid interns from the local college of domestic science.

And what a find...

Known locally as 'Rannie's', after Elise Orange Randall, the domestic science teacher who founded the school a century earlier, the Eastbourne College of Food and Fashion occupied an imposing Victorian mansion on Eastbourne's genteel seafront promenade. It's now closed, but at the time it enjoyed the quaint accolade of being Britain's last residential finishing school for young ladies, and it was something of a national curio. Rannie's curriculum centred on what were considered to be the essential skills required in becoming a good wife. Lessons included cookery, nappy changing, baby bathing, dressmaking, soft furnishing, flower-arranging, sugar craft and fashioning table napkins into amusing shapes. Crucially, there was a module on managing one's household servants, in which students were expected to become proficient in ironing, bed-making, dusting, firelighting and toilet-cleaning (the latter task being performed to the strict mantra of Flush! Brush! Flush!) – if only to place them in a position to instruct someone else to do it. Taken to its logical extreme, Rannie's should really have included a module on how to satisfy one's husband in the bedroom, but in 1907 when the curriculum was conceived this clearly was not thought to be a necessary wifely attribute.

If intellectual rigour was not a priority it was with good reason, for while Rannie's girls may have come from refined backgrounds (predominantly of expatriate parents stationed overseas with the armed forces, diplomatic corps or the Church), they were in the main academic throwbacks. They'd failed their exams, left school with few, if any, qualifications and their parents were at a loss to know what to do with them. With no prospect of going to university or entering an occupation worthy of their social status, and with their families ensconced in far-off lands, their one remaining hope was to find a husband. Rannie's offered the perfect commonsense compromise. But there was a problem. In 1907 it may well have been possible to keep a lid on the concupiscent impulses of some 200 post-pubescent debutantes confined beneath one roof. But by the late 1970s Rannie's had achieved a reputation locally as being a hot-bed of depravity, and with some justification. The girls, it seemed, had thrown off the shackles of their repressive bourgeois upbringings and were now hell-bent on losing their virginity, and more besides. For the town's male population it was manna from the gods. Clusters of sexually charged young men would gather nightly on the college steps, jostling for their share of the action while the girls showered them with

The Mousse and the Man from the Michelin

notes of supplication from their windows above, like so many maidens incarcerated inside a tower. The more determined of the men would even shimmy up the drainpipes after lights out to spend the night in the dorms. Many of the girls' admirers came from Eastbourne's dwindling fisherman community (who, by virtue of their proximity on the beach opposite the college, had claimed an unchallenged priority in the pecking order). Vulgar, libidinous and wreaking of decayed fish, they were in all likelihood not what parents had had in mind as suitors for their daughters when they enrolled them at an exclusive finishing school. But for the girls themselves it was apparently a match made in heaven.

As part of the college's cordon bleu cookery syllabus, the Rannie's board of governors had brokered a mutually beneficial arrangement with Gerald, whereby each of their students spent two days working in the Mute Swan kitchens. The official line was that the students furthered their culinary education in a professional environment. In practice, however, it was a means for the college to offload their students on the cheap, while for us it provided a limitless source of free labour that could be employed to perform any number of menial tasks around the kitchen. Even more importantly, at least from the point of view of the male kitchen staff, it allowed privileged access to a succession of sexually active young women who, for reasons upon which we could only speculate, seemed in awe of any man in chef's whites with a gift for filthy language and a large knife in his hand. (Even Kevin enjoyed a degree of success.) Another spin-off of this arrangement was that it allowed us to select the more promising students from each year's intake and offer them a full-time internship. Gerald had a particular fondness for the term 'internship' because, unlike the term 'job', it implied a legitimate excuse for paying minimum wages in return for maximum work and, as interns are technically still in education, their parents seemed happy to subsidise their meagre incomes. So cheap were our Rannie's interns that we could afford to have three on the go at once and still be in pocket.

The trouble now was that our ever-expanding kitchen brigade meant we soon ran out of space, and half the staff had nowhere to work. We clearly needed a new kitchen. Not a few years earlier, after much nagging and cajoling, Mark and I had finally persuaded Gerald to build an extension to our kitchen; but no sooner had the paint dried then we'd outgrown it. We were now obliged to build a second new kitchen, tacked on to the first one in record time. From our early days of working out of a shoe box, we were now rattling around in some 200 square metres of floor space. This provided a further advantage, in that we now had room for some essential new items of equipment, the most important of which was a food processor.

The Mousse and the Man from the Michelin

Nowadays we take these run-of-the mill gadgets for granted, but at the time it was a revelation and completely transformed the way we worked. Previously labour-intensive jobs – purees, soufflés, fruit coulis, soups, pâtés, mash, fondants, quenelles, sorbets, ice creams – could now be completed in the blink of an eye. The Magimix Professional commercial food processor, our chosen model, was the original forerunner of the far smaller machines of all makes and sizes that now form part of any domestic kitchen, and it was indisputably the Big Bertha of the breed. This heavy-duty beast could dispatch a kilo of chicken flesh to the consistency of wallpaper paste with just a few pulses of its machete-proportioned blade. But, as with most labour-saving innovations, there was a downside, which in the case of the food processor was the 'mousseification' of our nation's menus. In common with so many other chefs with misguided aspirations to greatness, I embarked on a love affair with the mousse. Mousses were now the height of fashion, and if I was ever to be taken seriously by the food guides, I reasoned, it would be by embracing them, in all their bland and ethereal glory. Mousses, of course, were hardly a new idea; Escoffier himself, the godfather of French cuisine (who I'm convinced was just looking for an ingenious way of catering for a nation without teeth), had been busy making mousses more than a century earlier. And from the hands of a master, a skilfully produced mousse can be a fine thing (especially if you're short of a few teeth). The problem was that the electric food blender made it all too easy. There was a time when making a mousse had been a labour of love, demanding the use of hand-operated moulis, sieves, ladles, much fiddly preparation and a spirit of dogged dedication. With the aid of a blender, however, it was overkill. Now any cowboy could knock up a mousse in moments. And I confess I was among the worst offenders. I began tentatively – stuffing chicken fillets with chicken mousse, salmon fillets with salmon mousse... Growing in confidence, I progressed to more adventurous combinations. I stuffed duck eggs with duck liver mousse, mushrooms with spinach mousse, artichokes with lobster mousse... I moved onto harder stuff (I thought I could handle it). I stuffed beetroots with goat's cheese mousse, tomatoes with Bloody Mary mousse... When I wasn't inventing mousses, I was busy experimenting with their close relative, the puree. At the height of my excesses, much of my culinary output resembled a bad copy of a Jackson Pollock – the ultimate expression of this trend being a dish I'd stolen from the Swiss chef Anton Mossiman, which went by the imperious name of 'Symphony of Fruits'. It was essentially a plate smeared with an assortment of fruit purees. The idea was to then fashion it into a kind of psychedelic Catherine wheel using the point of a knife,

The Mousse and the Man from the Michelin

but I never quite mastered the technique. Anton Mossiman's version was pretty impressive – even if it didn't look like food – whereas my own efforts resembled the daubing of a neurotic primate. By 1980 I like to think I'd long since hung up my Stetson hat in favour of becoming a serious chef, but, I'm ashamed to admit, there remained a distinct whiff of the OK Corral about my cooking at this time. The root of the problem, however, was not the food processor itself; the food processor just allowed me to commit my crimes against food with greater efficiency. No, the real offender was ignorance...ignorance and nouvelle cuisine.

The term nouvelle cuisine is said to have been coined in 1969 by Christian Millau and Henri Gault, originators of the *Gault et Millau* restaurant guide, apparently as a reaction to what they viewed as the stifling conformity of French classical cooking. In the 1970s the conservative-leaning *Michelin Guide* continued to promote traditional cuisine *classique*, while the iconoclastic new kids in town, Gault and Millau, championed a new generation of French chefs. These included such rising stars as Paul Bocuse, Alain Chapel, Jean and Pierre Troisgros, Michel Guérard, Roger Vergé and Raymond Oliver, most of whom were former protégés of the granddaddy of modern French cooking, Fernand Point. (I know this now in retrospect. I admit that at the time I'd never heard of any of these people.) And they brought with them some new ideas, many of which seem like common sense to our modern mindset, but at the time seemed the height of subversion.

Nouvelle cuisine is to haut cuisine what a pair of seven-inch stilettos is to a pair of sensible brogues. Where one is authoritatively functional the other is frivolously impractical (albeit more sexy). But at its best nouvelle cuisine did much to improve the food we eat, and its influence is felt to this day. It replaced heavy, flour-thickened sauces – such as the ubiquitous espagnole and béchamel – with delicate infusions and stocks, thickened with butter and flavoured with fruit vinegars. The long and ostentatious menus of the old cuisine were exchanged for the short (though on occasions equally ostentatious) menus of the new cuisine. There was a strong Japanese influence: complication gave way to simplicity; cooking times were drastically reduced and there was an emphasis on steaming and poaching; portions grew smaller, while the plates on which they were served grew proportionately larger.

And in France, and a handful of the world's more sophisticated capitals, that's pretty much all there was to it, and, being French, everyone instinctively understood what was going on. Here in Britain, however, nouvelle cuisine was the culinary equivalent of communism, in that it began life as a noble ideal but by the time people got wise to its

The Mousse and the Man from the Michelin

flaws it was too late. The British culinary establishment had always looked to France for authority and as such felt duty-bound to adopt nouvelle cuisine without question. It took to the task with the blinkered zeal of a religious convert and, as to be expected, the results were mixed. Some restaurants, such as the exclusive Brown's Hotel in Mayfair, abandoned their classical menus and went full-on 'nouvelle', literally overnight, seemingly without missing a beat. They could afford to; they catered for a moneyed international set that was happy to embrace any new fad to distract from the boredom of dining out seven nights a week. But while the new minimalist portions may have been great news for millionaire film stars and anorexic supermodels on a mission to preserve their figures, for the average diner it felt suspiciously like being short-changed. Because this radical new brand of cooking came with an equally radical new price tag, despite a typical main course now consisting of a nugget of meat or fish no bigger than a 50 pence piece. If you were lucky, this might arrive with a couple of elaborately sculpted potatoes, each the size of a marble, and a few shards of blanched and glazed vegetables, stacked vertically like a log cabin constructed from Pick-a-Sticks. This would be accompanied by a sauce, 'drizzled' in a floral motif across an otherwise empty plate the diameter of a dustbin lid. When touched with a knife and fork, the whole fragile edifice would collapse, ruining what artistry as might exist.

For my own part, marooned in the depths of the provinces, the adoption of nouvelle cuisine was a more circumspect affair. My knowledge of classical French cooking at the time could have been scribbled on the back of a pack of Gauloises. Being largely self taught, I'd yet to properly understand the 'old' cuisine, so giving me a new one to master only served to baffle. Aside from a vague idea that it had something to do with serving eccentric combinations of food in infinitesimal portions, I had no idea what I was doing, or indeed what I was supposed to be reacting *against*. It was like a clog dancer attempting to master the rudiments of modern ballet.

But I wasn't about to allow such trifling details stand in my way as a champion of progress, despite my early attempts at nouvelle cuisine resembling the product of a disturbed mind. These included such instantly memorable (for all the wrong reasons) dishes as compote of calf's liver with frozen grapes and Pernod mayonnaise; twice-piped avocado with glazed turbot mousse; hot crusted camembert with prawn jam; beef fillet with vanilla and bone marrow foam; white pudding on a bed of minced kiwi; cod with raspberries, quail with raspberries – in fact everything with raspberries.

The Mousse and the Man from the Michelin

To reinforce my modernist credentials, I also set about mastering the art of the Japanese garnish – which, along with the mousse, was now the height of fashion and an essential part of every chef's repertoire. Armed with the definitive book on the subject, *Japanese Garnishes,* by Yukiko and Bob Haydock, I would sit up in bed nights, a chopping board on my knees, cigarette in mouth, working diligently on my creations, which I preserved in a bucket of iced water kept beside the bed, before transporting them to work the following morning. In no time at all I was producing textbook cucumber chrysanthemums, radish lilies, carrot butterflies, apple bunnies, parsnip frogs, celeriac stars, turnip anemones, sweet potato fans... and any number of other pointless, twee and superfluous gimmicks that had no business being on a plate of food, all with just a few deft flicks of a paring knife. I would then decorate each main course with a selection of these miniature masterpieces, regardless of its appropriateness, before sending it to the table. I particularly prided myself on the witty flourish, such as the positioning of a parsnip frog peeping coyly from beneath a sugar-frosted daffodil. Who said art and humour don't mix? By the time I reached the end of my book and had worked my way through all the designs, however, I'd become heartily sick of Japanese garnishes and vowed never to make another as long as I lived. It was then that Gerald and Arabella, in the touching belief that they were filling a void in my life, bought me as a gift for my birthday the newly published sequel to *Japanese Garnishes*, the imaginatively titled *More Japanese Garnishes*. Concerned not to hurt their feelings, I renewed my efforts and soon created my first tomato rose. It was a turning point.

Sadly it was a turning point that coincided with an unexpected visit to the restaurant by one of the country's foremost food critics.

It all began when one of our Rannie's interns – whose name might have been Jocasta – received a telephone call from her mother. 'Mummy's reserved a table to dine at the restaurant tonight with my uncle Egon,' announced Jocasta when she got off the phone. 'She says they're coming to try us out.'

'Not *the* Egon?' I quipped.

Jocasta appeared puzzled, as was her tendency. 'Why, how many Egons are there?'

'Egon Ronay, of course. You know, the Egon Ronay Guide?'

Jocasta thought for a while before replying matter of factly, 'Yes, that's him. Why do you ask?'

Why did I ask? It's said that Egon Ronay, who died in

The Mousse and the Man from the Michelin

2010, did more to improve cooking in Britain than any other person. With the possible exception of the Michelin star, the Egon Ronay Restaurant of the Year Award was the most coveted accolade in the industry. Egon Ronay was probably the country's single most influential food critic.

'Why do I ask?' I said. 'Egon Ronay is probably the country's single most influential food critic. Are you sure we're talking about the same person?'

Upon further interrogation it became clear that Jocasta and I were indeed talking about the same person.

'The problem is though I don't believe her,' said Gerald, when I phoned to tell him the news. 'If her uncle is Egon Ronay, as she claims, then why hasn't she thought to mention it before? She's been with us three months.'

'Well, you know what Jocasta's like?'

'Do I?'

'You know, head in the clouds, out of touch and all that? She probably didn't think it important.'

'No, I'm not about to get caught out by that old chestnut again. It was bad enough moving heaven and earth for a non-existent Clement Freud.'

'But suppose she's telling the truth?'

'Take it from me, Kento, she isn't. Egon Ronay never inspects a restaurant in person. He's far too important. The girl's clearly a fantasist. If I were you I'd just humour her and carry on as normal.'

So I just humoured Jocasta and carried on as normal.

And when Egon Ronay showed up for dinner that night no one could say I wasn't warned. The worst part was that no one noticed his arrival, as we hadn't been expecting him (and wouldn't have recognised him even if we had). It wasn't until the great man came to leave that he finally revealed his presence, at which point he politely paid his bill and departed without a word. To this day I've no idea whether he enjoyed his meal, or even whether he appreciated the perfectly crafted tomato rose that adorned his plate. Nor could I say whether the two incidents were in any way connected when the following year The Mute Swan was quietly dropped from the *Egon Ronay Guide*.

Not that it mattered because it was around this time that Gerald inherited a fortune from his great aunt Hermione. Nobody knew the exact sum because, of course, it was vulgar to discuss money and we didn't ask, but it was understood to be in the millions. Gerald responded to his newfound wealth in typically understated fashion and refused to allow it affect his lifestyle. Other than treating himself to a few mod-

The Mousse and the Man from the Michelin

est essentials – which included the purchase of a Georgian manor house with tennis courts and pool, a new apartment in Chelsea, a Moody 44' ocean-going luxury yacht, a top-of-the-range Porsche 911 Carrera, a pilot's licence and a Cessna 172 Skyhawk – it was life as usual, which for the Golightlys meant winters spent skiing in the French Alps and summers at the family farmhouse in Provence. *Plus ça change*. Even at a time when he could have claimed to have needed the money, Gerald had taken an admirably low-key approach to his role as a businessman. But now, with any vestige of financial incentive removed, he was so laid back as to be comatose. Most of the time you wouldn't have known he was there, mainly because most of the time he *wasn't* there. There were periods when we saw nothing of Gerald and Arabella for months at a stretch. They simply managed the restaurant remotely via the telephone, calling home sporadically from whichever exotic foreign location they happened to be visiting at the time.

With Gerald and Arabella safely out of the picture, the staff began to enjoy their own, albeit more modest, version of the high life. After the restaurant had closed for the night and the final customers dispatched, we would push back the tables, turn up the music and dance. Gerald had recently invested in a new state-of-the-art sound system, ostensibly for the purpose of playing music in the dining room. When cranked up to full volume, however, it made the floor shake and could be heard at the opposite end of the village, the result being that we became extremely unpopular with our neighbours. When we tired of dancing we played risqué games, our favourite being strip poker. It wasn't unusual to find the entire staff gathered in one of the lounges in various states of undress, ranging from mild dishevelment to complete nudity. Betsie and Tabitha were always up for a game, as were several newcomers to the team, including two shapely young Brazilian interns, both of whom were named Maria. The two Marias were working for a year at the restaurant with a view to improving their English and promoting cultural solidarity. Happy to take part in any activity that would allow them a better insight into the British way of life, they had no reservations about removing their clothes along with the rest of us.

Then there was our version of the popular children's party game, Murder in the Dark – specially modified for adult tastes. The rules, such as they existed, were simple: a 'murderer' and a 'detective' would be appointed by drawing cards. The murderer then counted to one hundred while, amid fits of giggles, everyone else ran off to hide. Nowhere was out of bounds, including wardrobes and broom cupboards – in fact especially wardrobes and broom cupboards. We killed the lights by throwing the mains switch. This way

The Mousse and the Man from the Michelin

there was no possibility of people cheating by turning on a light until the murderer had 'killed' the last of their victims and it was time for the detective to solve the case (although, depending on our level of inebriation, we didn't always bother with this last bit). The only way to negotiate one's way around the labyrinthine building was by groping, hands outstretched. At this time the village had no street lighting, so we were operating in total blackness. It was hugely exciting, not least because, either by chance or intention, it was common to find oneself sharing a hiding place (for instance, a wardrobe or broom cupboard) with a member of the opposite sex, often with no clue as to their identity – guessing was all part of the fun. Of course, it was only a matter of time before our games degenerated into an excuse for a gratuitous petting session. Sordid as this may seem, before you rush to judge I would point out in our defence that as an activity it had much in common with the Venetian masque. During the masque, a noble tradition dating back centuries, the inhabitants of Venice were free to wander the city's darkened streets and canals in disguise and engage in all manner of licentious encounters with impunity. Being officially sanctioned by the state, the masque enjoyed a veneer of respectability and, being anonymous, remained both uncomplicated and gloriously guilt-free. Don't knock it until you've tried it.

Things could go wrong, though. On one occasion, while hiding in a cupboard beneath the stairs – where I'd carved out an intimate space behind a vacuum cleaner and a floor polisher – I was pleasantly surprised to find myself joined by Betsie (readily identified by the telltale fumes of cigarettes and schnapps). In an ideal world I would have preferred to be hiding with one or other of the Brazilian Marias, but in the dark and following a few drinks I wasn't about to complain. Besides, you could say what you liked about Betsie but she was all woman. Although, I had to admit, I couldn't recall her having quite such large hands, nor, come to think of it, quite so much hair on her chin. And yet her breasts and buttocks were as voluptuous as I'd remembered them. What strange hermaphrodite creature had I latched upon in the darkness?

'Kevin, it's you isn't it? Please tell me it isn't you.'

'Yeah, I'm here,' chuckled Kevin lasciviously. 'Did you wanna 'ave first go or do I? I'm easy.'

'Oh, Jezusaitchchrist,' gasped Betsie, her breasts heaving like bellows, 'zere ist two of zem. Ist meine lucky night, ist es nicht? Zwei Männe! Not vun but two!'

Our parties were destined to come to an abrupt end, and all because of a bizarre incident that no one could have anticipated. In the restaurant bar there was an inglenook fire-

The Mousse and the Man from the Michelin

place with a chimney so big it could accommodate a man. So it was that one of our more drink-addled guests had the idea of using it as a hiding place during one of our games. Sadly, he hadn't allowed for the fact that in the summer months, when the fire wasn't lit, the entrance to the chimney was blocked off with a wooden board to capture falling soot. While clambering up he dislodged the board, unwittingly disgorging a six-month accumulation of soot – the equivalent of half a bathtub full – into the bar below. And here's the best bit. Soot, we were to discover, is as silent as falling snow and so delicate that it's all but undetectable to the touch. It wasn't until we switched on the lights that we discovered what had happened, by which time the soot had been trailed throughout the building – carpets, furniture, walls, paintings, curtains, all smothered. Panicked, we attempted to clear it up, but our frantic sweeping and scrubbing only dispersed the soot and made it worse; the restaurant resembled a coal mine, and we the miners. Our only option was to call out an industrial cleaning company to deal with the mess the following morning. We couldn't very well charge it to the restaurant account, so we footed the bill ourselves. It wasn't cheap.

Fearing for her job, Betsie exercised her authority as manageress and, in a rare show of assertiveness, banned all further parties. Looking back, this was probably a good idea. Left unchecked, we'd been behaving like spoilt teenagers with expense accounts, all while standards in the restaurant continued to nosedive. And the worrying part was that no one cared.

Deprived of our parties, we took to enjoying unauthorised late-night dips in the Golightys' swimming pool, which was located at the top of the village just a few minutes' walk from the restaurant. Fuelled by large quantities of champagne, we would cast our inhibitions aside along with our clothes and dive in naked, splashing and squealing ecstatically like over-endowed toddlers. We even devised our own unique water sport. Called Purple Polo, it combined the grace and poise of water polo with the rough and tumble of conventional polo – the men performing the role of the horse, with the women taking it in turns to ride astride their shoulders with the ball. The sensation of a wet naked woman straddling the nape of one's bare neck by moonlight is impossible to describe (at least without resorting to crude similes), but as distractions go it comes highly recommended. Unsurprisingly, Purple Polo was an instant hit, at least among our little coterie of bathers (and to this day I have no doubt that it could rival beach volleyball as a spectator event). But like all contact sports it was not without its hazards, the most dangerous of which was to venture too far into the deep end of the pool with a woman on one's

The Mousse and the Man from the Michelin

shoulders. The combination of the extra weight together with having one's neck trapped in the pincer-like grip of her animated thighs made it impossible to surface. On one occasion – anchored as I was to the pool floor beneath Tabitha's fulsome buttocks – I swear I almost drowned, only making good my escape by pinching her inner thigh hard between finger and thumb until she self-ejected, her breasts ricocheting off the surface of the water like a pair of Barnes Wallis bombs as she landed.

Our al fresco lifestyle ended with the arrival of winter. For the rich, however, the English winter presents no such inconvenience. It is merely the interlude that occurs between the fading of the Mediterranean summer and the beginning of the European ski season. And so it was that at this time of year the Golightlys would make a whistle-stop call to UK shores to take stock of their social calendar. And there was much stock of which to take: Christmas gifts to buy, parties to arrange, holidays to organise, including a Caribbean sojourn for March or April – the latter being essential for escaping those final dregs of winter that linger on so tiresomely when the best of the skiing is exhausted and the Provençal spring has yet to arrive.

In fairness to Gerald and Arabella, they offset their charmed lifestyle by spreading their wealth around. This included the setting up and financing of a charitable trust that provided disadvantaged inner-city children with a summer holiday in the country. There was also the Oldies' Christmas Eve Lunch. This involved providing a free turkey lunch for Bovington's needier pensioners – the Golightlys giving of their hospitality, and the restaurant staff giving of their time. Deserving guests were selected on our behalf by the local Anglican diocese from among its Sunday brethren, apparently on the basis of their church attendance. One can only presume that any elderly atheists or lapsed churchgoers among the community were destined to spend a lonely Christmas.

As head chef, it fell upon me to cook the turkey. This presented a problem, in that the bird I'd acquired for the occasion weighed in at over forty pounds. The oldies were scheduled to arrive at the restaurant by midday on Christmas Eve. To have any hope of being ready on time, I calculated, I would need to begin cooking the turkey at around 4am. Overhearing me lamenting this prospect, it was Gerald who came to my rescue.

'Oh, no civilised chap should have to be abroad at that hour, Kento. No, you must do what my mother did on these occasions. Just wrap the turkey in foil, set the oven thermostat at a quarter and leave it to slow-cook overnight. In the morning it'll be roasted to perfection. We do our turkey this way every Christmas. Take it from me, Kento, problem

The Mousse and the Man from the Michelin

solved.'

Eager to embrace any plan that would allow me to remain in bed as long as possible, I took Gerald at his word. I slept well that night, oblivious to the inexorable machinations of Sod's Law as it conspired to wreck my day. I've since learned that in kitchens, as at sea, anything that can go wrong will, eventually, go wrong – and just when you're relying on it most. On this occasion it was the thermostat on the oven, for when I arrived in the kitchen that morning an acrid blue haze hung in the air. Despite being set on its lowest possible temperature, the oven had been operating on maximum heat for some 10 hours. Even without looking I knew my turkey was ruined. The foil had prevented the skin from blackening, but to describe the flesh as dry would be understating it. It was Death Valley at noon. So arid was this bird when I took it from the oven, so completely void of moisture and elasticity, that when I prodded it with a finger it collapsed into an incoherent heap.

It was now 10 am. The oldies would be arriving in two hours. With no prospect of finding and cooking a replacement turkey in so little time, I phoned Gerald and told him that I had no alternative but to cancel the lunch.

'Oh, nonsense, Kento. Don't overreact. I'm sure we can salvage it... Can't you just slice it up and pour gravy over it or something? I mean, these old folks are used to making do. They lived through the war for goodness sake. They aren't fussy. And besides, we can't let them down. Just think how disappointed they'd be.'

'No, Gerald, you don't understand, this turkey is beyond slicing. It's like...I'm not quite sure how to describe it...powdered cardboard?'

'Hmm, powdered cardboard, you say?' Ah, well, no worries. Then you should do what my mother did on these occasions. Just boil up some rice and turn it into a turkey curry. Take it from me, Kento, problem solved.'

'Curry? But this is supposed to be a traditional Christmas lunch. We can't give them curry.'

'Why on earth not? There's nothing wrong with curry. Why be a slave to tradition? And besides, beggars can't be choosers. It's not as if we're asking them to pay for it or anything.'

Left with no alternative, I turned what remained of the turkey into an approximation of a curry. The cremated meat was so fragile that it disintegrated on contact with the sauce to form a fibrous yellow-green slurry that precisely resembled a freshly excreted cow pat. I hadn't the stomach to taste it, so I instructed Kevin to try it on my behalf.

The Mousse and the Man from the Michelin

'Uuuuum, not too bad, considering,' said Kevin, smacking his lips appreciatively and helping himself to a second spoonful. 'Not too bad at all. I think you're onto a winner there with a few poppadoms and a bit of chutney on the side.'

'Really? Are you sure?'

'Yep, almost as good as my mum's vindaloo, that is.'

Having not personally tasted Kevin's mum's vindaloo, I was unsure whether this was a good or a bad thing. I suspected the latter.

Predictably, the pensioners weren't happy with the revised menu. Their initial response when the curry was served was puzzlement. A few made a game attempt at eating it, if only out of politeness. One or two people even cleaned their plates. But the mood soon turned ugly, as disappointment gave way to revolt. 'Zey are not 'appy rabbits,' said Betsie, returning to the kitchen with an armful of plates, still groaning with untouched food. 'And I do not to blame zem. Zey complain it eez 'orrible... grauenhaft. Zey complain zare are no Brussel sprout and voast potato and schtuffing. Zey complain it tastes burned. Zey complain they never to come here again.'

'Never come here again? How's that for gratitude,' I said, piqued. 'It's not as though we're asking them to pay for it or anything. And besides, beggars can't be choosers.'

'Not to worry, Kento,' said Gerald, breezing into the kitchen with a champagne flute in one hand and a bottle of Dom Pérignon in the other. 'Can't get it right every time. Anyway, on these occasions it's the thought that counts. So don't go blaming yourself.'

'Oh, don't worry, Gerald, I'm not blaming myself. I'm blaming a combination of bad advice from you and defective equipment.'

'Well, Daddy says a bad workman always blames his tools,' said Tabitha, who had followed Gerald into the kitchen.

'Hear, hear, Tabso, you tell him,' said Gerald, recharging his glass of champagne. 'No passing the buck, eh.'

'Kento, I told zem vot you shed zat beggars cannot to be choosers,' said Betsie, returning from the dining room with yet another pile of curry-laden plates, 'and zey shay zey are not beggars. Zey shay vee invited zem for lunch. Zey are our guests. Zey shay zat zey write to ze newspapers to complain about how zey are offended and wrongly tret.'

'Did you really refer to our guests as beggars, Kento? That's hardly in the spirit of the season, I must say,' said Gerald.

The Mousse and the Man from the Michelin

'And besides, Kento, how can you go blaming poor Gerald for your carelessness?' continued Tabitha. 'After all the good he's doing in feeding the poor and needy and whatnot... I mean, why didn't you just put the turkey in the oven at the proper hour, for goodness sake?'

'It would have meant me getting out of bed at three thirty in the morning, that's why.'

'And what, indeed, is so difficult about that? You wouldn't have lasted very long in the army, young man, that's all I can say. When Daddy was stationed in the veldt he thought nothing of rising before dawn to brave the crocodiles and shoot a hog at the waterhole. And skin it. And cook it over an open fire for his men, and all before first light. And mister softy pants here can't even get his carcass out of bed to pop a turkey into the oven. What does that tell you about the state of the nation? Daddy says they should bring back conscription, and I agree with him.'

'Hear, hear, you tell him, Tabso,' said Gerald, swaying slightly on his feet and belching discreetly into a handkerchief. 'Bring back the bloody draft, that's what I say. The whole damn country's lost its backbone.'

CHAPTER 10

Perhaps Tabitha was right. I had gone soft. If indeed I'd ever been anything but. Whatever my problem, there was no doubt I'd become accustomed to the good life. My relationship with Gerald, who by now had taken me under his wing like a big brother, had allowed me to feast on the crumbs from his golden table for too long. Over time I'd acquired a sense of entitlement which, since Gerald had inherited his new wealth, had merely intensified. If only by proxy I felt rich. Considering my lifestyle this was hardly surprising: summer holidays were spent sailing the Brittany coast with the Golightlys on their yacht; I drove fast cars, took frequent ski holidays, thought nothing of flying to France for lunch with Gerald on his plane (a nail-biting experience, being that Gerald, as pilot and navigator, frequently became lost, especially on the homeward leg and following a few glasses of burgundy). At least once a week we would eat a Prolonged Wine-Fuelled Lunch (or 'PWFL') in any one of London's finest restaurants. It was now the mid 1980s. The Big Bang had recently transformed the financial markets, spawning in the process a new class of big spender. The town was awash with bankers' silly money and it was making its mark on restaurants. London was no longer a culinary backwater in thrall to Paris; it now had an identity of its own. Michelin stars were as abundant as parking tickets and world-class restaurants were opening on every corner: Albert and Michel Roux's Le Gavroche, Pierre Koffmann's La Tante Claire, Nico Ladenis' Chez Nico, Antony Worrall Thompson's Ménage a Trois, Marco Pierre White's Harveys, Anton Mosimann at the Dorchester, Bruno Loubet at the Four Seasons... And these are just the ones I can remember. We frequented them all, working on a perpetual loop so that when we'd exhausted our list of Michelin-starred restaurants we'd simply begin again from the top. An unfortunate side effect of the Prolonged Wine-Fuelled Lunch (so fashionable in the 80s) is that it renders one more or less useless for the remainder of the day. We coped by dozing off the effects on the 90-minute train ride home from London Victoria to Polegate. I say 'dozing', but mostly we just slumped into a bibulous coma. More than once we missed our stop and awoke dazed and confused ten stops down the line when the train terminated at Hastings.

There was, of course, never any question of my picking up the tab on these occasions. This was 'work', and written off by Gerald accordingly. Because, decadent as they may sound, there was a motive behind our lunchtime expeditions. It was Gerald's way of keeping me on my toes and warding off complacency. And, for a while at least, it

The Mousse and the Man from the Michelin

worked. There is no better way, I discovered, of learning what is involved in winning a Michelin star than to experience it firsthand. And, I admit it, I was impressed. Because these weren't restaurants as I'd previously known them. These were temples dedicated to the art of gastronomy. One thing has to be understood: when cooking attains this level the chef becomes more important than the customer and, like it or not, you are subordinate to his ego. You either accept this inconvenient truth, or you eat elsewhere. The reverence afforded these culinary superstars was, and remains, extraordinary. The implication is that one should feel, and indeed behave, honoured to be in their presence, and this is driven home from the moment one walks through the door of the restaurant. Until now I'd had no idea that something so humdrum as the food we put in our mouths and excrete so casually from the other end could be taken so seriously: the forensic precision with which the maître d' explains the dishes on the menu when taking one's order; the reverential hush when the food is delivered to the table; the gasps of admiration from the diners when they appraise their plates; the orgasmic groans of pleasure as they commence eating. But should anything not meet with your approval, don't even think about asserting your rights as a paying customer, because the capriciousness of these stars is legendary. When a diner at Chez Nico asked the waiter for salt and pepper, chef-proprietor Nico Ladenis was so affronted that he threw a hissy fit and ejected him from the premises. (Ladenis made a point of refusing to place salt and pepper on the tables, as one would expect in any normal restaurant, as it was understood that the food would arrive seasoned to perfection, and diners could not be trusted to adjust the seasoning to their own taste.) Noted narcissist and epic tantrum thrower Marco Pierre White once ordered a party of diners, who'd had the temerity to complain about their food, to leave his restaurant immediately. When they refused to go, White instructed his waiting staff to physically remove the table at which they were dining from under their noses, complete with contents, leaving the still seated customers staring at a bare carpet. You didn't mess with these people.

Gerald's plan, ambitiously, was that I imitate the masters. If I sampled their food often enough, so his thinking went, then a little of their genius would rub off on me and I too would acquire the skills to win a Michelin star. His plan was flawed, of course. For by this logic an amateur watercolourist visiting the National Gallery a sufficient number of times would emerge to paint Van Gough's *Sunflowers*. Compared with these culinary wunderkinds I was a dabbler at best. Experiencing their cooking merely served to highlight my own mediocrity and expose the holes in my knowledge. Being a self-taught, 'gentleman' chef may have had its vir-

The Mousse and the Man from the Michelin

tues, but it was no substitute for learning from the masters. Because these chefs came from a privileged caste, with all roads, unsurprisingly, leading to France. It was the French-trained Roux brothers who are credited with producing the 80s generation of London chefs and bringing a new respectability to British cooking. Along with other notable French émigré chefs, such as Pierre Koffman, they mentored a new generation of home-grown talent – this included the likes of Marco Pierre White and other ambitious newcomers – who in turn nurtured the next generation. White's best known protégée was Gordon Ramsay; Ramsay went on to mentor Marcus Wareing, among others, and so on to the present day.

But it was never a bed of roses. The London restaurant scene in the 1980s resembled something between the Wild West and a bedroom farce – a gang of ruthlessly motivated young chefs, flitting promiscuously between the capital's best kitchens, greedy to steal recipes, win power, nurture contacts and drum-up patronage to further their careers. It was natural selection at its most brutal. For those who could survive the heat, the stress, the backstabbing, the bigotry, the bullying and the punishing 18-hour days, the reward was an accumulation of knowledge that no self-taught chef, however dedicated, could acquire in a lifetime of trial and error. Few stayed the course, and for those who did there was still no guarantee of making the big time. A handful of chefs, as we know, went on to become wealthy entrepreneurs, some hugely so: Gordon Ramsay's restaurant empire is said to be worth in excess of £60 million. Not bad for a working class boy with an itinerant alcoholic for a father and who left school aged 16.

With hindsight, it seems naive that I ever hoped to compete in this league. But I felt obliged to try. The good news was that by this time many of these chefs had produced cookbooks: The Roux brothers' *New Classic Cuisine*, Anton Mosimann's *Cuisine Naturelle,* Marco Pierre White's *White Heat,* Raymond Blanc's *Recipes From Le Manoir Aux Quat' Saisons,* Nico Ladenis' *My Gastronomy...*I went out and bought the lot. All I need do to emulate these chefs' successes, I reasoned, was to follow their recipes. What could be easier? Building a space rocket from a blueprint with no prior knowledge of astrophysics, perhaps? Because in my experience the recipes in these books fell into one of three categories: 1/ worked, and could be usefully adapted to include on the menu (10%); 2/ worked, but were too fussy, time-consuming or pretentious to attempt more than once (45%); 3/ didn't work at all (45%). To this day I'm convinced there was a conspiracy among these chefs-turned-cookbook-writers to deliberately mislead their readers. It makes sense: what better way of sabotaging the competition than to include intentional errors in one's recipes? This

The Mousse and the Man from the Michelin

way the author gets to enjoy all the rewards of publishing a bestselling cookbook while also demoralising his imitators.

Of course, I couldn't rule out the possibility that my worryingly high failure rate with recipes was due to my own ineptitude, rather than the author's. With this in mind I embarked on a self-taught re-education programme, beginning by reading a book called *On Food and Cooking – The Science and Lore of the Kitchen,* by Harold McGee, an updated version of which is still selling well to this day. This one's definitely for the geeks. Unlike normal cookery books, that tell us *what* to cook, McGee goes beneath the surface to show us, in painstaking technical detail, the *how* and the *why.* For instance, why do emulsified sauces such as hollandaise and mayonnaise curdle? How do you prevent it and what do you do if it happens? Why does cream go sour? Why does fish smell fishy, why does it go off quicker than meat, and how do you slow the decomposition process? How do you tell a stale egg from a fresh one? Why is it important to leave pancake batter to rest? How do you prevent a cheesecake from cracking when it's baked? Why do Jerusalem artichokes make you fart? Why does asparagus make your pee smell odd? (Pointless to know, but a good ice-breaker at dinner parties.) McGee covers it all – from the structure of wheat grains, the elemental processes that convert milk to cheese or butter, why soufflés rise (and why they don't), why prawns turn pink when cooked, and why pH and trace metals affect the colour of cooked fruit and vegetables. He tells us what chemical changes occur in an egg when it is cooked, and, if you're interested, how this knowledge will help you make a perfect sabayonne. For bakers there's a chapter devoted to the science of cake making, and even a section on how not to poison one's guests. However, this latter advice was no doubt lost on TV chef Heston Blumenthal (a self-confessed fan of Howard McGee) who, at the time of writing, has seen one of his Michelin-starred restaurants closed by the health authorities as a result of a norovirus contamination – the second such time it's happened. (On the first occasion it was found that uncooked oysters had become infected with the bug, most likely through raw sewage leaked into the sea.) Blumenthal cites Harold McGee as a major influence on his trademark molecular gastronomy. In 2005 his flagship restaurant – The Fat Duck, in Bray – was voted number one in the World's 50 Best Restaurant Awards, so it's clearly served him well. Sadly for me, at the time – and clearly lacking Heston Blumenthal's unquestionable talents – the possibilities of exploiting Harold McGee's research to such lucrative ends were destined to pass me by. Indeed, I'm not even convinced that knowing this stuff made me a better cook. But it certainly made me *sound* like I was a better cook, which when endeavouring to impress

The Mousse and the Man from the Michelin

is always half the battle. Unfortunately for me, it also gave Gerald an idea.

Gerald's lust for critical approval had returned with a vengeance. His plan this time was that I deliver a series of cookery classes. They would take place in the restaurant kitchens in front of a paying audience. They would also be filmed and made into videos for general distribution to complement our existing series of bestselling cookbooks. With the resulting publicity and a good agent, it was only a matter of time before we'd be on the right side of a bidding war for a TV series. Once more, so Gerald claimed, fame beckoned, and this time it would be on our own terms.

Gerald was confident of success. He'd thought it through. The classes would happen twice weekly, on Tuesday and Wednesday mornings, for five weeks. I had no idea how I'd cope, as it added several hours to my already crammed working day, but if it was going to serve as a launch pad to my new celebrity status, I had to be there. There was also the money to consider. Because the deal was that we split the profits 50/50. The plan was to have 10 paying guests per class, at £20 a head. I would therefore be earning, so I estimated, an additional £200 each week, in addition to my regular wage. Hardly a fortune, but in the 1980s nor was it a sum to be sniffed at, and all for just two mornings' extra work.

Kent Austin

But first I had to get myself kitted out. The current fashion among chefs was to have your name and rank embroidered on your jacket. But up until now I hadn't bothered, because while it might make sense in the kitchens of, say, a large hotel, to distinguish between various members of a brigade of chefs, such an affectation served no purpose in a small restaurant (other than to massage the chef's vanity). If people didn't know who I was by now, I clearly had a problem. But according to Gerald it was important that I look the part. Perception was everything. So I bought a classy new chef's jacket and had my name embroidered in ornate swirly blue font on the upper left breast, along with the words 'chef de cuisine', a Union Jack motif and a row of five gold stars (such as nowadays they award staff in McDonald's to denote faithful service). I felt like a million dollars; I looked like a complete arsehole. It had been decided that during the classes Kevin would by my assistant, acting as an usher, runner and general dogsbody. It was therefore important that he be similarly attired. Though, to denote his lowlier position in the kitchen hierarchy, his name was to be embroidered in a smaller, less flamboyant font, and without the Union Jack and only a single gold star.

Our first series of classes was an instant sell-out. The students were a mixed bag: bored housewives, cookery writers, restaurateurs, keen amateurs, aspiring chefs and the

The Mousse and the Man from the Michelin

just plain curious. I presumed they'd signed up because they wanted to become better cooks. But when asked, most said they were there to see how Banoffi Pie was made, The Mute Swan being the home of this now ubiquitous dessert. The history of Banoffi Pie is an odd one, in that for many years Mark and Gerald have been locked in an ongoing, and occasionally acrimonious, dispute over who actually thought of it first, as both claim credit for its invention. You would think it impossible to fall out over something as innocuous as a pudding, but of course this was no ordinary pudding. At the time no one could have predicted that Banoffi Pie was destined to become so universally popular. (Its fame extends as far as the USA, Russia, China and even the upper reaches of the British Establishment: both Margaret Thatcher and Princess Diana cited it as their favourite pudding.) Personally, I thought it was a cheap confection that had no place on the menu of a serious restaurant. Alas, I was in a minority, because whenever I attempted to drop it from the menu I encountered a revolt from all sides. Like it or not, Banoffi Pie was here to stay. Nowadays, of course, it's a staple on pub menus and supermarket shelves the length of the land. Had Gerald been able to glimpse the future, he would have patented the name, opened the world's first Banoffi Pie factory and made a lot of money. That said, he was never one to knowingly pass a bandwagon by, and when it became evident that he had a hit on his hands, he set about exploiting the Banoffi phenomenon to the full. So proud was Gerald of 'his' invention that he even had a specially made commemorative blue plaque attached to the outside wall of the restaurant, naming The Mute Swan as 'The Birthplace of Banoffi Pie, 1972'.

On the morning of my first class I was in the kitchen at 7am, busy preparing ingredients and, for the first time, giving some thought to practicalities. Because until now it hadn't occurred to me to plan my cookery classes (other than scribble a few ideas on the back of an envelope) nor iron out any potential problems by rehearsing with a dummy run. I would simply improvise, like any true artist. It was of course a recipe for disaster. Because – unlike TV chefs who have the luxury of stopping the camera and editing the final take to iron out delays in continuity – I was cooking in real time. And this demands much forward planning. My first demonstration that day, ambitiously, involved boning, stuffing and roasting a whole suckling pig. The boning and stuffing part went well, but I hadn't considered how I might entertain my students for the remaining two hours while we waited for the pig to roast in the oven. I managed to fill some time with a couple of other recipes I'd had planned – namely grapefruit sorbet and veal stock – but, like the suckling pig, these were quick to prepare but long in the

The Mousse and the Man from the Michelin

waiting. I'd run out of planned recipes, I still had an hour to kill before the class was scheduled to end, and yet I hadn't a single completed dish to present to my students. What to do for an hour? I felt like a musician who has run out of songs before the end of his set. But at least he can start again from the beginning. All I had to fall back on was the art of conversation. And, sadly, this was never my strong suit. What do I say to these people? I'm socially awkward in the best of circumstances. Give me an audience and I become tongue tied. Throw a video camera into the mix and I'm a quivering mess. To frustrate matters (and I've been told this even by those who profess to love me), I've a tendency to come across as arrogant and aloof. This did little to ease my predicament. Most of my students were genial enough, but it quickly became clear that there was a subversive element – the dissenters at the back of the room who would insist on picking holes in my recipes or asking awkward questions that I was unable to answer. I was rattled and struggled to disguise the fact, especially after a few glasses of wine – which was another problem.

The plan was that when the demonstration ended, the audience would have an opportunity to sample the food, accompanied by a glass of wine. But right now, with nothing to do and no food ready to sample, people were becoming listless. Unable to think of an alternative, my only resort was to break out the wine prematurely. Part of Kevin's remit as my assistant was to keep people's glasses replenished, a task he now took to with some zeal. A few of my students entered into the spirit of the occasion and even became quite voluble as a result. Following my third or fourth glass of Sancerre, I too was feeling distinctly mellow. I was inebriated and it wasn't yet lunchtime. Being drunk in charge of a commercial kitchen is not without its hazards, but with a degree of self-discipline it can be perfectly workable. Sharp knives and meat cleavers aside, at some time or another my cookery demonstrations demanded the use of a blowtorch, a salamander (a red-hot branding iron used for caramelising sugar) and an oyster opening machine (a vicious contrivance incorporating a spike and lever arm that could be mistaken for a medieval instrument of torture), a mincing machine and an industrial food processor, all of which had the potential to inflict horrible injury. However, having been operating these devices while under the influence for some years now without serious incident, I could see no problem. If anything, I'd come to believe that a few drinks served to steady the nerves and even reduced the likelihood of an accident. Sadly, this wasn't how one of my students saw it.

Our altercation began harmlessly enough. Still determined to address my continuity problem, I'd decided to fill time while my pig was cooking by showing off a selection

The Mousse and the Man from the Michelin

of cutting and slicing techniques. All went well until I came to puree some garlic. The method involves dicing the garlic finely on a chopping board and, using salt as an abrasive, crushing it repeatedly with the side of a knife until it becomes a puree.

'Well I don't like the look of that.' The voice came from the back of the room, a man in his early forties wearing a greying pony tail and black nylon polo neck. 'He's using the wrong chopping board...Look at him', repeated the man indignantly, 'he's using the wrong board – '

'I do have a name, you know,' I said, affronted at being so rudely interrupted.

'Surely a chef with your experience must know that chopping boards are colour coded to prevent cross contamination,' continued the man, unabashed. 'We watched you prepare an uncooked pig on that same board that you're now using to prepare raw vegetables. You should have used a red board for the raw meat and a brown board for the vegetables.'

'I think you'll find my assistant washed the board thoroughly between uses,' I said with an air of finality.

'Yeah, said Kevin,' nodding vigorously. 'I scrubbed it with bleach.'

'Bleach!' exclaimed the man. 'Bleach? On an absorbent wooden board? You shouldn't be using bleach, not on an absorbent wooden board.'

'Yeah, well, it kills germs and stuff,' said Kevin sullenly.

'Besides, you should be using nylon chopping boards,' continued the man. 'Not wood.'

'I would no sooner use a nylon chopping board than I would wear nylon underpants,' I said, with as much dignity as I could muster. 'Now, if I may continue with the class?'

'But it's no longer permissible to use wooden boards in a commercial kitchen,' said the man, who had no intention of backing down.

This was news to me. 'I'm aware of the guideline,' I lied, beginning to feel outflanked, 'but being a purist I prefer to use a wooden board. So can we leave it there, please?'

'It's not a guideline,' said the man imperiously. 'It's the law. What you're doing is breaking the law. Yellow is for cooked meats, which, incidentally, you'll need to use when it comes to slicing the suckling pig; blue is for raw fish, green for salads and fruits, white for –'

'He has a point,' said a woman in the front row. Look at that pureed garlic. It's all full of specks...looks like bits of wood mixed in with it.'

The Mousse and the Man from the Michelin

Our chopping board at The Mute Swan was regarded more as an heirloom than an item of equipment: a broad tranche of oak that dated back to Victorian times, it not only had history on its side, it had personality, and we looked upon it with some affection. That it might now be getting a bit tired was no cause to dispose of it. It did indeed shed minuscule wood fragments into the food from time to time, but we couldn't see how this did any harm. In fact we'd long held a theory that it achieved quite the opposite, and that a small quantity of seasoned oak actually acted as a subtle flavour enhancer, in much the same way an ancient oaken barrel adds depth and character to a fine wine.

'In fact I think you'll find that most of your kitchen constitutes an illegal hazard,' continued the man with the pony tail. He'd risen from his seat and was surveying the room with exaggerated thoroughness. 'Fire exits not marked. Fire extinguisher not coded for specific types of fire. No fire blanket. No visible first aid kit. Inadequate ventilation. The wrong floor tiles – '

'The wrong floor tiles?' I said incredulously. 'But this is a brand new kitchen. What on earth could be wrong with the floor tiles?'

'These tiles are class four smooth-type engineering tiles,' said the man authoritatively, while emphasising his point by stamping a foot on the floor, 'and as such constitute a slipping hazard. According to the Health and Safety Act of 1985, the correct floor tiles for a kitchen should be class six dimpled-type industrial.'

'Dimpled?'

'Yes, dimpled. Dimpled tiles are specified because they afford greater purchase underfoot due to the – '

'Why are you here?' I interrupted.

'I beg your pardon?' said the man.

'Why are you here? I really want to know, because it clearly isn't to bring cheer and happiness. Oh wait, don't tell me, is it that you were bullied at school, or simply that you have a small penis and you're determined to take it out on the world?'

At least this is what I wished I'd said, with the luxury of reflection. In reality, the best I could manage was to repeat myself. 'Why are you here?' I asked again. 'I really want to know.'

'Well, since you insist on asking,' said the man, 'I enrolled on this cookery programme because I thought I might learn something useful, but frankly I'm unimpressed. I'd even go so far as to say that I've never witnessed such a display of amateurishness in my life.'

The Mousse and the Man from the Michelin

'Nor have I, I'm very disappointed,' said the woman at the front,' to a chorus of affirmative grunts and much spirited nodding from several of the other students.

'Although I have to say that roasting pig smells pretty damn good,' said another student chirpily, clearly attempting to defuse the situation. I at least had one supporter. 'Weren't we supposed to get a taste of it before we're done?'

'It will never be cooked in time,' said the man with the pony tail with an air of certainty. 'I told you, we're dealing with amateurs.'

'But I am an amateur,' I said proudly, puffing out my chest as I spoke. 'And I wouldn't have it any other way.' I don't know why I said it. I must have looked and sounded ridiculous, but by now my dignity was in tatters.

'Well I certainly don't need any convincing on that point,' said ponytail man. 'A drunken amateur, too, so it would seem. I myself own and run a restaurant. Drinking alcohol is strictly forbidden in the kitchen on health and safety grounds, and any member of staff who broke this rule would be instantly dismissed.'

An awkward silence ensued while I struggled to formulate a suitably withering response. It was Kevin who eventually stepped in to fill the void: 'Top-up anyone?' he said brightly, brandishing a freshly uncorked bottle of Sancerre.

Kent Austin

My cookery classes could not be considered a success. Even after I'd ironed out my continuity problems, I still lacked the common touch. Try as I might, my attempts at repartee fell as flat as my jokes. By the time I'd completed the five-week series I was a nervous wreck and had succeeded in offending or alienating a majority of my paying students. Nor had I accounted for my dismal screen presence. Most of the time I just came across as diffident and tongue tied, and Gerald's amateur film footage – taken from a static camera, mounted on a tripod at the back of the room, with no zooming for detail – had all the visual appeal of a jihadist suicide-bomber's farewell video. It was beyond rescuing. Even an optimist such as Gerald was forced to conclude that the project was doomed. All further cookery classes were deferred indefinitely. But at least I had the money to look forward to.

However, not for the first time in my dealings with Gerald, the devil was in the detail. Because it was now time to deduct what he referred to as 'sundries' from the gross profit. This included the cost of ingredients, student refreshments, wine, staff, gas, electricity, cleaning, laundry, a percentage of the business rates, and 'wear and tear of equipment and infrastructure'. (He charitably waived a surcharge for air breathed.) By the time he'd finished, my share of the profit had been slashed from a projected £1,000 to a paltry

The Mousse and the Man from the Michelin

£240, a sum I would happily have relinquished just to have been spared the trauma.

CHAPTER 11

Not to be beaten, Gerald took a different tack and called in a favour from his connections at the Chelsea Arts Club, who seemed only too happy to pull a few strings on his behalf among their journalist acquaintances. They were as good as their word, and within days we received our first phone call. It was the then food columnist and restaurant critic for *The Spectator*, Jennifer Paterson. She told us she was 'coming down to the country' to dine at the restaurant and write a review for the magazine, and thought it only right that she give us 'a bit of advance notice'. It was certainly an unconventional approach. In our experience, restaurant reviewers preferred to show up anonymously, presumably working on the assumption that announcing their arrival in advance could result in them receiving preferential treatment. They might, on rare occasions, reveal their identities when they came to pay the bill, although never in advance. But perhaps this was how things worked when you were in the know? In any case, we were hardly going to complain about being placed at an advantage, and were happy to collude.

Jennifer Paterson said she would be travelling from London the following Sunday. It was arranged that she would meet up with Gerald and Arabella at their house, where they would have lunch, then on to The Mute Swan to meet with the chefs, followed by dinner at the restaurant. With little difficulty, Gerald had also persuaded her to accept their hospitality and spend the night at their home as a guest. That this may be viewed as a conflict of interest was evidently not an issue.

It needs pointing out that at this time none of us had heard of Jennifer Paterson. Not so many years later she was destined to enjoy popular success, with Clarissa Dickson Wright, as one of the Two Fat Ladies, in the BBC TV cookery series of the same name, but at this stage in the brief flowering of her career she was a relatively unknown food writer. Had it been suggested that she would one day find fame as a celebrity chef we would have been as incredulous as the next person. By any prevailing standard, Jennifer was not television material: rotund, bespectacled, quite the wrong side of 60, and with the demeanour of a dotty spinster, she seemed more like a matron in a Carry On film than a media personality. Indeed, before becoming a professional chef – and cooking private dinner parties for Prince Charles among others – she'd worked as a matron at a boarding school for girls. *Two Fat Ladies* launched in 1996 and was an instant hit, attracting 3.5 million viewers. It has a cult following to this day, especially in the USA, where it seems

The Mousse and the Man from the Michelin

that British eccentrics continue to hold a place in viewers' affections. The programme cocked a snoot at every fashionable taboo to do with food, while the protagonists took it in turns to cook to camera. Unusually for a cookery show, it was also funny – mainly because it was unscripted and the cooks were allowed to adlib at will. Each episode began with Jennifer Paterson astride a motorbike (she was a keen biker) with the equally corpulent and oddball Clarissa Dickson Wright squeezed into a sidecar beside her, clad in helmets and goggles, careering through the countryside to their latest destination. Red meat was high on the menu, and the pair appeared to revel in their political incorrectness by creating cholesterol-soaked dishes based on all the fattiest cuts. Non-meat eaters were written-off scornfully as 'manky little vegetarians'. 'I blame Americans for this fear of red meat and fat that's spread all over England,' Jennifer Paterson once remarked in an interview. 'They say our show tells Americans that it's OK to eat red meat and cook with butter. I don't know why they feel they need permission.' She attributed her own health and longevity to 'lots of meat, drink and cigarettes, and not giving in to things'. It was a comment, however ironically intended, that was to prove cruelly fateful, for shortly afterwards she was diagnosed with lung cancer and, in 1999, died, aged 71. She was midway through filming a fourth series.

Kent Austin

When Jennifer Paterson arrived at the restaurant that Sunday afternoon she was in an expansive mood. A prolonged liquid lunch courtesy of the Golightlys had left her a little unsteady on her feet, but when we gathered in the bar for coffee she was clearly in control of her faculties. In contrast to my previous one-sided encounter with Crispin Sutherland from the BBC, Jennifer was eager to talk shop and interrogated me at length about my menu, bouncing gamely from subject to subject while sipping brandy and puffing on an unbroken chain of un-tipped Woodbines. Quick-witted and engaging, Jennifer was a natural raconteur and, just as importantly, seemed genuinely interested in what I had to say. But flattered and entertained as I was, I had more pressing concerns. Time was running out and to have any chance of being ready for service I had to return to the kitchen and begin cooking. To complicate matters further, Gerald's London contacts had arranged an interview with another magazine which clashed precisely with Jennifer Paterson's visit. We'd phoned and tried to cancel, but it was too late, a journalist and photographer had already been dispatched and they would be arriving at the restaurant later that afternoon. The magazine was called *Restaurant Business,* a respected but low circulation trade monthly aimed at catering professionals. Alongside the usual articles and industry gossip, it would run as its centrepiece a restaurant

The Mousse and the Man from the Michelin

review. This included a profile and potted history of the featured restaurant and an interview with the chef, who would then be photographed with a selection of his or her signature dishes arrayed tastefully in the foreground. The picture was to feature on the magazine's front cover, resulting, we were assured, in much positive PR – among whom and to what purpose was unclear, as it all seemed a bit incestuous, but we went along with it anyway, if only to spite the competition.

I also had a plan. Rather than use individual plated dishes for the photo-shoot, which, I'd noted, was the preferred approach of most chefs, for maximum visual impact I would prepare a completely over-the-top buffet. The centrepiece was to be a spectacular dressed salmon, around which would be arranged an array of dishes, each selected for its photogenic appeal, including a scallop tart, a game terrine, assorted canapés and a tower of chocolate-coated profiteroles adorned with spun sugar. As was so often the case with my menu planning, it was hopelessly ambitious, and I was now faced with the near-impossible task of completing both the buffet and preparing for the coming restaurant service, all in five hours. To add to the stress, Gerald and Arabella had arranged a post-photo-shoot soirée. This way the buffet would be put to good use, and the restaurant would also benefit from the local publicity. It was to be a select affair.

Kent Austin

On the guest list were several politicians – including former chancellor of the exchequer Denis Healey, who lived in nearby Alfriston – a retired cabinet minister, a smattering of writers, artists and academics, a chief magistrate and the cream of the county's landed gentry.

The first job on my list was to dress the salmon – which I'd cooked and left cooling on the prep room table earlier that day – and I now went to retrieve it. In my haste when leaving I'd obviously neglected to close the prep room door behind me, because I returned to find a wild cat (one of many that continued to dwell in our garden) squatting on top of the salmon and feasting greedily on its flesh. The cat was so intent on gorging itself that it failed to notice me approach, and a second or two passed before it became aware of my presence. When eventually it looked up and met my gaze I expected it to panic and make a dash for the door, in the manner of any normal cat. But to my surprise it stood its ground. It even snarled in defiance, as if to warn me off its kill. In my experience, such boldness in a cat was unprecedented. On one level I could see his point. When you've spent a life subsisting on rancid scraps scavenged from bins, supplemented only by the occasional mouse or crippled songbird, the chance discovery of a perfectly poached Scottish salmon must be akin to winning first prize in a lottery. You aren't about to give it up without a fight. But facing

The Mousse and the Man from the Michelin

off with a human? Surely this was a conceit too far. But then again this wasn't just any cat. It was a vicious black tom known to the restaurant staff as Bent Ear, so named because one of his ears had been left badly deformed after a fight, giving him a distinctly sinister appearance. Bent Ear was indisputably the king of the pride, and was well-known around the village for his practice of violently raping any female cat that crossed his path. (On one occasion he'd even pursued a victim into the restaurant dining room, where in panic she'd fled for shelter, and nonchalantly raped her in full view of the customers.) And pity the fate of any rival tomcat foolhardy enough to stand his ground. Imagine, if you're able, a feline equivalent of the boxer Mike Tyson and you have some idea of what we were dealing with. Mad, bad and built like a panther on testosterone, Bent Ear was a perfectly evolved killing machine. He wasn't just undomesticated; he was, in every sense of the word, wild; twice as big as any ordinary cat and genuinely dangerous. And now here I was pitted against the full force of his primal rage.

He had, however, seriously underestimated not just the gravity of the situation and my determination to resolve it, but also his inherent handicap as a species. Thankfully, one of the superior traits that set man apart from the beasts is his ability to use a weapon, and I was about to take full advantage of the fact. My chosen weapon on this occasion was a heavy stiff-bristled broom, which just happened to be propped against a wall within convenient reach. Wielding it before me like a war hammer, I took aim, my intention being to strike a wide, lateral blow that would propel my adversary from his perch without damaging the salmon. Remarkably it worked, but only up to a point, because although Bent Ear was sent flying by my perfectly judged sidewinder, his claws remained firmly embedded in the flesh of the salmon, and as such much of it was destined to travel through the air with him. He hit the floor in a blur of fish flakes and flailing limbs. Anticipating retaliation, I raised my broom to deliver the knockout blow. But while Bent Ear continued to hiss and spit, any fight had been knocked out of him in the first round, and he now fled through the open door into the garden, defeated and, I like to think, humiliated.

I inspected the damage. It wasn't good. The cat had eaten a circular hole in the salmon some fifteen centimetres in diameter and three centimetres deep. There were also several deep gashes in the flesh caused by its claws, as well as a sticky residue of dust and fur adhering to the skin where it had been sitting. If there was any glimmer of hope, it was that the damage was confined to the middle third of the fish, the head and tail ends having somehow escaped unscathed. The salmon was salvageable. Under any other circumstances I would have binned it and put the loss down to experience.

The Mousse and the Man from the Michelin

But I wasn't about to forego the centrepiece of my buffet, and I didn't have a replacement. I did, however, have some spare salmon fillets. All I need do was clean up the fish using a vodka-soaked napkin to kill any bacteria, carefully excise the offending area around where the cat had been eating, and then patch the hole with the newly poached fillets. And as the entire salmon was going to be finished with cucumber scales and glazed with aspic, the repaired area would be concealed and no one would be any the wiser. It was a time-consuming pain in the arse, true, but it was feasible.

By a miracle of effort, when the journalist and photographer from *Restaurant Business* arrived, the buffet was finished and laid out on display in one of the restaurant lounges, salmon included. And the general opinion was that it looked pretty damned good. My interview, on the other hand, turned out to be not so good. The journalist was a London foody type. Even before we'd begun, his body language told me that nothing I was about to say was going to impress him. Perhaps he was bored with interviewing his umpteenth chef, or felt he was destined for better things. Whatever his problem, he seemed determined to take it out on me. None of my answers chimed with what he wanted me to say, and he made no effort to strike a rapport or put me at my ease. By the time we'd finished the interview I felt belittled and patronised. My final embarrassment was when he asked me to describe my style of cooking.

'Eclectic,' I answered promptly. I'm not sure why I used this word. Perhaps I'd read it somewhere.

'All chefs say that these days,' drawled the journalist. 'It's probably the most widely flogged cliché in the business. Couldn't you perhaps think of a more original term?'

'Er, diverse?'

The journalist rolled his eyes.

'Varied?'

'We'll stick with eclectic.' The journalist snapped shut his notebook and consulted his watch. 'Anyway, I think we're done now. We'll just get some shots of the food then we'll pack up.'

'Where do you want me to stand?' I asked. 'Or would you prefer me to remain seated?'

The journalist furrowed his brow. 'Erm, I don't think you're in the shoot, actually. We're using Gerald.'

'No, you're photographing me. I'm the chef.'

'That's not what we were told.'

Gerald had up until this point been keeping a low profile and chatting with Jennifer Paterson at the back of the room.

The Mousse and the Man from the Michelin

Now, as if on cue, he straightened his cravat, smoothed his hair and proceeded to strike a distinguished pose – directly behind my buffet. I was dumbfounded.

'But wasn't it me who's supposed to be in the photo?' I asked Gerald when the photographer had finished and was packing away his equipment. I found it hard to disguise my disappointment.

Gerald seemed surprised. 'No cause to be peevish, Kento, it's my restaurant. It's up to me if I want a photograph taken.'

'Yes, but surely it's the chef who should be photographed, if he's the one who, you know, cooked the food? That's the way it normally works.'

'I can't see what you're complaining about, Kento. Besides, I allowed you the interview. Speaking of which, you really shouldn't have described your cooking as eclectic. Terrible cliché.

The buffet was a success. Everyone turned up and my food was swiftly demolished, including the salmon, which was stripped to the bone. Compliments flowed in proportion to the wine.

It was only after the final guest had departed that I told Gerald about the incident with the salmon and the cat. With hindsight it was a mistake. I'd meant it to come across as an amusing anecdote of the *you'll never guess what happened earlier but I got away with it* variety, but, sadly, this wasn't how it was to be received.

'But what if you've infected somebody, Kento?' said Gerald, his face having turned instantly pale.

I laughed. 'Oh, come on, Gerald, you can't be serious?'

'I couldn't be more serious, Kento. Did you not consider the host of lethal diseases this insanitary beast might be harbouring before taking chances with people's lives? How could you be so thoughtless? You should have thrown the whole thing away and been done with it.'

'I think you might be overreacting, Gerald. I cleaned it up as best I could.'

'Overreacting? Cleaned it up? As best you could? What guarantee is that? The food hygiene wallahs will throw the bloody book at us. We'll be put out of business. That's all it takes. And they won't have forgotten the worms, you know, the worms they found in our freezer. They keep a record of these things. And this puts the bloody worms in the shade. We could have a case of mass poisoning on our hands. It'll be like Jonestown revisited. I'll be ruined, sued for every last penny.'

The Mousse and the Man from the Michelin

The prospect of being held responsible for the deaths of not one but two former cabinet ministers, not to mention the decimation of a majority of the county's chattering classes, was for Gerald a scandal too far. 'It's no good,' he said, 'I need to take expert advice. I'll phone my doctor. He'll know what to do – '

'Wouldn't it be better to just sit tight and expect the best?' I said. 'I mean what are the odds of anyone being poisoned?'

'That's my very point, Kento. What *are* the odds? We need to know. Perhaps there's an antidote or something that can be administered to prevent people from falling sick.'

Gerald phoned his doctor, while taking care not to reveal the precise nature of his concern. The doctor was of the opinion that there was a risk, but not a significant one. Cats, apparently, carry relatively few harmful bacteria in their mouths (unlike dogs' mouths, which are crawling with bugs). The most likely infection, if any, to occur as a result of my negligence was salmonella enteritis. Symptoms include diarrhoea with bleeding, fever and abdominal cramps. Most sufferers recover well, although salmonella is responsible for some 80 deaths in the UK each year. The incubation period is 12–72 hours.

'Oh, so that's alright then,' said Gerald when he came

off the phone, 'only a mere eighty deaths a year, so clearly nothing to worry about there. And I've only to endure three whole days and nights of torment before we know whether we're in the clear, so no problem there either. What an almighty cock-up. I can't believe this is happening. What were you thinking of, Kento?'

Gerald's panic was beginning to rub off on me, and now I too began imagining the worst. In my darker moments I could not rule out a charge of manslaughter, possibly even a jail term. Gerald was right. What, indeed, had I been thinking of?

I've no idea how I achieved it, given my frame of mind, but following the buffet I somehow found the wherewithal to prepare for that night's service and, without a hitch, fed a packed restaurant, Jennifer Paterson included. Here's how she described the meal in her column for *The Spectator* the following week:

***

The first courses included a fine soup of devilled squid, fragrant and filling, pink with peppers and tomato, an exquisite mousseline of scallops with tiny halved langoustines. I had duckling in aspic, which consisted of the leg meat chopped and served in its own jellied stock with some tiny slices of pink duck breast and citrus fruit on the side: an

The Mousse and the Man from the Michelin

excellent combination. There was also a croustade of quail eggs sitting on a nest of asparagus bathed in hollandaise sauce...succulent breast of duck with a marsala and passion fruit sauce (first class)...a noble dish of fillets of salmon and turbot with scallops and a beurre blanc sauce (extremely rich and rightly so). I had a dear little maize-fed poussin stuffed with lobster and ginger served with a choron sauce (very good indeed). The most lovely scent of tarragon and ginger assailed the nostrils when unplugging the first piece of lobster from the bird's cavity.

Tiny perfectly cooked vegetables arrived in plenty, boiled new potatoes for the fish and crisp–topped dauphinoise for the others, carrot purée, broccoli, beans and midget corn cobs. All the helpings were very generous...The list of puddings was formidable and so tempting that we bravely ploughed on after a bit of a pause. This is the place that invented Banoffi Pie 22 years ago, though its fame has spread far and wide, even to the Royals and No. 10 I believe. I had never heard of it but it is a great slice of pie of sliced bananas topped with whipped cream on a thick layer of soft toffee sitting in a shortcrust pastry case. Outrageous! The toffee layer is made by boiling tinned sweetened condensed milk in its unopened tin, but covered all the time by boiling water or it explodes. Takes five hours; imagine the excitement and the danger.

Kent Austin

Another killer was hot chocolate cake with ice cream and hot chocolate sauce. Marvellous almost black chocolate cake and sauce steaming with heat accompanied with creamy golden

homemade ice cream. Everyone had a plunge into this. Wow! Then there was a nice simple praline and raisin ice cream and superb cheesecake in a pool of blackcurrant sauce. We declined a free glass of port but had a lot of good coffee and homemade bitter mints straight from the freezer, icy and brittle, a good foil. A very respectable dinner most charmingly served by a bevy of beautiful girls radiating good humour, professionalism and pleasure. What more could you ask? There are two chefs... We had Kent Austin, so many congratulations to him. It was a thoroughly nice place, I loved it. The restaurant is open for dinner every night of the week and also for Sunday lunch. It seemed very full so I should think booking would be advisable. You may purchase a very good little book of their receipts which I shall unfold to you on my cooking page in the future...

Jennifer Paterson

Jennifer had delivered – although to this day I've no idea whether her enthusiasm for my cooking was heartfelt or merely dutiful. Either way, Gerald and Arabella were delighted with the write-up and, amid much back slapping and

The Mousse and the Man from the Michelin

popping of corks, I was heartily congratulated for my efforts. And there was more good news: seventy-two hours had now passed since the 'Jonestown Buffet' (as it had become known) and we'd received no word of sickness or sudden death among the attendees. Still sceptical, however, Gerald was unable to resist phoning each of our buffet guests personally, on the pretext of it being a routine social call and enquiring, very casually, after the state of their health. This turned out to be a mistake. Because it transpired that a number of our guests had indeed been taken ill following the buffet, although, to Gerald's relief, none had thought to blame it on our food.

Or so we thought...

It was two days later when a man in a white coat showed up at the kitchen door announcing he was from the health department. It would seem that a disgruntled diner was holding the restaurant responsible for an apparent case of food poisoning, caused, so they claimed, not by salmon, but by eating my game terrine. Our accuser remained anonymous, so we had no way of telling whether he or she had been a guest at the buffet or was simply an ordinary diner, because game terrine featured on both menus. The man in the white coat announced that he had come to take a sample of the suspect foodstuff for analysis in the laboratory. 'Just as a formality so that it can be ruled out, you understand,' he said apologetically. 'It's not to suggest that we think it's necessarily the cause.'

I pointed out that the game terrine that was currently in our refrigerator was in fact an entirely different batch from the one I'd been serving the previous week, and as such testing it for contamination would be a pointless exercise and prove nothing.

'Quite,' agreed the man in the white coat. 'But I have been assigned by my superiors to take a sample, so take one I must. I do apologise for any inconvenience.'

Predictably, the sample tested as negative, but not before Gerald had suffered a further week of sleepless nights awaiting the result. To this day I'm convinced any illness our guests might have suffered was attributable to a vomiting bug that was prevalent at the time, and in no way connected to my buffet. But Gerald was not to be persuaded and even now holds me responsible for infecting our guests. That no one had died or been hospitalised he put down to good fortune and the general hardiness of our guests' constitutions (as I write, Dennis Healey continues to enjoy good health, aged 97). We were in the clear. The episode was consigned to history and it was back to business as usual.

But that was the problem.

I'd been running the kitchen single-handedly now for

The Mousse and the Man from the Michelin

two years, and I wasn't coping. True, I had some help from Kevin, who with much hand-holding was finally able to work unsupervised. I'd assigned him to cooking main courses on Sundays, which at least enabled me to get a day off. But the truth was that Mark's departure had heralded the demise of a golden era. Most significantly, it meant an end to my cushy three-day week and work-free weekends. It was a luxury I'd come to take for granted, and its loss came as a blow. Not only did I now have to work six days every week in the kitchen (like any normal chef) but I also had responsibility for managing a team of four trainee interns, planning and costing daily menus, ordering all produce and maintaining profitability and stock control. I was working an average 70-hour week. With Mark gone my workload was effectively doubled.

That was the downside to the new regime: Mark was no longer a part of it. I missed him, I admit it. Without Mark being there I had nothing in common with any of my work colleagues, and, Kevin aside, found myself bereft of male company. Worse still, I had no one to turn to for advice when things went wrong. There were times when I felt so miserable with Mark not being there that I was unable to make decisions. On more than one occasion I even considered phoning Mark and telling him how miserable I felt without him being there and that I couldn't make decisions without him. But then, irked by the thought of giving him the satisfaction of knowing how miserable I felt without him being there and that I couldn't make decisions without him, I would make the decision not to contact him. Unfailingly, I would then congratulate myself for having made a decision without Mark being there. Having made the decision, I felt much happier. Indeed I felt so much happier that I was in no doubt that I was quantifiably happier than I might have been had Mark still been there. I was enjoying an unprecedented surfeit of happiness and it was all because Mark wasn't there. Then I'd slowly begin missing him again and the cycle would repeat itself. I was in no doubt that I was cracking up.

CHAPTER 12

Help arrived in the unlikely guise of our latest Rannie's intern. Her name was Ophelia and, like most Rannie's girls, she had a wayward streak. The daughter of a five-star NATO general, she had resisted her father's attempts to marry her off to a young officer in the Bengal Lancers and, to her family's disappointment, not to say horror – and in keeping with what was now a tradition among Rannie's girls – had taken up with a local fisherman. His name was Frank, although people knew him as Frank the Fish. He lived in the hold of his fishing boat – a dilapidated clinker-built ketch moored permanently on the beach in Eastbourne's fishing quarter, a bleak expanse of scrub and shingle at the eastern extreme of the town. When she wasn't working at the restaurant, Ophelia would spend her time with Frank on his boat, the consequence being that she smelled permanently of decayed fish and diesel oil. We were offended by Ophelia's body odour and regularly told her so, but she remained unmoved by our protests, and even suggested that it was we, with our bourgeois notions of hygiene, who had the problem, not she. Why Ophelia – an attractive, well-bred girl who could doubtless take her pick among men from her own social caste – should prefer to dwell in an insanitary boat with a malodorous recluse twenty years her senior remained a mystery. But whatever Frank the Fish's allure, it was clearly worth smelling bad about. What, I wondered, could it be? I was about to find out.

'Frank says he wants to meet you,' Ophelia casually informed me one evening after work. 'He thought he might pop over some time and say hello, if that's alright?'

'Really? Why would he want to meet *me*?' I asked suspiciously. The prospect of coming face to face with the original source of Ophelia's body odour consumed me with dread.

'Well, there's no need to get all grumpy about it,' said Ophelia. 'Besides,' she continued darkly, 'he may have something you want.'

'Something I want? Like fish, you mean?'

'No, not fish, something else. Something you *want*.'

I couldn't imagine what Frank had that I could possibly want. But avoiding him was not to be an option.

For someone with a reputation as a hermit, Frank turned out to be remarkably sociable. True to his word, the following night he turned up at the kitchen door of the restaurant, ostensibly to meet Ophelia from work, although his main aim, clearly, was to talk to (or at) me, and he was very good

The Mousse and the Man from the Michelin

at it – at least if one valued quantity over quality. Frank liked to amuse me with his anecdotes, which were seemingly limitless and of dubious veracity. Along the way I wasn't surprised to learn that he was a drug dealer. He looked the part: gold hoop earrings; shoulder-length hair and a porkpie hat, sat at a jaunty angle on the back of his head. He had abnormally green eyes which gave him a feline appearance; and his teeth, broken and discoloured, appeared to be deliberately filed into points.

(Although I later discovered that this resulted from a dental condition called ectodermal dysplasia.) He also suffered from a pronounced curvature of the upper back which left him permanently hunched. Altogether he looked like a cross between Bill Sykes and Quasimodo and, in the right light, just a hint of Cat Woman.

In my experience, drug dealers are incapable of discretion. Just as anyone who went to Oxford or Cambridge will inevitably slip the fact into the first minute of any conversation, so a drug dealer cannot resist blowing his own trumpet. Within moments of our meeting, Frank had offered to procure for me a quantity of any drug I'd ever heard of, as well as several I hadn't. At the time I wasn't interested. I didn't do drugs. I might have smoked a joint on the rare occasions when I went to a party, but apart from this drugs played no role in my life. This was about to change. It happened at the end of an especially hard day. I was tired and overworked and complaining about it volubly to Frank over a beer and a cigarette in the kitchen garden. He nodded attentively and seemed genuinely sympathetic. 'Well, I think what you need me old son is a little pick-me-up,' he said, after I'd finished pouring my heart out. And with a conspiratorial tap of the nose he reached into his pocket and produced a sachet of white powder, a sharpened credit card and a small mirror. It was almost as if he'd been anticipating his moment. 'This'll make you perky. See if I'm not wrong.'

There are people out there whom we instinctively know to be bad news, and yet there's something about them that charms us into ignoring the fact. And unavoidably we end up regretting it. So it was that I began buying cocaine from Frank the Fish.

It was the answer to all my problems. Such was my exhaustion and ennui at the time that I'd been struggling to crawl out of bed in the mornings. But with the aid of a line or two of cocaine on waking (repeated as necessary on the hour) I became instantly alert. I could work a twelve-hour day and party on into the night without missing a beat. Not only this, but I was mentally alert, decisive, gregarious, boundlessly energetic, full of marvellous ideas and very, very (very!) witty. In fact all the things I wasn't in real life. It was as if my troubles had never existed. How on earth

The Mousse and the Man from the Michelin

had I ever got by without this stuff? Frank was very clearly quite a find.

Frank worked with two business partners. I say 'worked', but I use the term loosely, because in Frank's case work consisted of little more than waiting for a two-kilo consignment of cocaine to arrive in his possession, bulking it out with a roughly equal quantity of horse tranquiliser and laxative powder, and dividing it into smaller packages. These would then be passed on for a healthy profit to the legion of street-level dealers who relied on him for their supply. (Demand always exceeded supply by a wide margin.) End to end the entire process took no longer than four hours. Frank would repeat this ritual once a fortnight. The rest of his time was his own, which in the main was spent getting stoned in the hold of his boat.

Frank's boat was called the Channel Queen, although locals knew it as the Coca Queen – such was its notoriety. It was equally familiar to the local drug squad, who had long suspected Frank of being a dealer. But despite repeated raids they'd been unable to pull off a decisive bust. Whenever they searched Frank's boat they would leave empty handed, or with a few grams of cannabis at best. There was a good reason for this, and the drug squad had so far failed to work it out. Frank took delivery of his contraband at sea, somewhere far out in the English Channel, where he would rendezvous with a boat from Holland under cover of darkness. Not only did he receive his drugs at sea – and this is the clever bit – but he stored them at sea, in water-tight cylinders secured inside lobster pots. The lobster pots were then tossed overboard a mile or two offshore, where they would sink to the seabed, marked only by a solitary buoy. He concealed his illicit cash by the same means. In recent times, according to Frank, the drug squad had all but given up trying to bust him, and he operated with de facto impunity. In fishing, it seemed, he'd found the perfect front.

Frank's first business partner was called Mickey Dredge, but everyone knew him as Laughing Gnome (if you'd met him you'd know why), and he was the most bizarre person I'd ever met. Short, squat, with a little protruding belly, he did indeed resemble a gnome. He wasn't a midget in the genetic sense, but at some time in his early teens he'd apparently stopped growing. He was now in his mid forties, yet struggled to reach four-foot-ten. Imagine a truncated version of Russell Brand, minus the wit and intellect, and permanently overdosed on helium, and you'll be close. The words verbal and diarrhoea had never been more aptly paired. People who knew Laughing Gnome coped by ignoring him, but anyone meeting him for the first time would find it a disconcerting experience. When Laughing Gnome wasn't talking – a staccato chatter more akin to white noise

The Mousse and the Man from the Michelin

than communication – he occupied the gaps with laughter. This was no ordinary laughter; it was the zoo at feeding time, the din of bedlam – cackling, hooting, screeching, incoherent jabber. Ten minutes in his company and you were exhausted. Laughing Gnome was terminally amused. That's not to say he was funny. Most of the time, he wasn't. He was amused, not amusing (at least not wittingly so). Whatever the occasion, whatever the subject, he would extract a laugh from it, even if – as was generally the case – no one else in the room had the faintest idea what he was laughing *about*. That he was a victim of his dissipated lifestyle was a given. Drug dealers usually conform to one of two types: those who use and those who don't. Frank was nominally in the latter category (cannabis aside), while Laughing Gnome fell resolutely into the former.

Laughing Gnome led a colourful life, central to which was an obsession with sex and mind altering substances. The first time I met him, he confided that he was affected by a rare medical disorder called priapism, which had left him with a permanently erect penis. Noting my incredulity, he insisted on showing me, along with everyone else in the crowded pub in which we happened to be drinking at the time. His penis was indeed erect, tremulously so, and, judging by its livid beetroot hue, so engorged that it might haemorrhage at any time. He claimed to have been in this state for several months. His doctor, he told us, was gravely concerned and had recommended surgery to relieve the pressure. But Laughing Gnome declined to be treated. To his mind it was manna from heaven and, while it lasted, he was determined to use his erection to maximum advantage.

Frank's other business partner was called Speedy Sue (due to her profligate use of amphetamines). Speedy Sue cut a striking figure. Pale and pencil thin, she had a long, beaked nose and artificially black waist-length hair which gave her a witchlike appearance, an image she liked to nurture by wearing wide-brimmed hats and dressing exclusively in black. She had much in common with Laughing Gnome, in that she was a drug dealer, an addict, was borderline mad and never listened to a word anyone else said. She was also, albeit on a very casual basis, Frank's lover. Although at the time she'd been displaced by the much younger Ophelia.

Behind their addled exteriors, Laughing Gnome and Speedy Sue were canny operators. With Frank they ran a cartel which had Eastbourne's thriving drugs trade sewn-up (the duller the town, it is said, the more buoyant its drug market). I never quite worked out the complexities of their relationship, and still less the logic behind their business model: all three sold drugs; all three sold the same drugs, and to the same people, who were essentially the others'

The Mousse and the Man from the Michelin

customers. Yet they were partners in the same business. They were effectively competing with each other. As a system it bordered on surreal. It seemed to work. The three supplied drugs as far afield as London, and even boasted a number of celebrity customers. During the early 1970s, so it was alleged, Laughing Gnome had regularly supplied David Bowie with cannabis, which he would deliver personally to the singer's London flat. He'd first met the young, and hitherto undiscovered, Bowie in the late sixties when he played a gig at an Eastbourne club. (I say 'club', although this is really too flattering a term to describe such a low-life dump. Known as The Eastbourne Suite, it occupied a single dingy room above Burton Menswear in the high street. It didn't even serve alcohol.) The night was a flop and Bowie found himself playing to just a handful of people, one of whom was Laughing Gnome. To cheer the singer up after his depressing experience, he invited Bowie back to his bedsit to get high, and the two became friends. The legend locally was that Bowie had been so taken with his dealer – who at the time still went by the name of Mickey Dredge – he'd written a song in his honour, entitled *The Laughing Gnome,* which he included on his debut album. The name stuck. Unlikely as this story may sound, I'm inclined to think Laughing Gnome was telling the truth. The clue is in the lyrics:

Kent Austin

I was walking down the High Street

When I heard footsteps behind me

And there was a little old man (Hello)

In scarlet and grey, shuffling away (laughter)

Well he trotted back to my house

And he sat beside the telly (Oaah..)

With his tiny hands on his tummy

Chuckling away, laughing all day (laughter)

Oh, I ought to report you to the Gnome office

(Gnome Office)

Yes

Hahahahaha)

Ha ha ha, hee hee hee

"I'm a laughing Gnome and you can't catch me"

Ha ha ha, hee hee hee

"I'm a laughing Gnome and you can't catch me"

Said the laughing Gnome

Well I gave him roasted toadstools and a glass of dandelion wine (Burp, pardon)

The Mousse and the Man from the Michelin

Then I put him on a train to Eastbourne

Carried his bag and gave him a fag

(Haven't you got a light boy?)

"Here, where do you come from?"

(Gnome–man's land, hahihihi)

"Oh, really?"

And so it continues for several more verses. The clincher, according to Laughing Gnome, is the line: 'Then I put him on a train to Eastbourne'. Anyway, he had me convinced. As an aside, I think it's fair to argue that *The Laughing Gnome* is not just the worst song that David Bowie ever recorded, but very possibly the worst song in the entire history of popular music. And this is from the same songwriter who not long afterwards had a number-one hit with *Space Oddity*. I can only put it down to a temporary lapse of judgement. Laughing Gnome could have that effect on people.

Meanwhile, my cocaine habit had reached its silly phase. There is of course a downside to using cocaine, although it can take a little time to reveal itself. Now, after relying on the drug more or less continuously for six months, it had finally caught up with me. First, there was the loss of judgement. Cocaine is to rational thought as an oil slick is to an albatross, yet such is the nature of the drug that it deludes one into believing the precise opposite. My management of the kitchen was becoming increasingly erratic, but to my mind I was still functioning normally. I'd lost my appetite: the thought of eating was abhorrent, and even when I could bring myself to try some food my sense of taste was non-existent – not ideal if one is a chef. I was losing weight, and yet I failed to see it as a problem. Sleep became a luxury: I would eventually get to bed at dawn, only to stare numbly at the ceiling for six hours with the sound of jet engines roaring inside my head. Frank prescribed cannabis, assuring me that it would counter the effects of the cocaine. When this failed to send me to sleep, Laughing Gnome placed me on Mogadon tablets. They worked. The problem was they worked too well, and I would remain unconscious until mid-afternoon. This made me late for work, which in turn meant that I struggled to be ready in time for service. Standards slipped. I was running out of money: at the height of my habit I was spending upwards of £300 a week on cocaine. Then there was the pendulum effect to contend with – this dictates that when using a drug, any euphoria attained on the upward swing will be succeeded by a precisely corresponding depression on the downward swing, as the effect of the drug wears off: the higher the high, the lower the low. The only reprieve is to take more cocaine, and so it continues, while the dose needed to maintain this equilibrium increases

The Mousse and the Man from the Michelin

incrementally, as the body acquires a tolerance to the drug. Apart from this, and apart from the compulsive jaw clenching, the mood swings, the unnatural sweats, the paranoid delusions, the suicidal thoughts, the sexual dysfunction, the loss of proportion and an overwhelming suspicion that everyone I knew was plotting against me, I was coping just fine. I could handle it all – all, that was, apart from the anal leakage. Because when you're suffering from anal leakage it tends to put your other problems in perspective. Frank's cocaine contained a high proportion of laxative powder, a medium used commonly by dealers to 'cut' their product and maximise profits. It's for this reason they say that people with a cocaine habit should never wear white trousers (Nigella Lawson take note). I'd add to this by saying that people with a cocaine habit should always – and I mean *always* – resist an urge to fart.

While this was happening – and via some subtle manoeuvring that had somehow escaped my notice – Frank had moved into my home. I could see the appeal: winter had arrived, and my cottage – with its log fire, comfy sofas, stereo, TV, well-stocked fridge and wine rack – was doubtless preferable to living in the hold of a dank boat without power or sanitation. Frank was also at a loose end: Ophelia had recently been kidnapped by her parents and whisked away to live overseas, the upshot being that he had even more time to kill than usual. The situation had arisen because I'd mentioned to Frank that he should drop by sometime. With hindsight, it was a mistake. I'd intended it as a politeness, a passing remark. I certainly hadn't expected him to take me up on the offer. Anyone with the least grasp of English manners knows that an invitation to 'drop by' should always be inferred to mean the opposite. It's fundamental. But clearly I'd been consorting with the middle classes for too long, because that same night Frank showed up at my door. Not only this, but he brought Laughing Gnome along with him. They stayed for two hours, rolled a joint, drank a case of my beer and left. The following evening they arrived again, this time extending their visit indefinitely by passing out together on the sofa. Try as I might, I couldn't stir them. They remained comatose until the early hours of the morning, at which point they recovered sufficiently to raid my fridge and smoke a bong before slumping into a resumed coma. They were still unconscious when I left for work the next day. I returned home some twelve hours later to find them seated around the kitchen table with Mildred. They were playing a game of pinochle and, judging by their animated conversation, all getting along like a house on fire – encouraged in no small measure by a fresh consignment of cocaine that had fallen into Frank's possession that very afternoon (just recently there had been a shortage).

The Mousse and the Man from the Michelin

Frank welcomed me warmly. 'Come in, come in, man, yeahhhh, we've been missing you. What can I get you to drink?' He rose unsteadily from his seat and opened the fridge. 'Let's see now, we have beer...wine...'

I of course knew this, because I'd put it in the fridge myself. 'Oh, thanks,' I said. 'I'll have a glass of wine, if you don't mind?'

'We're playing cards,' said Mildred unnecessarily, as Frank uncorked a seventh bottle of my Pouilly Fuisse Grande Reserve.

'Yes, I can see,' I replied. 'Would that be my Pouilly Fuisse Grande Reserve you're drinking or, should I say, have drunk?' My remark caused Laughing Gnome to disintegrate into a spasm of giggles.

'We knew you wouldn't mind,' said Mildred, beaming munificently. Her pupils were dilated, and a faint white ring showed beneath each of her nostrils. 'We're celebrating.'

'She's a great girl, this one,' said Frank. He took Mildred by the shoulder and gave her an all-enveloping hug. 'Why didn't you tell me about her? You're a lucky bloke to have an old lady like this, make no mistake.'

'Hey, less of the old, Frank, if you don't mind,' laughed Mildred, at the same time giving Frank a playful punch on the arm.

'Ouch! Enough already!' said Frank, feigning outrage. He then pretended to fall from his chair, while he and Mildred laughed so hard that I found it impossible not to join in.

'Celebrating?' I asked, wiping the tears from my eyes. 'Celebrating what?'

'Frank's going to be moving in with us. He's renting our spare room,' announced Mildred. 'Isn't that good news?'

This was the same Mildred, you will recall, with whom I'd been cohabiting since my teens. That we were still together after all these years was due more to inertia than compatibility. The trick, we'd discovered long ago, was to live independent lives while respectfully tolerating the other's existence: each of us did as we pleased, when we pleased, no questions asked, no lies told. It was rare, if ever, that we shared time together socially, and rarer still romantically. Central to our arrangement was that, in exchange for her looking after the home, Mildred need not go to work, whereas my part of the deal was to pay the bills. (This included the cost of feeding and stabling Mildred's two horses, as well as the purchase and upkeep of a twin horsebox and a 3-litre Opel Commodore with which to tow it.) Neither one of us would have described our situation as perfect, but we were at least comfortable in the other's company, just as one

The Mousse and the Man from the Michelin

is comfortable in, say, an old and well-worn pair of shoes: you know you should really replace them, but somehow you never quite get around to it.

But here was something new. Over the years I'd formed an idea of Mildred and set it in stone, all the while blind to the possibility that I might have got it wrong. For had I at any time been asked to describe Mildred's personality – and had I answered honestly – I would have said she was morose, unsociable, humourless and generally lacking in empathy and affection. Very clearly, however, I would have been wrong on all counts, because here before me was a different woman. All I'd ever known, it would seem, was a version of Mildred. Even allowing for the socially lubricating properties of the cocaine, her transformation was extraordinary. It was as if Mildred had emerged from a decade-long coma.

While Mildred organised practicalities such as rent and bills, Frank wasted no time in making himself at home. The arrangement, I was informed, included us providing occasional accommodation for Speedy Sue, who, in Ophelia's absence, appeared to have resumed a relationship with Frank, albeit in the very loosest sense. Had she been someone else – someone normal – her presence might have caused a problem, because our spare room was barely large enough for one person, let alone two. But thankfully Speedy Sue had little need of a room, or indeed a bed, because she seldom actually slept, at least not in the conventional manner. She simply lost consciousness wherever she happened to be at the time, without any warning and typically mid-sentence. This tended to occur on a four-day cycle: 72 hours of consciousness succeeded by 24 hours of unconsciousness – during which time she would remain immovable and impossible to rouse. Periodically she would urinate in her sleep. This played havoc with the soft furnishings, as well as adding to the already offensive odour that had pervaded the cottage since Frank's arrival. To limit the damage, we would slide a plastic bin liner between her buttocks and the sofa cushion, but it simply displaced the problem by channelling the urine onto the carpet. Other than this one inconvenience, however, Speedy Sue was surprisingly little trouble to have around. I even grew to like her.

Mildred and Frank, meanwhile, had become good friends. It seemed they had much in common – not least an open-ended amount of leisure time that required filling. They'd taken to spending their days together, travelling about the countryside in the Opel Commodore, horsebox in tow. Mildred clearly enjoyed Frank's knockabout sense of humour, and appeared to have no difficulty with the smell of fish or his rudimentary approach to personal hygiene. Apparently, Frank shared Mildred's passion for horses. I found this odd, because he'd never struck me as a horse loving

The Mousse and the Man from the Michelin

type, but it turned out he was from gypsy stock. Horses, he said, were in his blood.

Mildred and Frank would disappear together for days at a time. Following one such absence, I returned home one afternoon to discover three strange men in my living room. They were sitting on the sofa and watching an episode of *Tom and Jerry* on the television. Who were these people? And, more to the point, what were they doing in my house? There was something distinctly sinister about their appearance – not least because they were dressed uniformly in black (although on closer scrutiny it was clear their clothes had begun life in a variety of shades that over time had turned consistently black through lack of washing). And then there was the hair. I'd never seen so much hair in one place: it exploded from heads, jutted from chins, sprouted obscenely from ears and nostrils. So hairy were my visitors, and so grimy, that it was impossible to determine their ages. They made me think of troglodytes, surfaced from the bowels of the earth, perhaps to perform some foul deed upon my person. 'Who are you?' I said. 'And, more to the point, what are you doing in my house?' The troglodytes declined to answer. They just ignored me, their eyes fixed on the TV screen.

'We knew you wouldn't mind,' said Mildred, emerging from the kitchen. She was carrying a tray laden with bottles of beer and a dish containing a mountain of chocolate brownies, which she placed before our visitors. 'Frank always says it's important to look after your crew.'

'Yeah, we knew you wouldn't mind, mate,' said Frank, his head appearing around the kitchen door. He was wearing a floral pinafore apron which I recognised as belonging to Mildred. 'We brought the crew along with us. It's important to look after your crew. That's what I always say.'

'Oh, right,' I said, unsure how else to respond, 'yes, of course.'

Frank introduced me to his crew. Their names were Matt the Hat (so called for reasons unknown), Slim (so called, presumably, because he wasn't) and Mad Andy (so called, presumably, because he was –he definitely had that look about him). They were fishermen, but earned their money, Frank informed me, by working as his foot soldiers, dropping off consignments of drugs, collecting payment and, where necessary, punishing non-payment – if not with threats of violence then with actual violence. Their favoured way of communicating appeared to consist of three primary noises: the affirmative grunt, the negative grunt and the neutral grunt, complemented by the occasional nod of the head or a raised finger for emphasis. But despite their uncivilised demeanour, they at least had the good manners to have re-

The Mousse and the Man from the Michelin

moved their boots before entering the cottage. The smell was terrible, but I appreciated the gesture.

'It's just that the guys was feeling a bit left out down there on the beach all by themselves, and whatever,' continued Frank. 'Felt they was missing out, like. You can't blame 'em. Thought I'd bake some cakes. Cheer 'em up a bit.'

'You've been baking cakes?' I said. Here was another surprise. As far as I knew, Mildred had never baked a cake in her life. And Frank had certainly not struck me as the cake baking type (no more than he'd struck me as the horse loving type).

'Yeah-I-have,' said Frank proudly. 'Hash cakes. Best you'll ever taste. Here, try one.' Frank wiped his floury hands down his apron and handed me a hash cake. 'Excuse my fingers. And be careful, they're still hot.'

'Best you'll ever taste,' echoed Mildred, passing round the dish.

I took a bite. It was surprisingly good. 'That's surprisingly good,' I said, taking a second bite.

'Well, what do you think, guys?' said Frank, addressing his crew. 'Do you agree with our main man here? He should know. He's a fuckin' professional cook. Are they good or what?'

Kent Austin

The three troglodytes said nothing. They just munched impassively, their jaws churning in unison like so many grazing llamas. *Tom and Jerry* had ended and they were now engrossed in an episode of *Skippy the Bush Kangaroo*.

Frank looked on anxiously. 'It creeps up on you,' he explained. 'Subtle like. Take your time and report back when you're ready, okay, guys? No rush.'

An hour passed by, as well as two further episodes of *Skippy*. Eventually, one after the other, the troglodytes grunted their approval and reached for a second hash cake.

Frank was visibly relieved. 'One tip, mate,' he said, addressing me, 'you've gotta trust the opinion of the experts in this business. Quality control, there's no other way. Now we can go into full production.'

'Production?' I asked. 'Production of what?

'Hash cakes, of course. Can't sell enough of 'em, mate. Right little earner.'

'A hash cake factory? Here? In my kitchen?'

'Don't worry, mate' said Frank, noting my alarm. 'I'll bung you something extra to cover the gas and electric. As I say, I always look after my crew.'

Between us we finished off the remainder of the hash

The Mousse and the Man from the Michelin

cakes. It wasn't long before Frank's crew had passed out on the sofa. They slept like babies, snoring in harmony. From time to time one would let rip an explosive fart which would disrupt the rhythm of their sleep. But inevitably they would settle down again and their snoring would revert to its synchronised pattern. Lulled by the sound of the troglodytes' snores, and with the psychoactive effect of the hash cakes now peaking, it wasn't long before I too slipped from consciousness. I've no idea how long I was out. But I do recall having erotic dreams, and they were of an oddly intense and unsettling nature. I awoke to discover Frank and Mildred fucking doggy style on the carpet next to where I lay. I re-closed my eyes and pretended to be asleep.

I was pondering the significance of this latest turn of events when happily it resolved itself. Just days later, news arrived that Speedy Sue had been murdered. She'd been in bed at the time, holed-up in a Margate boarding house while attempting (unsuccessfully as it turned out) to lie low. Her assailant, a drug dealer to whom she owed money, had smashed his way through the door of her room with an axe (Jack Nicholson fashion), and then used it to equally brutal effect on her skull. For good measure he did the same to her lover, who'd had the misfortune of being in the same bed. And, in case you were wondering, Laughing Gnome *did* manage to squeeze a laugh out of it – the amusing angle being that Frank wasn't there in bed with her when it happened and '*it was the arsehole what was shagging her what got the chopper instead*'. I've no idea whether he and Frank attended Speedy Sue's funeral, or, if so, whether Laughing Gnome managed to see its funny side, because I was destined never to see either of them again. Like passing locusts, Frank and his entourage were to depart from my world as abruptly as they had arrived.

The effect was dramatic. On learning of Speedy Sue's death, Frank announced he would be leaving immediately. He was headed for Ireland, he said, to 'to run with the gypsies' (whatever this entailed). With an axe-wielding maniac on the loose, I could well understand why Frank might be in a hurry to flee the country; for reasons he declined to explain, he seemed convinced that he was next on the hit list. Although I admit that it caught me off guard when Mildred said she would be joining him.

'It just happened, mate,' said Frank, after Mildred had broken the news to me. 'We knew you'd understand. It's nothing personal, like.'

'Yes, it just happened,' echoed Mildred. 'Frank and I have feelings for each other which cannot be denied. I hope we can all be mature about this and just move on with our lives.' As she spoke she was busy loading the back of

The Mousse and the Man from the Michelin

the Opel Commodore with her final few belongings and, somewhat bizarrely under the circumstances, as much of our kitchen equipment as she could squeeze in around the edges including, to my distress, a set of Le Creuset casseroles which I'd been adding to over a number of years at considerable expense. Since Mildred didn't cook, I thought this was an injustice too far.

'Look, since you don't cook,' I said, 'would you at least mind leaving behind the Le Creuset? It cost me a fortune.'

'Frank and I will be setting up home together in Ireland,' said Mildred angrily (and to my mind a little too angrily, considering we were only discussing kitchen utensils), 'and it's never too late for me to learn to cook, is it? Besides, I'm leaving you the furniture.'

I didn't see it this way, and told her so. And when she still refused to part with my treasured casseroles, I lost my temper and called her a grabbing whore. She responded by calling me a control freak and a bully and that she couldn't wait to see the back of me. And so it came to pass that my last ever conversation with my fiancé of ten years was destined to be a petty squabble over a set of cooking pots – although with hindsight I suspect there may have been deeper issues at play.

'Come on, Grides, we need to be moving!' Grides was

Frank's pet name for Mildred and, apparently, an old gypsy term of endearment. Frank was seated behind the wheel of the Opel Commodore – which was parked in front of the cottage, trailer attached and loaded with Mildred's horses. He was becoming more agitated by the minute, glancing anxiously up and down the lane and revving the accelerator impatiently. 'Are you coming then, Grides, or what?'

'Yes, alright, Frank, I'm on my way!' Mildred made to leave, one last item of Le Creuset clutched tightly to her breast, as if fearful that it might be snatched from her possession. Before she walked out of my life for good, however, I couldn't resist one final question: what was it, I asked her, that she found so appealing about Frank? It had been playing on my mind for some time, and so far I'd been unable to arrive at a satisfactory explanation. My best guess was that she was beguiled by his swashbuckling lifestyle. But now when I put this idea to Mildred she scoffed at my naivety. No, the truth was altogether more prosaic. According to Mildred, she was attracted to Frank for the simple reason that, unlike me, he liked horses. Also, unlike me, he made her laugh with his jokes. And, last – but, judging by the gleam in Mildred's eye when she informed me, by no means least – unlike me, he knew the exact location of her G-spot and, so she claimed, had a knack for giving her orgasms of unparalleled duration and intensity, apparently by

The Mousse and the Man from the Michelin

employing a rare finger technique taught to him by a Moroccan prostitute.

So now at least I knew. On this note, we shook hands and parted.

If I learned anything that day, it was that one should never jump to conclusions.

PART THREE

THE MAN FROM THE MICHELIN

'Gordon Ramsay told recently how he wept openly when his New York establishment, Gordon Ramsay at the London, lost its second star. "It's a very emotional thing for any chef," he said… "It's like losing a girlfriend… You want her back…"'

Quoted in *The Week*

I was having one of my 'bad' nights. It had come on the back of an equally bad day, during which I'd suffered a string of disasters, beginning with an explosion...

I'd been boiling toffee to make Banoffi Pie. As the birthplace of Banoffi Pie, the restaurant had become something of a pilgrimage for its many devotees. It was our best-selling pudding by far and we produced it on an industrial scale. In the unlikely event that you're unfamiliar with this now ubiquitous confection, one of its key ingredients is caramel toffee. Nowadays it comes conveniently premade in ring-pull cans, but at the time we made the toffee by placing unopened cans of sweetened condensed milk in a pan of water and boiling them on full heat for several hours. To save energy, we would boil four dozen cans at a time, using a vast pan specially reserved for the purpose. To prevent the pan from boiling dry, it was important to top up the water at regular intervals. The consequences of not doing so could result in carnage – as many cooks have learned from painful experience. Without adequate water, the pan becomes a literal time bomb, as the caramel inside the cans continues to heat and expand out of control (the boiling point of sugar being significantly higher than that of water). If left unchecked, the cans eventually explode in rapid succession, like a salvo of cluster grenades going off. But instead of shrapnel, the air is filled with a million droplets of molten sugar, any one of which has the capacity to burn its way into the flesh or eyes, causing scarring or even blindness. Despite being aware of the danger, we had a record of laxness in this area, and explosive episodes were so commonplace that we'd almost become blasé about them. On this occasion no one was injured, but several cans exploded before we managed to subdue the remainder by dousing them with cold water. The worst part, as always, was the mess, because by the time the content of the cans reaches exploding point it has become a viscous black lacquer which hardens to the consistency of glass and sticks fast the instant it makes contact with any surface. Attempting to remove it is like scraping faeces from a blanket and about as effective. For one night at least, Banoffi Pie was off the menu.

The Mousse and the Man from the Michelin

My next setback occurred when the fish I'd ordered from the wholesaler failed to arrive. Finding myself short of a fish course, I decided to use a turbot from the freezer. I generally avoided using frozen fish, but on this occasion I had no alternative. It was late afternoon, and I was running out of time. So to speed up the defrosting process, I threw the turbot (a vast specimen weighing some ten pounds) into a sink of cold water in the kitchen scullery. With a bit of luck, it might just be soft enough for me to fillet and skin by the time service arrived. Sadly, I hadn't bargained for the ineptitude of my second-in-command. It was a big sink, more than a metre deep. Failing to notice the submerged turbot lurking at the bottom, Kevin proceeded to fill it with dirty pots and run a hot tap over them. By the time I realised what had happened and pulled the fish from the hot water, a layer of flesh some five millimetres deep had begun to cook and flake away from the main body, while the rest of the fish remained frozen hard. It looked as if it had been flayed and subjected to some form of torture. Disgusted, I tossed the turbot into a bucket in the corner of the kitchen and struck it from the menu.

By way of a hat trick, not minutes later I somehow succeeded in decanting a kilo of peeled cooked shrimps into a pan of chocolate sauce. They were intended for a fish soup I was making at the same time, but by now I was working frantically against the clock and in my haste had confused the two pans. Unsure of what I was attempting to achieve, I strained the chocolate sauce through a sieve. I was left with a pot of fishy-flavoured chocolate sauce and a pile of chocolate coated shrimps (and if I'm not mistaken, a culinary first on two counts). Never one to baulk at a gustatory challenge, Kevin popped one into his mouth. 'Ummm, they don't taste bad, actually,' he said, helping himself to a second and a third shrimp. 'Try one.' I tried one. Kevin was right. It was not at all unpleasant, moreish even. Perhaps I'd inadvertently hit on something. If Heston Blumenthal can get away with serving egg and bacon ice cream and snail porridge, then surely this wasn't so outlandish? The fishy chocolate sauce, on the other hand, was judged less successful, and it made perfect sense to pour it down the sink, all four litres of it – prepared from the finest Belgian chocolate, laced with brandy. This left me with a problem. I needed chocolate sauce to serve with my profiteroles, which were a big seller, but I'd run out of chocolate with which to make more. I sent an intern to the local pub to borrow some chocolate. She returned with something called 'Kake Brand Covering'. Made from sugar and palm oil, it contained so little by way of cocoa solids that it didn't qualify to be called chocolate, and was described on the packet as a 'chocolate-flavoured confection'. It clearly predated the inception of the sell-by

The Mousse and the Man from the Michelin

date system by some years and, judging by its fossilised appearance, had been languishing in the pub storeroom since the days of wartime rationing. Accepting defeat, I took profiteroles off the menu.

The setbacks of the day had put me behind, and when the first orders came in that night I was unprepared. This, as every chef knows, is a road to ruin. We got off to a bad start and never really recovered, yet somehow we served a full restaurant three times over in the space of three hours. By the time service was over, the kitchen looked as if there'd been an explosion (which of course there had). Kevin and I were sitting on the wall outside the kitchen, taking a cigarette break, exhausted and, as was our habit, well on our way to becoming inebriated. We were contemplating the prospect of tackling the chaos in the kitchen when Betsie appeared from the dining room. 'Zere is a man 'ere in ze restaurant who vonts to speak viz the chef. Can you to come out pliz?'

My heart sank. 'Must I?' I groaned. 'What does he want?' It wasn't uncommon for customers to ask to meet the chef, usually for no other reason than to compliment me on their meal and buy me a drink. Inevitably I would decline, citing that I was too busy, but it was mainly down to shyness

"E sez 'e vonts to speak viz you. I sink 'e's an inspector

person.'

'An inspector? Why didn't you tell me we had an inspector in the restaurant?'

'I didn't to know. Don't to go taking it out on me. 'E vos viz ozer people.'

'What sort of inspector?'

"Ow should I to know?'

'Tell him I've left for the night –'

But before I'd completed the sentence the door to the dining room opened and a man marched into the kitchen. 'Please excuse my intrusion, gentlemen, but I was wondering whether I might have a word with the chef...unless of course he's *left* for the night?'

How do you spot a Michelin inspector?

As with all other restaurant inspectors, they are supposed to operate incognito. But in practice they might just as well arrive clad in a suit of inner tubes emblazoned with the Michelin logo, such is their cavalier approach to anonymity. The first and most obvious giveaway is that inspectors generally dine alone. Lone diners at The Mute Swan were a rarity and as such whenever we received a table reservation for one person it was safe to assume we were dealing with an

The Mousse and the Man from the Michelin

inspector. The real problem was in establishing which guide they were working for, (If it transpired they were with the AA, Ackerman or some such lesser guide, then they could be safely disregarded.) although very often they would helpfully oblige us by carrying a copy of the selfsame guide under their arm when they arrived at the restaurant. Once ensconced at their table, the suspect would then be spied upon by the waiting staff at every opportunity, in an effort to spot further tell-tale signs as to their identity. For instance, the presence of a spiral notepad, lodged indiscreetly next to their plate, or a tendency to dissect each course of their meal with a forensic thoroughness while leaving most of the food uneaten. Although by far the most important characteristic to look for when identifying a restaurant inspector is the general malaise of spirit that inevitably results from dining out alone some 300 times a year. I've no idea of the life expectancy of a restaurant inspector, but I suspect that as a career choice it can only lead to despondency, flatulence and, ultimately, an untimely death.

For once, the Man from the Michelin had succeeded in slipping beneath our radar, simply because he wasn't dining alone. Now, for those who aren't involved in the restaurant trade, I have to point out that for a Michelin inspector to break cover was a rare – and in our experience unprecedented – event. But now here He was, the Man from the

Michelin – His mythical self – marching bold as life into my kitchen. Why was He here and, most importantly, what did He want? Something was afoot. Could it possibly be that...?

They say that it's never a good idea to meet your heroes. So it was when I finally came face to face with the Man from the Michelin. I'm not sure what I'd expected him to look like, but it wasn't this (and in truth, of course, he isn't a single person but an imaginary construct, comprising any number of faceless Michelin inspectors the world over). Squat and round, he reminded me of my deputy headmaster at secondary school, complete with a little bow tie, dandruff lapels and the identical officious manner. The Man from the Michelin shook me by the hand and gave me his calling card. Without missing a beat, he then produced a pencil and notepad and proceeded to interrogate me. What were my culinary influences? What did I consider to be my signature dishes? Did I plan to introduce a 'menu *dégustation*' any time soon? Did I have any influence over the wine list...? I responded to the best of my ability, but for the most part I was too tired, too drunk and too anxious to deliver a coherent answer. I tried to disguise the fact by saying as little as possible, but this only made me sound monosyllabic. The Man from the Michelin continued as if nothing was untoward, but I could tell he was unimpressed. When he asked me what steps I had in place, if any, for 'succession

The Mousse and the Man from the Michelin

and continuity', I answered that I had no idea what he was talking about. 'Well, in the event that you weren't here,' he continued patiently, 'who would take up your mantel as *chef de cuisine*?'

'Yeah, well, that would be me, as it happens,' interrupted Kevin, who had been hovering at my shoulder throughout our interview.

'And your name is...?' said the Man from the Michelin, turning to Kevin.

'Well, erm, actually, it wouldn't necessarily be you who would take my place, Kevin,' I said. 'Besides,' I continued, fixing the Man from the Michelin with what was intended as a reassuring smile, 'I have no plans to go anywhere in the foreseeable future – '

'The name's Wilkes,' answered Kevin, while making no effort to suppress a triumphant smirk. 'Kevin Wilkes.'

'Ke...vin...Wil...kes,' repeated the Man from the Michelin, jotting Kevin's name into his notepad before snapping it shut. 'Well, thank you for your time, gentlemen, and, once again, please excuse my intrusion. I'll be on my way.'

Before he left, however, the Man from the Michelin took a step back and made one final, leisurely – and seemingly intensely critical – appraisal of the kitchen. His face said it all. In turn, I felt his eye settle upon the cheap chocolate cake covering, still in its packet on the table; the flayed turbot disintegrating forlornly in its bucket of water; the myriad scraps of food littering the floor; the charcoal droplets of caramel adhering to the walls and ceiling; the embarrassing number of empty lager bottles cluttering the kitchen doorstep; the chaotic mess that pervaded the entire kitchen; the obvious break down of any kind of organisation. And what he must have made of the chocolate coated shrimps is anybody's guess...

Whatever else might have been passing through his mind, I remain convinced that at that moment we'd been on the verge of a breakthrough, and that had the Man from the Michelin arrived on a different night, a 'good' night, when things had gone according to plan, the outcome might have been different. But as it was I'd just blown my one and, as it turned out, only opportunity to win a Michelin star. The game was over. And I'd lost.

It had taken me the best part of fifteen years, but finally it was time to concede defeat. The harder I strived for recognition, the more wholeheartedly it eluded me. Apart from a folder full of fading press clippings and one fleeting appearance on the BBC, my quest for fame had been an unqualified failure. The seeds of greatness that Gerald claimed to have identified in me all those years ago remained dead in

The Mousse and the Man from the Michelin

the ground. It was time to face the truth: I just wasn't celebrity material. I lacked the talent and, perhaps even more importantly, the sheer bloody-mindedness required to claw my way to the top. I was by definition mediocre, and destined to remain that way, the restaurant world's equivalent of Cliff Richard – despised by the critics, applauded by those who should know better: easy listening for the palate.

***

The day I decided to quit cooking we were on the homeward leg of a gastronomic mini-tour of the West Country. Over the course of a long weekend, we dined at Cranes in Salisbury, The Carved Angel in Dartmouth, Thornbury Castle in Devon, and The Hole in the Wall in Bath – all restaurants which, at the time, were regarded as being among the best in the country. The trip had been Gerald's idea, his reasoning being, as ever, that it would serve as an inspiration and 'drive us on to the next level', as he put it. It should have been fun, a treat; it felt like anything but. The downside, for me at least, was that we were accompanied by the entire restaurant staff (Gerald had hired a minibus for the occasion). I find the art of dinner conversation a trial at the best of times. But, fond of my work colleagues as I was, dining out with the same people four times in succession (and that's not counting breakfast and lunch) had stretched my powers of geniality to their limit. Besides, by now we knew each other so well that the probability of any one of us saying something original or amusing was pretty much zero. There was also the food to contend with. I enjoy eating as much as anyone, but I'm no gastronome. By the end of the weekend I was so heartily tired of dissecting, commenting upon and stomaching the contents of my plate that I was fit to vomit into the nearest aspidistra. And had I been obliged to set foot in one more restaurant, rub shoulders with one more flatulent, greasy-chinned *bon vivant* (his self-satisfied paunch inevitably swathed in a voluminous white napkin); been fawned over and patronised by one more unctuously over-attentive waiter...

For reasons which now escape me, on the final leg of our trip we took a detour via London to visit the trade show of the international mineral water industry (the name of which I forget). I think it was at Earl's Court, or possibly Olympia. It was a surreal affair: aisle upon aisle, a hundred stands, each staffed by a team of chirpily enthusiastic sales people, gamely promoting the virtues of their respective water – its unique mineral balance, its distinctive creaminess on the palate, the explicit texture of its gaseous bubbles, which when discharged serve subtly to enhance the flavour of whatever one is eating... You had to admire their dedication, because if any among them suspected that the distinction between their own brand of water and the next was so negligible as

The Mousse and the Man from the Michelin

to be meaningless (as I'm sure they must), they certainly didn't show it. There was something of the Emperor's New Clothes about it. Duly complicit, we quaffed our way self-consciously through thimble-cupful after thimble-cupful of mineral water, rolling it around our mouths, nodding appreciatively, groping for appropriate adjectives. We took in every stand, until eventually our critical faculties, along with our bladders, could bear no more.

Any civilisation possessed of the will to fly water in bottles at vast cost from the four corners of the planet, for no other reason than to agonise over its peculiarities has either: a/ disappeared so far up its own decadent arse as to be on the verge of extinction, or: b/ solved all life's pressing problems, and therefore reserves the right to act as self-indulgently as it chooses. I couldn't decide which. At least this was the gist of my thinking as we left the exhibition hall. On our walk back to the Tube we passed a homeless man, sheltering in a shop doorway. He was young, no older than twenty, a grimy sleeping bag pulled up to his neck for warmth. I couldn't help wondering whether his preference might be for Perrier or Pellegrino.

SIX MONTHS LATER...

Closing my front door behind me, I knelt down and pushed the keys through the letter box. There, the deed was done. No turning back. I tossed my suitcase onto the back seat of my car. I was travelling light: a change of clothes, a handful of books, and a folder containing my passport and an open-ended plane ticket to Asia. It was a fine morning in early summer. The air was alive with birdsong and sweet with the scent of flowers. I looked back one final time at the home I was leaving behind. With its rose-clad stucco walls and rickety red-tiled roof, it was almost too picturesque for its own good. (It wasn't uncommon for me to rise in the morning to find myself surrounded by a semi-circle of amateur artists, all busy painting my home. I swear there must have been a watercolour of my cottage hanging in every tearoom and doctor's surgery across the county.) It was an enviable place in which to live, and now here I was about to abandon it for good. I suppressed a pang of regret. It was never too late to change my mind, tell Gerald that it had all been a dreadful mistake. Ask him to take me back... But no! I could do this. It was a new beginning, the fresh start I'd been promising myself for so long. I was feeling good about the future. I hadn't used drugs for the best part of a year. I was drinking less, taking regular exercise. It was a fragile optimism but it was optimism nevertheless... No looking back...

I got into the car. I started the engine. I drove the 300 or so metres to the end of the lane. So far so good, no looking back... I was about to pull out onto the main road next to The Mute Swan, when I spotted Gerald in my driver's mirror. He was running behind the car, waving and signalling for me to stop. I pulled over and rolled down my window.

'Ah, there you are, Kento.' Gerald was ruddy faced, breathless from his exertion. He was carrying a large gift-wrapped box. 'Going somewhere?'

'I'm off today. You know, to Japan?'

'Good heavens, so soon! You'll have to forgive me, but, yes, I'd forgotten. My, you're travelling light, aren't you?' Gerald was peering through the driver's window, gesturing at my suitcase on the back seat. 'Just the one case?'

'Yes, just the one.'

'Ah, anyway, Kento, I've something for you. It probably isn't the most appropriate time, what with you about to fly off into the blue yonder and whatnot, but I might not get another opportunity. So here you are, a small token of my... our...appreciation for all your hard work.'

The Mousse and the Man from the Michelin

Gerald presented me with the box he'd been holding. I had trouble pulling it through the car window, but with some manoeuvring I managed to get it onto my lap. 'Oh, er, thank you. Shall I open it now?'

'Yes, of course, Kento.'

I tore away the wrapping. Inside was a Hitachi CD player.

To place this in perspective – albeit with the benefit of hindsight – in December 2012, the then director general of the BBC George Entwhistle resigned. His alleged mishandling of the Jimmy Savile sex abuse scandal had made his position untenable. After just 55 days in the post he walked away with a severance payment of £450,000, plus an additional £200,000 to cover legal and PR expenses. And this was in exchange for doing his job badly. Such arrangements nowadays are commonplace, especially in senior management posts. Even allowing for inflation and the comparative lowliness of my station, I still can't help feeling short changed. I may not have been a director of a corporation, or indeed anyone of note, but, even in my lowest moments, throughout my years at The Mute Swan I'd always hoped I might be worth more than a bottom-of-the-range electrical appliance.

'Oh, well, thank you,' I said, 'just what I needed, in fact.'

What else could I say? I placed the CD player, still in its box, next to my suitcase on the backseat of the car. It then struck me that I had a problem. My furniture, and indeed everything else I owned, was in storage. I was on my way to the airport; my plane was scheduled to take off in three hours. I would have to take my new CD player with me to Japan, which was kind of ironic seeing it had come from there in the first place. Like taking kippers to Grimsby. I was just reflecting on the absurdity of this situation when I noticed that Gerald seemed mildly agitated. 'Is everything okay?' I asked.

'*I'm* okay, yes, Kento, never felt better, tickety-boo, in fact. It's *you* I'm concerned about.'

'Me?'

'You know what, Kento... Now I don't want you to take this the wrong way...But the way I see it you've come full circle.'

'Full circle? How do you mean?'

Gerald gestured towards my suitcase on the backseat for a second time. 'Just think about it. Fifteen years ago. You arrived with a suitcase...all your worldly possessions in a single suitcase. And now, after all these years, you're leaving with...a suitcase.'

The Mousse and the Man from the Michelin

I felt like reminding Gerald that in addition to a suitcase I was at least now the proud owner of an entry-level CD player, but suppressed the urge.

'It's a full circle you see...all those years and nothing to show for it but a single suitcase. Think about it. You've lost it all...woman...home...livelihood...career...future...All gone. I mean how are you *ever* going to recover from this, Kento?'

'I, erm, I suppose something will present itself, Gerald. Life has a way of throwing us new opportunities. I'm looking forward to a fresh, you know, start...in Japan –'

'Do you honestly think that running away to Japan is about to change anything, Kento? That's my point, you see, you can't run away from *yourself*. No, you know what I'd do if I were in your position, don't you?'

I had no idea what Gerald would do if he were in my position, but could hazard a guess. 'I don't know,' Gerald, 'cash in a few shares, perhaps? Take a long holiday? Start a llama farm in Patagonia?'

'I'd top myself. That's what I'd do.'

'Top yourself? You mean...?'

'Yes, no compunction.' Gerald made a slashing gesture across his throat. 'All over. Done with. Wouldn't be able to live with myself, you see.'

As Gerald spoke, I could feel my increasingly fragile optimism begin to evaporate. It was palpable, like steam escaping from a punctured soufflé. We lapsed into an uneasy silence, neither of us sure of what to do next. Gerald appeared to be on the brink of saying something when he was interrupted by the distant ringing of his office phone. 'Ah, must get that! Do excuse me, Kento, I'm expecting a call.' And with this he was gone. Although he did find time for a parting shot, delivered over the shoulder as he turned to leave: 'And you do realise, don't you, Kento? You're an absolute fucking bastard for leaving me like this.'

While we'd been speaking the sky had become overcast. As I started the car engine, the first heavy drops of rain exploded on the windscreen.

POSTSCRIPT

'It's changed everything. It's given me a way to look at the genome of gastronomy and reflect on it. Honey, for example: so simple, but where taxonomically would you place it? If people don't understand that honey is an elaboration that animals are cooking for you, people will not understand the process of cooking.'

Ferran Adria, chef-director, El Bulli, Catalonia, (3 Michelin stars) quoted in *Time Magazine*

***

Known to her followers as the 'Diva', Park Seo-Yeon is South Korea's leading exponent of *muk-bang* (meaning literally 'eating rooms'). Every night at 8pm sharp, she sits down in her tiny Seoul apartment and eats a meal, which is streamed live via webcam to some seven thousand gastronomic voyeurs. Seo-Yeon's devotees pay a subscription to access her website, which also entitles them to chat with her online while she eats. This earns her around £6,000 a month and has enabled her to give up her day job and eat full time. Much of Seo-Yeon's appeal, apparently, has to do with her ability to consume vast amounts of food while remaining effortlessly slim. A typical online meal – which can last several hours – comprises four large pizzas with a bucket of chicken wings, or thirty fried eggs and a box of crabs' legs, or five packets of noodles and four kilos of beef. The waif-like thirty-three-year-old is said to have the appetite of an elephant and the metabolism of a humming bird. Many of her viewers are on diets, and they claim that 'eating' vicariously through The Diva helps them stay off food. Another factor in her popularity, says Seo-Yeon, is loneliness, because her viewers can talk with like-minded people while they watch her eat. Quite what they talk *about* while the Diva is filling her face is unclear.

What is clear, however, is that our relationship with food is deeply ambivalent. Like sex, we obsess over it and yet equally we are shamed by it. In his book *A Cook's Tour,* chef and author Anthony Bourdain embarks on a worldwide gastronomic odyssey in search of the 'perfect meal'. It is food porn at its most lurid: Bourdain visits Saigon where he eats the still-beating heart of a live cobra, before sampling a soft-boiled duck embryo with half formed bones and feathers; takes part in a 'pig feast' in Portugal; munches on roasted sheep's testicles with the Tuaregs in Morocco ('crispy and veiny'); attends a ritualised multi-course kaiseki banquet in Japan; eulogises upon the virtues of such dishes as pork-blood cake, goat's head soup, lemongrass tripe... He even braves scalding his mouth on a deep-fried Mars bar in a

The Mousse and the Man from the Michelin

Glasgow fish and chip shop. In the process, unsurprisingly, he suffers multiple bouts of vomiting and some serious abdominal upsets – and despite his suffering, never does quite decide on his perfect meal.

But what is the perfect meal? And where would you go to find it? It is of course a highly subjective notion: one man's delectable sheep's testicle is the next man's chewy reproductive organ. Until recently, however, the critics' – pretty much unanimous – choice was El Bulli, in Catalonia. (I say 'was' because, despite having been awarded three Michelin stars, the restaurant closed in 2012, claiming, remarkably, that it was losing money.) Hailed as the most 'controversial and experimental' restaurant in the world, it is said to have received reservation requests from some two million people each year, only 8,000 of whom managed to get a table. Chef Ferran Adria's 35-course molecular gastronomy dinner – a snip at €350 a head – included such delicacies as 'Smoke Foam', 'Carrot Air with Coconut Milk', 'Gorgonzola Balloon', 'Mint Pond', 'Spice Plate', 'Trumpet Carpaccio', 'Chocolate Donuts', 'Puff Pastry Web'... Clearly some of the poetry is lost in translation, but you get the idea. I never had the pleasure of dining at El Bulli, but had I done so I'm in no doubt that I would have been as awe struck as the next person. But does such a rarefied experience really add-up to the 'perfect meal'? At the end of a long day, tired and hungry, can I really hear myself saying, *'I could murder a gorgonzola balloon, and maybe a side order of smoke foam and carrot air to help it down.'*? (Indeed, I suspect this very deficiency is the reason why I never made the big time as a chef: my inability to take food seriously – or at least not seriously enough.) Perhaps Heston Blumenthal – himself a noted dabbler in molecular gastronomy – is closer to the truth, at least where the British palate is concerned. In his book *In Search of Perfection*, he deconstructs some of the nation's most enduring staple meals and subjects them to a painstaking scientific analysis before reinventing them to arrive at the definitive version of each dish. The meals, in case you were wondering, are roast chicken and roast potatoes, pizza, bangers and mash, steak, spaghetti Bolognese, fish and chips, Black Forest gateau and treacle tart with ice cream. I bought the book when it came out in 2006, having watched the TV series by the same name. And, I suspect, like most others who bought it, I've yet to open it. It's all too much like hard work.

I'm not alone. Cooking is on the decline. We may be hooked on watching *MasterChef*, and indeed entire TV channels devoted to showing cookery programmes; spend millions each year on cookbooks and state-of-the-art kitchens, yet most of us appear not to actually *do* any cooking. If the polls are to be believed, Britons now spend half as

The Mousse and the Man from the Michelin

long cooking their evening meal as in the 1980s – typically just 34 minutes – and, on average, know just four recipes. Despite our preoccupation with exotic food, our favourite meal remains the roast dinner, followed by pizza. (Heston Blumenthal has clearly done his research). We are, in the main, a nation of non-cooks. We'd rather eat out.

Quite *where* we eat out is another matter...

The Mute Swan closed its doors for the last time in January 2012, (some 22 years after my departure, and proving beyond any doubt that it could survive perfectly well without me). Having weathered the idiosyncrasies of popular British taste for more than 40 years, it finally gave in to the inevitable and, like the kipper tie and the platform shoe before it, fell from fashion – the product of another more innocent, more forgiving age. As one particularly spiteful critic observed at the time, the only thing about the restaurant to have changed significantly since the 70s was the waistline of the waitresses. The Mute Swan may not have been the best restaurant in the world. And it never did win a Michelin star, and probably never deserved to. But for all its faults the name lives on. The Mute Swan Restaurant – the former monastic dwelling fronting onto the dusty B-road that snakes its way through the village of Bovington – has once again metamorphosed, to be reborn as 'Mute Swan Cottages' – a row of tastefully converted holiday homes, the blue plaque commemorating the birthplace of Banoffi Pie still nailed proudly to one wall.

***

'Awarded "Chef of the Century" by the *Gault Millau Guide*, Joël Robuchon operates a dozen restaurants in cities such as Paris, Tokyo, New York and Hong Kong. His restaurants have garnered a total of 25 Michelin stars – more than any other chef in the world...'

joelrobuchon.co.uk

Made in the USA
Middletown, DE
24 May 2018